Architectural Design 55 7/8-1985

Editorial Offices: 42 Leinster Gardens, London W2 Telephone: 01-402 2141 Subscriptions: 7/8 Holland Street London W8

EDITOR
Dr Andreas C Papadakis
HOUSE EDITOR: Frank Russell
CONSULTANTS: Catherine Cooke, Dennis Crompton, Terry Farrell, Kenneth Frampton, Charles Jencks, Leon Krier, Robert Maxwell, Demetri Porphyrios, Colin Rowe, Derek Walker

Architectural Design Profile 60

DRAWINGS FROM THE
LE CORBUSIER ARCHIVE

Guest-edited by Alexander Tzonis

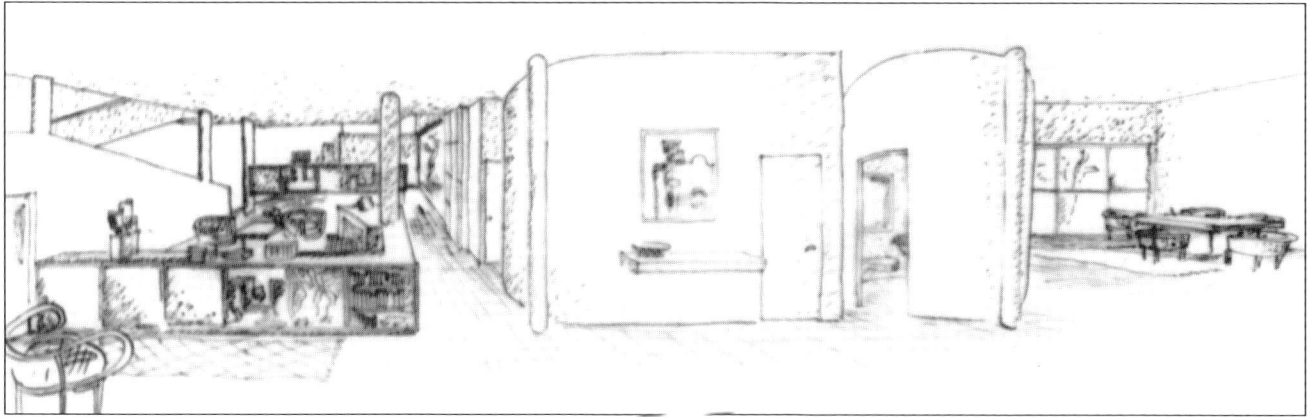

Villa Meyer, Neuilly-sur-Seine, France, 1925. Interior perspective (FLC 31.514).

Guest-editor Alexander Tzonis has specially selected for this issue drawings from the Fondation Le Corbusier in Paris together with a number of introductory essays by Tim Benton, Danièle Pauly, Kenneth Frampton, Peter Serenyi and Tzonis himself which discuss specific themes in Le Corbusier's work and demonstrate the architect's syncretist and critical approach. These are extracted from the thirty-two volumes of the *Le Corbusier Archive* published by Garland Architectural Archives and the Fondation Le Corbusier, the largest publication of architectural drawings ever undertaken.

© 1986 AD Editions Ltd. All rights reserved. No part of this publication may be reproduced or transmitted in any form or by any means, electronic or mechanical, including photocopying, recording or any information storage or retrieval system without permission in writing from the Publisher. Neither the Editor nor AD Editions Ltd hold themselves responsible for the opinions expressed by writers of articles or letters in this magazine. The Editor will give careful consideration to unsolicited articles, photographs and drawings; please enclose a stamped addressed envelope for their return (if required). Payment for material appearing in AD is not normally made except by prior arrangement. All reasonable care will be taken of material in the possession of AD and agents and printers, but we regret that we cannot be held responsible for any loss or damage. *Subscription rates for 1986* (including p&p). Annual rate: UK only £45.00, Europe £55.00, Overseas US$79.50 or UK sterling equiv. Student rates: UK only £39.50, Europe £50.00, Overseas US$69.50 or UK sterling equiv. Double issues £7.95/US$14.95. Single issues £3.95/US$7.50. Please add £1.00/US$2.00 per issue ordered for p&p. All 1986 subscribers will receive *Art & Design* as part of their subscription. Printed in Great Britain by G A Pindar & Son Ltd, London. [ISSN: 0003-8504]

Bookshop distribution: Academy Editions, 7 Holland Street, London W8 4NA   Distributed in the United States of America by St Martin's Press, 175 Fifth Avenue, New York, NY 10010

Villa Savoye (Le Corbusier, *Précisions*, p.139)

Architectural Design Profile 60

DRAWINGS FROM THE
LE CORBUSIER ARCHIVE

FONDATION LE CORBUSIER IN PARIS

PUBLISHED BY GARLAND ARCHITECTURAL ARCHIVES

Guest-edited by Alexander Tzonis

INTRODUCTION
Alexander Tzonis 5

SYNCRETISM AND THE CRITICAL OUTLOOK IN LE CORBUSIER'S WORK
Alexander Tzonis & Liane Lefaivre 7

VILLA SAVOYE AND THE ARCHITECT'S PRACTICE
Tim Benton 9
Maison La Roche-Jeanneret 20 Villa Meyer 21
Villa Cook 23 Villa Ternisien 23 Villa les
Terasses 24 Villa Planeix 25 Villa Ocampo 26
Villa Baizeau 26 Villa Savoye 27

THE CHAPEL OF RONCHAMP AS AN EXAMPLE OF LE CORBUSIER'S CREATIVE PROCESS
Danièle Pauly 31

THE LEAGUE OF NATIONS, THE CENTROSOYUS AND THE PALACE OF THE SOVIETS, 1926-1931
Kenneth Frampton 41
Centrosoyus 51 Palace of the Soviets 54

TIMELESS, BUT OF ITS TIME LE CORBUSIER'S ARCHITECTURE IN INDIA
Peter Serenyi 55
Chandigarh: High Court 76 Capitole 77
Assembly Building 77 Secretariat 81
Ahmedabad: Association of Mill Owners 83
Museum 85 Villa Sarabhai 86
Villa Shodan 87

THE FONDATION LE CORBUSIER 88

© Copyright for all the drawings in this volume lies with the Fondation Le Corbusier.
All the material in this volume is reproduced by permission of the Garland Architectural Archive.

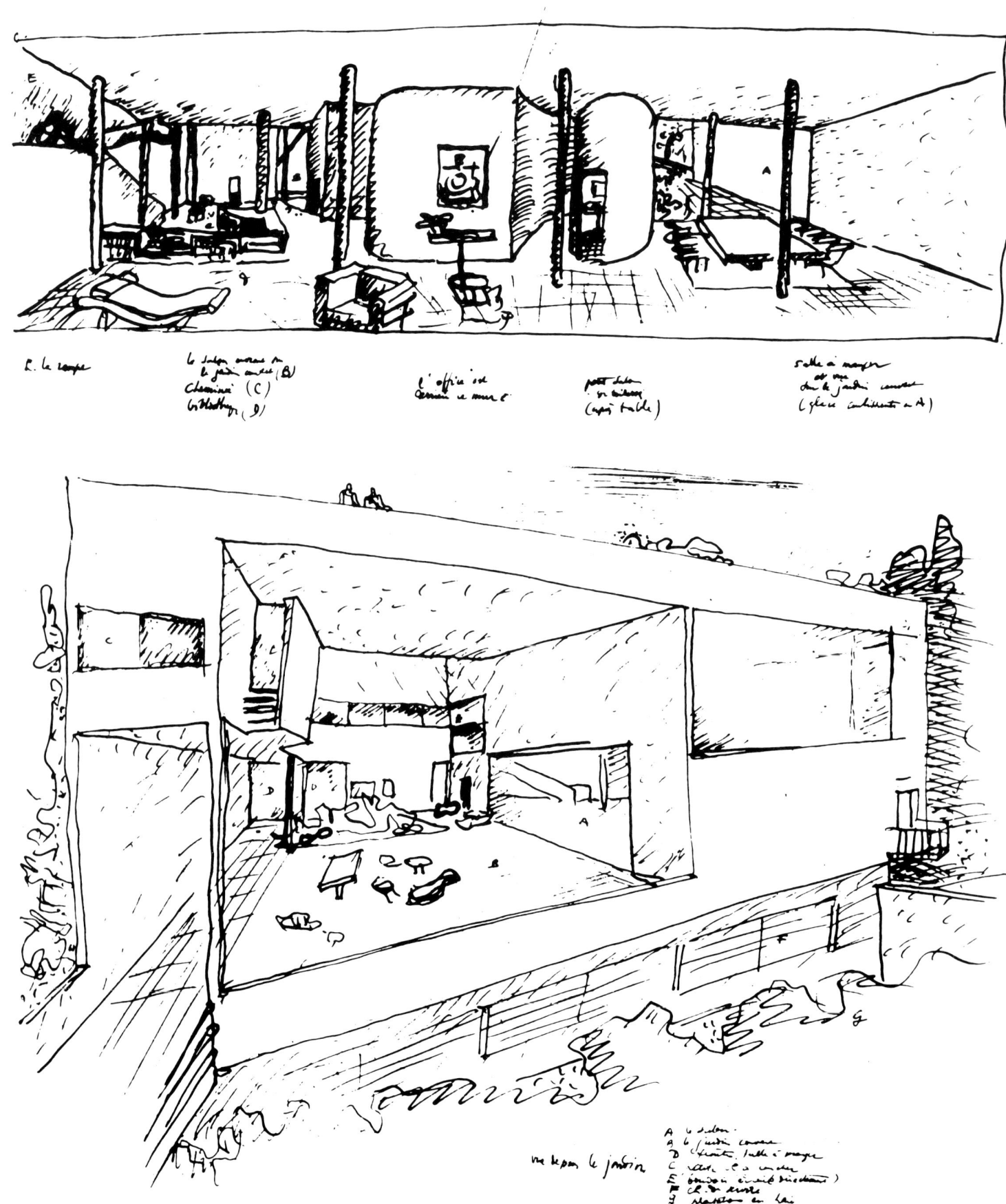

Study sketches for Villa Ocampo, Buenos Aires, Argentina, 1928 (FLC 24.235)

Introduction
ALEXANDER TZONIS

Perspective of the Palais des Nations, Geneva, Switzerland, 1927 (FLC 23.194)

ARCHITECTURE HAS TRADITIONALLY RECEIVED less attention than literature or art as a shaper of culture. Moreover, the end product, the building, has attracted greater interest than the creative process forming it. As a result, architectural drawings, the most revealing documents of this process, have tended to be seen as poor relations to the poet's notes or the sculptor's sketches, and architectural archives as secondary in comparison with the manuscript and drawing collections of libraries and museums.

This situation has changed dramatically over the last two generations. Major documentation centres of architecture have emerged around the world to house architects' archives, and the number of scholars devoted to the study of architectural thinking as a process has been mounting. From there, the idea of publishing architectural archives in their entirety was a natural step.

The publication of the archives of the Fondation Le Corbusier in Paris was the result of a growing demand by users of the archives and mounting difficulties in terms of their accessibility. It was also the outcome of the enviable success, in 1978, of another Garland publication, the sixty-three volumes of the *James Joyce Archive*. Why shouldn't an architect who was a contemporary of Joyce, and a person of equivalent cultural status, have the same treatment?

Just eight years later, in 1986, the thirty-two volumes of the *Le Corbusier Archive*, the largest publication of architectural drawings ever undertaken, are reaching all parts of the world. The publication contains all the presentation and working drawings owned by the Foundation. It also includes all the conceptual drawings and diagrams, even of those projects which never materialised; these, like drafts of a novel or incomplete sketches of a painting, help us reconstruct the context out of which an individual finished product emerged. Such fragments can be invaluable in understanding the life work of the architect and – as in the case of the novelist, the poet, the painter – in seeing it as a total project. They allow us to comprehend more deeply the world within which the work has evolved.

Soon, the *Louis Kahn Archive* and the MoMA *Mies van der Rohe Archive* will also be available. Many other similar projects are being contemplated. One hopes that the proliferation of this kind of material will make architectural thinking more accessible to a wider public; make it easier to see buildings in a less mystified, petrified manner; and assist the improvement of architectural quality.

The drawings and the introductory essays by Tim Benton, Danièle Pauly, Kenneth Frampton and Peter Serenyi which are included here represent only a small part of the whole publication. The selection has been made especially for *Architectural Design* with the aim of highlighting certain themes in Le Corbusier's work and demonstrating the syncretist and critical nature of his contribution. The short introductory essay which follows tries also to prepare the ground for these topics. *AT*

Rez de Chaussée

18 juin 1931

Syncretism and the Critical Outlook in Le Corbusier's Work
ALEXANDER TZONIS & LIANE LEFAIVRE

AS THE TWENTIETH CENTURY BEGINS TO DRAW to a close, Le Corbusier emerges more and more clearly as the key figure of the Modern Movement in architecture. This prominence is due less to his adherence to a unique position than to his capacity to create an image of modern architecture through synthesising the planning concepts and programmatic visions of many disparate groups and figures. Although Le Corbusier's work radiates the same revolutionary fervour and aura of polemics that one finds in Sant'Elia, Van Doesburg, El Lissitsky and Buckminster Fuller, he did not share their monistic and reductive tendency. On the contrary, like Stravinsky and Picasso in their respective fields, his approach was syncretic, that is to say, uniquely polyphonic, universal and inclusive, and like the composer and painter, he is both praised and condemned in the name of the modernity which he appears to represent.

Le Corbusier's syncretic approach affected the manner of his professional practice. His atelier served as a receptor for young architects who brought to it their inquisitive energy and capacity for resolving problems. At the same time, Le Corbusier was well known for dispensing with the services of his most productive personnel. These 'attritions' came about as much from the tensions which arose between different members of the team as from Le Corbusier's own fears that his studio was becoming stultified and parochial. Before others could attempt to challenge his position, he would dispute it himself by adopting a new approach reflecting the changing spectrum of modern perception. Thus while Ronchamp was his response to the Neo-expressionism and Neo-monumentalism of the early 1950s, the Philips Pavilion was his answer to the Neo-technological aspirations of the late 1950s. Towards the close of his life, his Venice Hospital project reiterated the hopes and aspirations of the younger generation of the 1960s, that is to say, it manifested the ideas of the Team X Group who, in response to a growing demand for a low-profile architecture capable of being integrated into the existing urban fabric, had openly criticised the CIAM principle of the 'functionalist' city. Many erstwhile collaborators of Le Corbusier contributed to this inter-generational debate within CIAM; figures such as Candilis, Soltan, Xénakis and Woods, to mention only a few of the prominent members of the atelier at 35 rue de Sèvres during the decade which followed the Second World War. The concept of the Venice Hospital was in fact closely linked to Shadrach Woods' 1963 project for the development of the razed Römerberg district in the centre of Frankfurt.

Le Corbusier's fear that he would lose touch with the active pursuits of the younger generation did not arise out of a vain desire to remain up-to-date but came instead out of a deep need to achieve a convincing level of synthesis in his work. Le Corbusier could not remain content with the reassuring company of a closed circle of faithful disciples. Although he favoured small avant-garde groups, little reviews and 'cafe-loci', he also promoted large international assemblies where the heterogeneous contributors would be compelled to confront one another and where he himself would be forced to question the value of his own position. Le Corbusier was able to derive the raw material for his compositions from these occasions. They provided him with the necessary opportunity to emerge as the great synthesiser. Aside from this, he was constantly travelling, restlessly discussing his projects wherever he went. While all of this might be regarded as nothing more than the typical behaviour of an ambitious architect in search of potential clients, there was more to it than that. On each of these trips, he always advanced his own ideas, but he also listened, observed, took note and acquired elements of knowledge with which to enrich his overall system. The material he brought back from his visits to New York, South America, Moscow, Northern Africa and India stacked up on his desk like the latest finds in a field under critical examination. These elements were soon incorporated into his changing and ever-expanding compendium of twentieth-century architecture and urbanism. And yet, important as such external stimuli undoubtedly were, they do not finally account for Le Corbusier's unique capability of synthesising aspects drawn from conflicting tendencies. Integral to his thought and character was an intrinsic method for conceiving and composing assemblages.

The first idea that the term 'assemblage' brings to mind is, of course, the collage, that is to say, that specific form of artistic expression which emerged with the Cubists at the beginning of the century. The technique of Cubist collage combined heterogeneous materials in a single composition. The choice of materials was determined fundamentally by formal rather than iconographic concerns. This technique generated colour, texture, rhythmic pattern, diverse scale effects, etc. And yet, while Le Corbusier's assemblages did derive in part from Cubist compositions, his intentions were functional and metaphoric; they were not devices which arose out of purely formal or visual considerations. Thus the project, the preparatory drawings and the justifying diagrams reveal different aspects of the same comprehensive search for a complex object. This multi-levelled synthesis was demonstrably different from the much simpler design strategies adopted by Ludwig Mies van der Rohe and Walter Gropius, to mention only two of Le Corbusier's contemporaries.

However, Le Corbusier's lifelong effort to achieve a complex synthesis should not be confused with mere eclecticism. In an eclectic work where pieces are taken out of different cultural contexts, the designer is usually motivated by a sense of nostalgia. The pieces are combined, one might say, out of the impossibility of recapturing a given past and out of narcissistic resignation in the face of this sense of loss. In his use of the work of other designers, Le Corbusier was not historicist in the same way as, say, Pound, Cavafy, or Eliot, who were in the habit of citing or referring to historical pieces, partly as a means of implying the incapacity of our epoch to construct a coherent culture of its own. By contrast, Le Corbusier plundered history and the works of his contemporaries in order to grasp, control and transform the given modern reality. He searched constantly for those elements with which one would have to construct the appropriate modern instrument.

At first glance it seems that Le Corbusier was only an ingenious problem-solver whose syncretic products emerged out of analogical thinking. An architect thinks analogically when he adduces a design by introducing into it elements which are derived from existing objects on the assumption that the new product and the prior object share certain functional or structural characteristics. In this way a new synthesis emerges out of pieces brought together through analogy. Under these conditions the new work seems to be a partial combination of these objects, a synthesis of their characteristics, a species of *bricolage*. Le Corbusier's analogical method led, however, to more intriguing results largely because his syncretic approach attained a more totally deconstructed and synthesised result. From this point of view, Le Corbusier can be likened to the Renaissance architects who, through analogical inference, wove together large, well-tempered theoretical constructions using ideas from movements as disparate as Vitruvianism, Neo-Platonism, Euclideanism and Neo-Ciceronianism tied with fragments of biblical exegesis and flotsam drawn from the antique masonic tradition. In a similar way Le Corbusier brought together a phenomenal number of tendencies drawn from the avant-garde movements of his time; from De Stijl, Constructivism, Dadaism, Surrealism, Expressionism, and from the technological advances exhibited by American industrial organisation and by early Soviet social experiments. In his use of analogical inference, Le Corbusier was far removed from the problem-solver. Instead, his synthetic approach led to a critical and programmatic outlook. To understand this better, we must refer to another contemporary method of analogical 'assemblage', namely, that of Dadaism, for Le Corbusier's work shares many of its characteristics.

Both Le Corbusier and the Dadaists created assemblages by removing objects from the context of their ordinary use and bringing them together in new forms of association. By forcing the objects to coexist in unprecedented contiguities, Le Corbusier, like the Dadaists, generated what have been called 'thing-signs', objects which carry new meanings, or complex statements which have a strong impact on the thought and emotions of the viewer.

This potential of objects to interact semantically was already observed by the Romantics. The poet Novalis outlined the process very clearly when he wrote: 'When completely unrelated things are brought together, by being in one place, at one time, or by some curious similarity, peculiar combinations and strange associations arise – and the thing brings to mind everything, [it] becomes the symbol of many things, and is itself signified and evoked by many things'.

Through the procedures of collision and collusion, Le Corbusier's assemblages produced not only new solutions but also new knowledge. A deeper understanding emerged about the objects which were combined together not only with regard to the form of analogy, but also with respect to the context from which the objects had been drawn. This was because each of the collected parts was seen through a different frame of reference provided by other conjunctions which were also present in the same composite. Thus distinctly different world views were merged and confronted with one another. Everyday routines were destroyed and common-sense practices, ordinarily taken for granted, were turned into extraordinary reflexive experiences. They compelled one to think *about* the objects rather than merely operate *through* them. In this way the user became conscious of larger entities and issues, such as the contemporary state of the human habitat and deeper questions underlying the problem of the habitat itself – such human dilemmas as deprivation and/or class opposition arising out of the act of dwelling in the modern world.

Like the Dada artists, Le Corbusier emerges through his analogies as an epistemologist and a moralist. And yet, unlike the Dadaists, his analogies are not nihilistic, paranoiac and destructive. They are optimistic, positive and constructive. For this reason they may be seen as legitimising new ways of living, or as giving authority to the new institutions of modern living – to working and leisure, as well as to the processes of socialisation and learning. They may thus be interpreted as operating in the manner of architectural analogies of the late Renaissance. These analogies permitted the new authority of the absolute prince to be perceived as a legitimate power by transferring to their domain – as represented by the palazzo and city – architectural elements taken from the buildings of antiquity. In this way they transferred the authority of the ancient world to the new condition. This transference implied that a common right to govern obtained between the old and the new authority since a common attribute could be found between these respective centres of power. Le Corbusier's analogical approach worked in a similar way, that is to say, it inserted elements taken from traditional living patterns into modern compositions which were destined to serve the new institutions. In this way they irrefutably legitimised the new way of life.

But this account gives only a reductive or partial view of Le Corbusier's achievement. His work when seen as a whole manifests his intention to underscore the distressing aspects of contemporary life, instead of simply masking its darker aspects. At one and the same time it was both critical and programmatic. It was optimistic and positive in the sense that it verified a collective aspiration to overcome our loss of involvement with the physical world. As the manifestation of an apparently general desire it attempted to overcome the dissolution of the community, the fragmentation of experience, and the dreariness of work. It sought to put joie de vivre back into contemporary experience; it tried to overcome the eclipse of the pleasure of seeing, walking, breathing; it attempted to slow the slaughter of the innocent in everyday life. To this end, *pilotis* and roofscapes served as a critical commentary on the present untenable conflict between culture and nature, and the irreconcilability of the public and private in the modern world. These critical allusions helped to inform the programmatic requirements of the future; they helped to establish new norms for the architects and the public.

When a building performs as a cultural object, as an icon, both critical and programmatic functions have to be fulfilled. As an icon, therefore, a building cannot simply be a graphic object; it cannot merely masquerade as an image to be looked at. In order for its full meaning to be appreciated, a building must be used; it must be consummated, so to speak, if it is to enter into the culture as a place-icon. A building is inevitably subject to many interpretations depending on the frame through which it is perceived. In theory these differing frames of reference can be applied one at a time or they can be superimposed, progressively affecting perception. In practice, however, they often compete and clash with one another, thereby engendering misfunctions, discomforts and incongruities. Le Corbusier welcomed these incongruities as a tragic testament with a cathartic potential. He saw no problem in the lack of comfort that often arose from such conflicts. An altogether different situation came into being, however, when his designs became disseminated throughout the world.

While Le Corbusier was often to be envied for his 'success', he was also frequently censured for his 'failure'. Above all he was taken to task for the poor quality of the environment that his imitators produced. These judgments as to his success or failure are ultimately irrelevant to an appreciation of his work. His elaborate projects were never intended as solutions to be duplicated. The mere re-enactment of his designs usually emphasised their disfunctional aspects while obscuring the critical and programmatic qualities inherent in his work as a whole.

Seen from this point of view, the work of Le Corbusier remains an unfinished project. His lasting contribution is to have put together a comprehensive modern framework for thinking and for posing the questions out of which many answers to contemporary problems can eventually emerge.

Villa Savoye and the Architect's Practice
TIM BENTON

L'Idée architecturale est un phénomène péremptoirement individuel, inaliénable. Il est bien de pousser l'idée jusqu'à l'état de pureté.[1]

SO EXTRAORDINARY AND ALMOST OTHERWORLDLY is the Villa Savoye in its appearance that it might seem hard to justify a reading of it that stresses the typical, the classic, or the standard. And yet, in many ways, the Villa Savoye can be shown to have resulted, at least in its general form, from a natural and spontaneous expression of the vocabulary, ideas and methodology of the work of the previous five years. But it is also essential to stress the uniqueness of the building and its particular moment in the changing attitudes of its architects.

In a lecture on October 11, 1929, in Buenos Aires, Le Corbusier himself drew attention to the place of the Villa Savoye as a culmination of a set of houses extending from the Maison La Roche-Jeanneret in 1923 via the Villas Stein and Baizeau. A drawing, included both in the Buenos Aires lecture and in the first volume of *L'Oeuvre complète* (Figure 1),[2] is designed to demonstrate the synthesis achieved in the Villa Savoye:

> The fourth type [the Villa Savoye] has the external purity of form of the second [the Villa Stein]; in the interiors, it combines the advantages and qualities of the first and third [La Roche and Baizeau]. A pure type, very generous, full of resources, too.[3]

In the lecture, he finished with a tour of the house, using two sheets of drawings to illustrate his analysis (Figures 2, 3). He noted:

> The house is a box in the air, pierced all around, without interruption, by a long window. No more hesitations about playing architectural games with space and mass. The box is in the middle of the prairies, dominating the orchard.
>
> From the interior of the vestibule, a gentle ramp leads up, almost without noticing it, to the first floor where the life of the owner is deployed: reception, bedrooms, etc. Taking their views and light from the regular perimeter of the box, these different rooms adjoin each other radially from a suspended garden which is there like a distributor of light appropriated from the sun. It is onto the suspended garden that the sliding walls of glass of the salon and several other rooms are opened in all freedom; thus the sun enters everywhere, to the very heart of the house.
>
> From the suspended garden, the ramp becomes external and leads to the roof and the solarium.
>
> The latter is also linked by three turns of a spiral staircase to the cellar dug into the earth below the *pilotis*. This spiral, pure vertical organ, is inserted freely into the horizontal composition.[4]

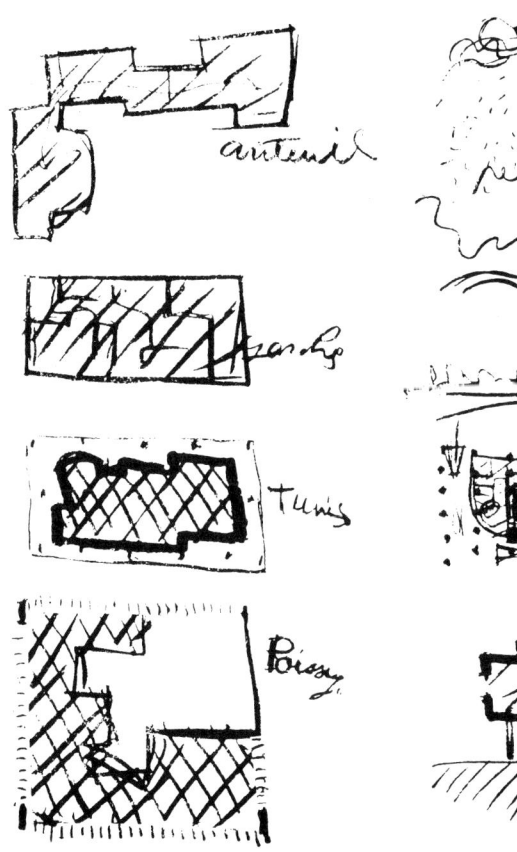

Figure 1. Four plans: Maison La Roche, Villa Stein, Villa Baizeau, and Villa Savoye (Le Corbusier, *Précisions*, p 135).

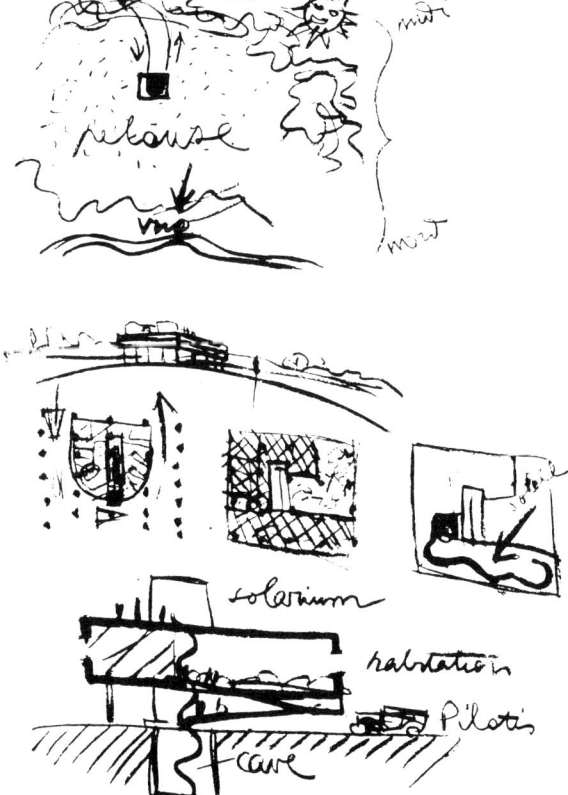

Figure 2. Sketch for Villa Savoye (Le Corbusier, *Précisions*, p 137).

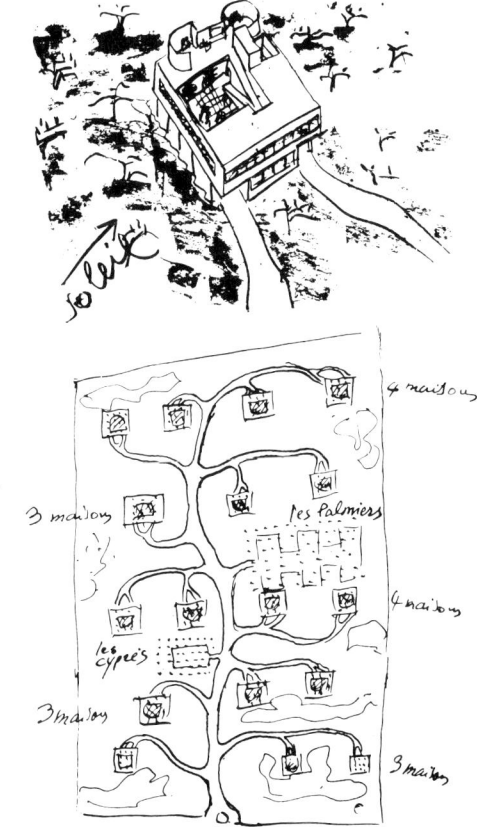

Figure 3. Sketch of Villa Savoye as a standard cell (Le Corbusier, *Précisions*, p 139).

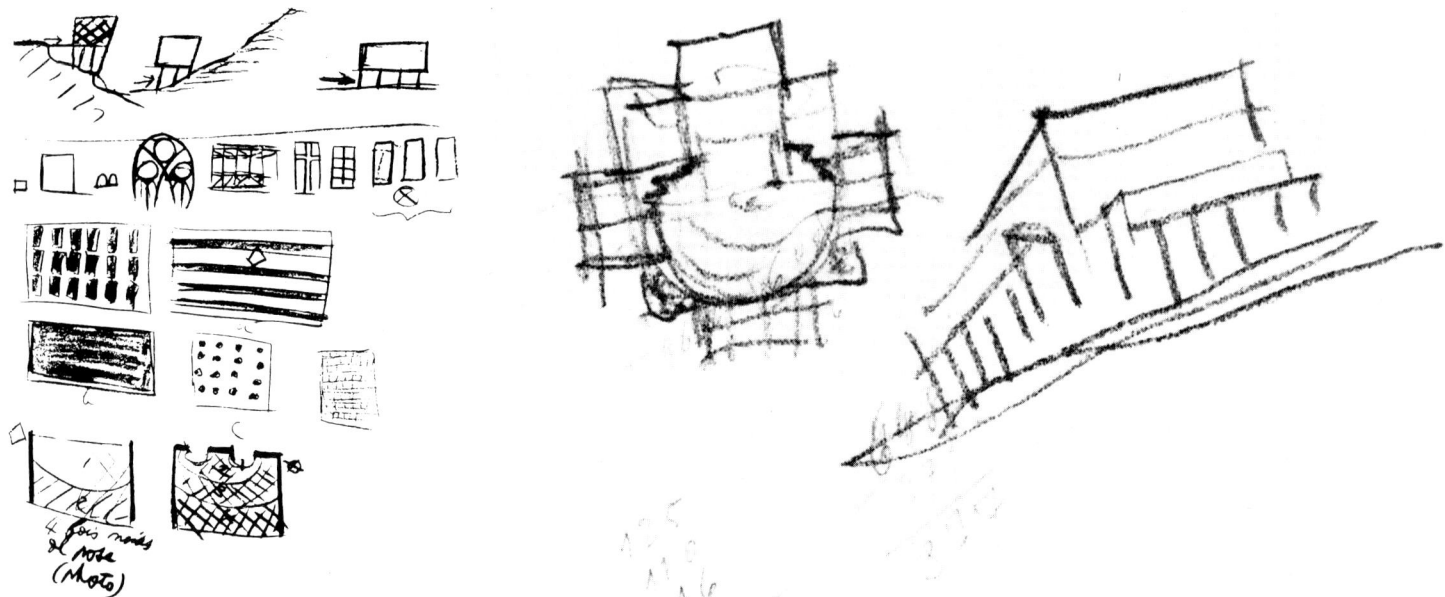

Figure 4. Studies for the window (Le Corbusier, *Précisions*, p 55).

Figure 5. Detail of marginal sketches, December 1928 (FLC 19.505).

He then went on to suggest that the house could be transplanted to Biarritz or even to the Argentinian pampas. A sketch (Figure 3) showed a tree-like formation of drives linking twenty standard Villa Savoye houses in the middle of the countryside, without spoiling it:

> The inhabitants, who will have come here because this countryside was beautiful with its country life, will contemplate it, preserved intact, from the height of their suspended garden or from the four sides of the long window. Their domestic life will be inserted into a Virgilian dream.
>
> I hope that you will not blame me for having deployed before your eyes this example of *taking liberties*. They have been taken because they have been acquired, seized from the living source of the stuff of modern life. Poetry, lyricism, produced by technology.[4]

It is worth extracting this passage in extenso because it not only sets the scene for an understanding of the design but also introduces the subtle balance between the ideal and the practical in Le Corbusier's ideas. Part of the description is specific to the site, but each feature of the house rests on standard solutions, 'certainties' acquired in Le Corbusier's 1920s practice, confirmed by the slogans in his writing. To cite only some from *Précisions*:

Architecture is circulation[5]
Architecture (more exactly, the house) consists of illuminated floors[6]
Free plan, free facade[7]
I compose with light[8]

And, as Figure 3 demonstrates, Le Corbusier saw no irony in treating the Villa Savoye as a prototype standard housing cell.

Compared with the earlier texts of the 1920s, the Buenos Aires lectures employ a relaxed and almost ecstatic vocabulary that betrays a moment of extreme confidence in the development of Le Corbusier's ideas. The repeated stress on freedom, on the body, on nature, on individuality and will, the relative lack of obsessive concern with the details of structure, materials and cost are remarkable.

Within a month of returning from South America, Le Corbusier was to embark on one of the last of his great houses, the Villa de Mandrot.[9] Here there was to be a dramatic shift in priorities – away from the hermetic purity of the box on stilts, the pure prism, the complete enclosure, the machine materials. Rough stone and plywood facings, an organic embedding in the split-level site, an extrusion of functions and, above all, a collaboration with a local Italian-born mason, Aimonetti, produced a building that, formally at least, seems to belong to a different world.

In trying to show how the Villa Savoye, at least in the first designs published in *L'Oeuvre complète 1910-1929*, emerged naturally from the imagery and dogmas of the 1920s, we will have to distinguish between the accumulated repertoire of forms in the earlier work and the arrival at certain received truths that carried a special status in his ideas. For example we might list features such as the ramp (already on show in the La Roche house), or the steel spiral staircase and the mushroom-shaped toilet extrusion on the first and second floors (both incorporated in the Stein house), or any number of details such as the fireplaces, the concrete 'tablettes', the partition walls incorporating built-in cupboards and wash basins on both sides, and so on. These, if you like, belong to the category 'tricks of the trade' and are described as such in his lectures.

But behind these devices lie the more universal discoveries; the first flat roof and roof garden, the terrace as an extension of the living area, the ideological association of vehicular circulation with the ground-floor plan, the *pilotis* as an expression not only of modern structure and a Platonic device to lift living away from the soil but also of the revolution in urban life that would follow from lifting whole cities off the plane of commercial and personal transportation. These are emblematic devices carrying 'proofs' at several levels at once. For example, the search for a standard window must be read on numerous levels (Figure 4).[10] The *fenêtre en longueur* served first as an expression of concrete structure; just as the medieval masons had a type of window related to stone pier and rib construction, so there were different windows in the Renaissance and the nineteenth century that, when 'honest', related to the nature of wall construction. But the *fenêtre en longueur* was also an interior solution, the most efficient way to distribute light. And it was a storage solution; underneath the long windows, whether in a house, or the Secretariat of the League of Nations, or the Centrosoyus building, built-in cupboards allowed for storage and concealed distribution channels for services. Finally, it was a technical solution; Le Corbusier and Pierre Jeanneret repeatedly tried to patent their sliding window, in different forms, in France and Switzerland. Furthermore, by 1928, the long window was one of two 'facade solutions' (the other being the *pan de verre* for larger buildings). The Villa Savoye showed that it had reached the status of a cliché, that is, a solution

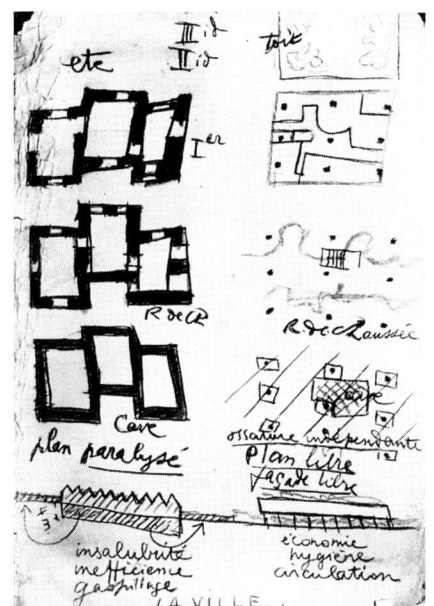 

Figure 6. Sketch made to illustrate Buenos Aires lecture, October 1929 (FLC).

Figure 7. Detail of marginal sketch for Villa Baizeau (FLC 24.983).

imposed on a problem of instinctive choice, overriding minor difficulties. Only this can explain the extension of the long southwest window across the empty first-floor terrace, and we have the evidence of the project of November 26, 1928 (Fondation Le Corbusier [FLC] 19.428), to show that Le Corbusier himself recognised some ironies in its deployment.

There are other features of the project published in *L'Oeuvre complète 1910-1929* that can be shown to have derived directly from the search for 'ideal' solutions. For example, the dimensions 5 m, 2.5 m, and 1.25 m inform the layout of the grid of *pilotis* and several other elements. And these dimensions are typical of the early design stages of other 1920s projects. Second, the functions of living on the first floor have been rigorously 'classified', in true Cartesian style: for each facade, a type of activity. To the northwest, with the beautiful view, a full-length salon; to the southwest, a sun-trap terrace; to the southeast, the bedrooms for his son and guests; to the northeast, the services. Third, Le Corbusier pursued his search for an ideal expression of circulation unifying car and man, city and country, more comprehensively than in any other project since the League of Nations drawings. The villa is linked to the Savoye town apartment at 105, rue de Courcelles, by a 30 km car drive, and this link is manifestly expressed in the plan. Furthermore, the scale of the house derives not only from Vitruvian man, but from what one must call the Vitruvian automobile: the ground-floor dimensions match the turning circle of a large car. Car circulation and human circulation meet in the hall. It will be no surprise to find a sketch (Figure 10), discussed below, that makes this identity of ramp and car circulation complete. Finally, we can perceive in the play of forms on the roof more than an expression of functions (solarium, bedroom, and associated rooms). They can also be read autonomously in Purist terms as an expression of the aesthetic certainties of the Phileban solids.

In the completed building, these 'type' solutions are less visible, or absent (Figures 14, 15). In the later stages of the design, the pressure of practical solutions introduced a more pragmatic and picturesque sequence of visual sensations which can be referred to the Corbusian notion of the *promenade architecturale*. The development from the Platonic to the phenomenological during the design process is itself characteristic of Le Corbusier's 1920s work.

A tension between the ideal and the pragmatic runs through all Le Corbusier's work and theory. Many of the 1920s houses were designed for relatively hard-up clients with difficult requirements and awkward urban sites that allowed for only one or two visible facades. The struggle to adapt the dogmas of his theory to these problematic circumstances lends much of the interest and some of the content of his work. The Villa Savoye appeared to offer an 'ideal' brief to design a perfect house in a perfect site for a perfect, or at least uncomplaining, client. The obvious parallel with the Villa Rotunda of Palladio is supported by an intriguing marginal sketch on a sheet of details datable to December 1928 (Figure 5). In both cases, the 'ideal' villa can be defined as a four-facade house on a hill; both stand in relation to the other work of the two architects in comparable ways. To put it another way, the Villa Savoye was an unconstrained response to the dogmas of the Five Points.[11] The sketches illustrating these in the Buenos Aires lectures provides a schema for the Villa Savoye more naturally than for any other house (Figure 6).

To support this analysis, it is important to recognise that key features of the Villa Savoye design can be shown to have emerged from the early stages of designing another house 'with a view', the Villa Baizeau in Tunis. The Baizeau site was a narrow one, a crucial constraint on the whole design. The 'natural plan', as Le Corbusier emphasised in *Une Maison – un palais*, was square.[12] But the first two projects for the Villa Baizeau also represented the problem of bringing cars across the front of the facade to offload passengers into the entrance hall before turning into a garage.[13] The sketches for the smaller second scheme even look superficially like the Villa Savoye.[14] This was in March 1928, and on one of the elevation drawings for this second scheme can be seen a selection of perspective sketches that are so strikingly like the Villa Savoye that they must be accounted for (Figures 7, 8).[15] My argument is not that there is any material connection between the two commissions at this stage, since there is no evidence that the architect had even met the Savoyes until six months later. Rather, these sketches represent doodles fantasising on the potential of the Baizeau scheme released from the constraints of site. The hovering first-floor living area, with its long window and extravagant sculptural extrusion on the roof are, it seems to me, purely an instinctive extrapolation of the Corbusian language, responding to the cliff-top site and the notion of free circulation at ground level.

Superimposed over part of another drawing for the Baizeau scheme (FLC 8.507), this time datable to around August 30, there is a square plan with garaging for three cars and a bullnosed vestibule (like the Maison Cook) adjoining what must be a ramp (Figure 9).[16] This time, I believe that the Savoye scheme was in his mind, since the dimensions would seem to be consistent.

Two sheets of sketchbook that appear to have been drawn during the adaptation of the Villa Meyer drawings for the Villa Ocampo (in September 1928) give a more explicit sign of the origins of the Villa Savoye (Figures 10, 11).[17] This time, the association with the Poissy site is much stronger. We see the trees, the domed site, the oblique angle of the boundary wall, the access from the southeast and, most significant of all, an indication of an orientation on the angle ('S' on the plan), all of which describe the Poissy site precisely.

What makes these drawings almost unique in the 1920s corpus is their vagueness and ambiguity. Le Corbusier is responding here to ideas at a high level of abstraction. They include scribbled outlines indicating little more than an L-shaped or Z-shaped configuration responding to the opposed pull of sun and view.[18] But they also include worked-out plans, section and site plans of a house whose most extraordinary feature is an access drive from the southeast that rises on *pilotis* to first-floor level and passes an L-shaped *porte-cochère* projecting from the first-floor plan before descending through the plan to ground level to a garage to the left and an exit drive to the right. So abstract and impractical is this idea that it involves running the cars through the corner supports of the building, indicated by two arrows on the plan.

And yet, the first-floor plan includes the essential features of the Villa Savoye today: salon to the northwest, terrace to the southwest, services to the northeast, and some kind of accommodation on the remaining side. The service staircase, as in the developed first project, runs parallel to the ramp. Another plan is more ambiguous about the cars, apparently relying on the fall of the land to allow pedestrian access to the first floor up a short ramp.

My contention, therefore, is that prefiguring ideas for the Villa Savoye can be found among the drawings for other schemes in 1928 and that these ideas emerged from a level of idealist abstraction based on a synthesis of the earlier work.

It is my view that, almost unique among the 1920s houses, the Villa Savoye is a 'free' design – an example, indeed, of 'taking liberties'.[19]

Before looking in any detail at the design history of the house, I would like to make some observations about reading architectural plans as evidence and about my own methodological assumptions. William Curtis, whose book on the Carpenter Center has set standards in the analysis of Corbusian drawings, wrote recently:[20] 'Unfortunately, the evidence of Le Corbusier's sketches for the Villa Savoye is incomplete, patchy, and not firmly dated'.[21] Having studied several buildings of this period, all with different kinds of lacunae in the evidence, I now feel confident that this is not accurate.[22] True, few of the 316 drawings for the villa and the lodge are dated, but only a handful cannot, I believe, be placed with accuracy (within a few days) into the order of things.

My own procedure has been to divide the drawings into five 'projects' for the main villa and one for the lodge (Projects A-E and Project L), each one subdivided into variants but fixed in relation to specific dated drawings. Thus, Project A can be dated to the period leading up to October 10, 1928; Project B to November 5-7, 1928; Project C to November 7-26, 1928; Project D to December 1928-February 1929; Project E to February 1929 onwards. The dated drawings for the lodge extend from April 27, 1929 to February 24, 1930.[23]

An object lesson in the pitfalls awaiting the historian who assembles drawings according to a plausible 'development' towards the finished design can be drawn from a study of a set of pencil numbers added to the corners of the key plans for the building. These arrange an 'order' that might seem logical but one that is contradicted by a weight of evidence and that cannot possibly be sustained. The first twenty-five pencil numbers refer to the drawings of the middle and end of November (Project C); the next group are from the first project of October (Project A), followed by drawings datable to November 6-7 (Project B).

There is no doubt about the main stages of the design and the causes for rejecting or modifying them. During September, the scheme eventually published in *L'Oeuvre complète, 1910-1929*[24] was developed through a number of minor variants to be presented to the client between October 6 and 14, 1928. That this project was taken seriously by the architects is shown by the number of detailed drawings, more even than for the design as built, and by a complete set of tenders and costings that were assembled during late October and early November.[25] Why was this project not built?

Here we must enter into a discussion of the client and of the economics of the enterprise. In many cases of Le Corbusier's domestic architecture, and the still-running saga of the Villa Baizeau was a case in point, the reasons for abandoning one design and starting again can be documented in terms of a straightforward conflict with the client's intention. For the Villa Savoye, we have two versions of the client's brief, a list of requirements by Madame Savoye herself and a sheet of notes of a meeting by Pierre Jeanneret. We also have a list of comments by Madame Savoye on the drawings of the October scheme.[26] Although there are several points in which Le Corbusier's design does little justice to Madame Savoye's original stipulations, she herself makes no mention of them. Instead, her remarks are mostly concerned with details of electric power points, the separation of the wine cellar from the fruit store, and so on.[27] On one matter that might have been substantive – her request that her bedroom should be oriented to the east – no effect can be seen in the intermediary designs of November, although the December project does indeed shift her bedroom accordingly. But if Madame Savoye was not the cause of the abandonment of the first project, where must we look for an explanation? Fortunately, the answer is straightforward and characteristic in kind of all Le Corbusier's houses.

The tenders for the first project came in at the beginning of November, and on November 5 Pierre Jeanneret began to total up the estimates. However he worked it out, and with whatever marginal cuts to individual tenders, the result came out at about 785,060 francs, and that was including a mere guess for the lodge and nothing for architect's fees.[28] That this sum was very much more than the Savoye family had intended to pay for a summer cottage is not a matter of guesswork. When, in December, Pierre Jeanneret wrote with the costings of what he called his third project, he was specific about the cuts that had been effected in response to the client's wishes.[29]

If there is one factor that unites every domestic design by Le Corbusier and Pierre Jeanneret that I have studied, it is that the first projects are always too expensive and always need trimming down. This was the case, for example, with the La Roche house, the Stein house, and the Baizeau house. But the remedy, in each case, was relatively obvious. La Roche lost the ground floor under the gallery, the Steins lost the service wing that had projected on one side, and for the second design for Lucien Baizeau, Le Corbusier simply chopped a bay off the length of the house. The Villa Savoye, however, was a different matter. The first project was not only based on the canonic 5 x 5 m grid, it was also founded on the dimension of the turning circle of a large car and the space required to bring a gently sloping ramp up through the house without dividing the plan in two. To reduce the area of the Villa Savoye by one bay in each direction, the obvious solution, would have rendered both features of the planned space inoperative. But Le Corbusier and Pierre Jeanneret embarked on a series of

Figure 8. Detail of marginal sketch for Villa Baizeau (FLC 24.983).

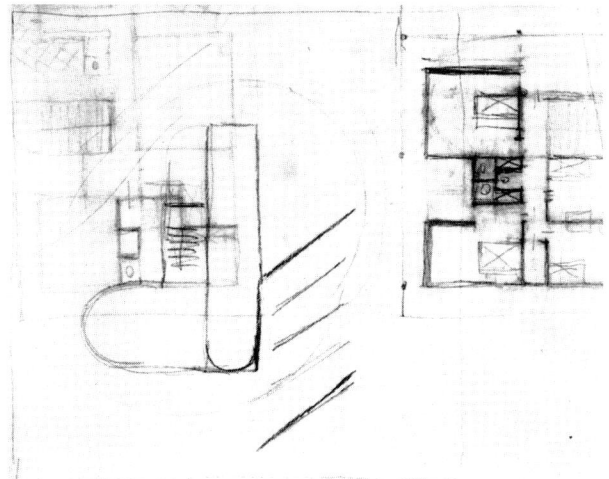

Figure 9. Detail of plan superimposed on plan for Villa Baizeau (FLC 8.507).

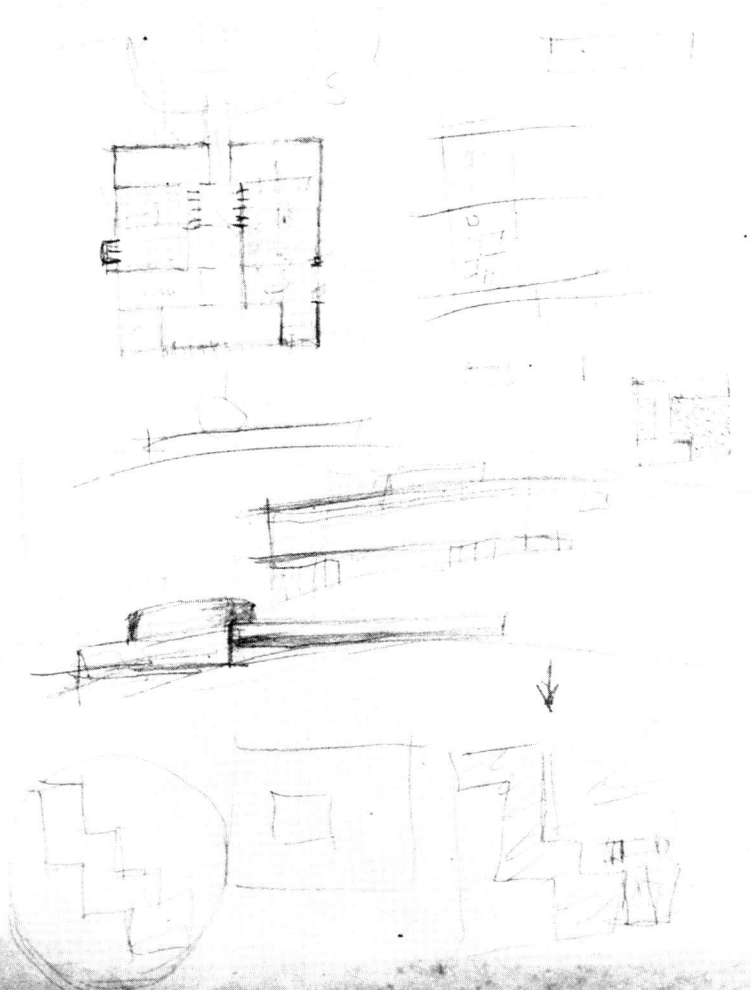

Figures 10 (above) and 11 (above right). Details of sketchbook pages, September 1928 (FLC 31.044)

designs (Project B) that, while retaining the basis of the first- and second-floor plans, dismantled virtually every other feature of the design that rendered it formally recognisable and intellectually unique.[30] The ramp, the U-shaped ground-floor plan with its free-flowing concept of circulation, the *fenêtre en longueur*, the image of the *boîte en l'air*, the whole horizontality and naturalness of the project were sacrificed. What emerged by November 26 (Project C) was an extraordinary play of volumes and spaces, incorporating a brutal juxtaposition of vertical staircase mass (with a *pan de verre* window) and horizontal planes.[31]

This was a short-lived episode in the design. What I have called Project B, including the designs of November 6 and 7 and associated drawings, includes only fourteen drawings, exclusively in plan, but it does incorporate calculations of areas from which an estimate of cost can be made (c 350,583 francs).[32] The next project went somewhat further. In thirty-seven drawings, for a preliminary idea and two variants, we find sections and elevations as well as plans and another set of calculations of areas that would have given a crude building cost of c 464,269 francs.[33] This project was submitted to the client on November 26 in four sheets incorporating plans, elevations and sections, but there is no record of the client's response to it or of the reasons for abandoning the scheme. It is fair to assume, however, that Le Corbusier had little enthusiasm for this extraordinary departure and that as soon as he and Pierre Jeanneret had thought through the original problem, that of reducing the cost of the first project, the solution quickly presented itself.

Three main ingredients were needed. First, instead of relying on the tender for the first project by his regular builder Summer (originally 482,000 francs, but reduced by negotiation to 433,000 francs),[34] Le Corbusier turned to a verbal estimate by C Cormier of 350,000 francs, noted on a page of sums dated November 5, 1928,[35] and proceeded to calculate as follows:

Cormier (1 Project)	350,000	
Suppression top storey	58,000	
	292,000	
Reduction 10% area	29,000	
	263,000	
The rest	150,000	
	413,000	
Lodge	30,000	
(Total)	443,000	
	44,000	(architect's honoraria)
(Grand Total)	487,000[36]	

On the basis of this ad hoc estimation, which turned out to be just over half the actual cost of completing the building, Le Corbusier presented a set of drawings to M Savoye on December 21.[37]

This was essentially the first project, reduced from a 5 m grid to 4.75 metres (giving an area of roughly 19 m x 21.5 m instead of 20 m x 22.5 m) and with the master bedroom squeezed into the first-floor plan, leaving only a staircase housing and solarium on the top floor.

Two points must be made about this exercise. First, there can be little doubt that Le Corbusier and Pierre Jeanneret practised a conscious deception on their client as to the actual cost. When the tenders for the new scheme came in, in February 1929, the total presented to M Savoye amounted to 558,690 francs.[38] In this total, no estimate was included for the entrance gate and driveway (c 20,000 francs), or for landscape gardening and planting (c 48,000 francs), nor was a proper tender for the lodge obtained (it was not even designed at this stage). At several points where tradesmen had submitted alternative estimates using cheaper materials, these had been adopted, although there can be no doubt that Le Corbusier always intended to use the more expensive versions. For example, Le Corbusier was so adamant about the use of plate glass for his windows that he had risked a major row with the client of the Cook house over this issue. And yet the February costings included ordinary glass and the use of distemper for internal walls and plaster render for external walls (both changed in the course of execution for the much more expensive use of oil paint and special 'jurassite' exterior finish and the use of Cimentol paint).[39] Furthermore, a month after the contracts to builder and tradesmen had been issued, the design was changed quite substantially, in a set of drawings that are sufficiently different to warrant the nomination of Project E.[40] The staircase was rotated and made open all round; there were substantial changes (two sets, in fact) to the apartment for the chauffeur on the ground floor; expensive alterations to the dimensions of the ground floor involved the addition of 9 cm to the height of the windows, which had already been manufactured; and repeated alterations to the plumbing and central heating conduits allowed the builder to put in for extras amounting to nearly double the contracted estimate.[41] The result was a building history more than usually fraught with wrangles over cost and depredations to the structure due to post hoc piercing of the brittle partition walls and floor slabs. A similar story can be told of the Villa Stein: again contracts were issued on plans that were not in their final form. We must conclude that Le Corbusier and Pierre Jeanneret had great difficulty completing the design process except under the urgent pressure of building activity in progress. Building work was already under way in April 1929, when the final set of plans was produced, and the production of drawings extended until June, by which time construction had reached the first floor.[42]

What use are we to make of this information? Building houses is a notoriously messy business, and there may well be architects who regularly experience the order of difficulties and stresses that seemed to accompany all Le Corbusier's undertakings. But there is no doubt that Le Corbusier had a peculiar horror of the practicalities of building, although he left all the routine supervision and designing work to Pierre Jeanneret and the assistants. Indeed, in 1934 he felt able to say:

> I must admit that I am not au fait with this [a complaint about the central heating], which was a matter between Mme Savoye and my associate Pierre Jeanneret . . . Never having followed this affair, it is difficult for me to offer an exact opinion . . . [43]

Le Corbusier's direct involvement with clients or tradesmen was restricted to the more forceful begging letters or threats, and his intervention in the design process was as much by scribbled comments and marginal sketches as by full-scale drafting. Again, however, I feel that in the case of the Villa Savoye, the main explanation for this is that, having worked out the main ideas at a very early stage, he had little interest in seeing the design through all of its ramifications. He was involved in the drawings for the abortive November projects and in the first sketches for the December scheme, but the bulk of the elaboration of the final version was by Pierre Jeanneret and the assistants, of whom the most consistent contributor was Albert Frey.[44] In Le Corbusier's dualistic dialectic between ideal and practical his own impact was invariably formal and generalising, adding breadth and depth to solutions and contributing the curved, flowing forms to Pierre Jeanneret's more patient elaboration of planning spaces.

But Le Corbusier also worked on dense, detailed drawings in which major decisions were taken and worked through. The sheet FLC 19.583, drawn to a scale of 1:100, embodies the essential features of the first project and is in Le Corbusier's hand. A

Figure 12. Villa Savoye, view from the northwest. (Photo Tim Benton)

Figure 13. Villa Savoye, view from the west. (Photo Tim Benton)

similar sheet, FLC 19.634, probably by Pierre Jeanneret, must have been drawn shortly after, incorporating some minor modifications and a first-floor plan at a larger scale of 1:50. Although it is possible that Le Corbusier made some preliminary sketches for 19.583 which have been lost, the evidence of other projects would not support it, as he declared: 'Now that I have appealed to your *spirit of truth*, I would like to give you architectural students the *hatred of drawings*. Architecture is created in the head'.[45]

There are some drawings of the site that may precede this one, and a curiously anomalous group of sections and perspectives that do not correspond exactly to any of the variants for the first project, but I assume that the latter must be explained by simple deviations among the assistants and a failure to read Le Corbusier's dense sketches on FLC 19.583 with sufficient accuracy. This key drawing incorporates a number of minor features that were altered before the definitive set of drawings for the first project was elaborated: square *pilotis*, a *fenêtre en longueur* instead of a full-height window to the hall, a three-quarter-height window to the salon on the terrace side, the characteristic addition of a spiral staircase from the second-floor terrace to the roof, and so forth. None of these changes represents a fundamental shift in the design concept. The forty-eight drawings of the final version of the first project include several sections, elevations and plans at a scale of 1:20, mostly intended to provide information for the fourteen interior details, elevations and axonometrics at this scale. The inked presentation plans, sections and elevations were invariably at a scale of 1:50. It is symbolic of the priorities in the design that the first of the stencil-numbered presentation drawings, FLC 19.412 (LC 1096), should have been for the first-floor plan and that, as in most of his schemes, this should have been labelled *rez-de-chaussée*, the real ground floor being labelled *soubassement*.

When we come to the decisive departure from the idea of the first project, around November 5, 1928, my judgment is that the first drawings are also of the first-floor plan. Three drawings (FLC 25.036, 25.043 and 25.039, among the Baizeau drawings) indicate a plan not dissimilar to that of the first project for the Villa Savoye, but on a grid of 3 m x 5 m (17.5 m x 15 m) and without the ramp. There follows a set of loosely drawn charcoal drawings of all three plans (FLC 19.659, 19.699, 19.698) in which the disastrous consequences for the ground-floor plan are first encountered and in which a partial remedy is sought by extending the cantilever to the sides (southwest and northeast) in order to add as much breadth to the salon as possible, so that room can be made for the kitchen and pantry. Another set, dated November 6, 1928, was then worked up from these charcoal sketches (FLC 19.660, 19.645, 19.636) probably by Pierre Jeanneret, followed by the November 7 variant (FLC 19.663, 19.662, 19.714, 19.523, 19.661) in which the cantilever is returned to the northwest and southeast facades. What emerges from studying the development of these sketches is that the residual curvature of the ground-floor plan and the awkward arrangement of the arrival and departure of cars become untenable. On the first floor, the plan becomes increasingly clearly divided into three slices, with the central portion given over to the staircase block. It is this theme, that of a dominant staircase mass, that led to the next solution.

A single drawing, FLC 19.700, with four plans on it, builds on the motif of a circular staircase rising through the house, scattering the organs of each floor plan on either side. The explosion of the ground-floor plan is indicated clearly. At this point, the clear articulation into a grid of 5 m bays loses clarity, and the next scheme abandons the regular grid almost completely.

Project C can be divided into two variants by some minor adjustments, such as the direction of the staircase (clockwise, then counterclockwise), some details of fenestration, and the provision of balconies on the roof of the second-floor rooms.

Figure 14. Villa Savoye, spiral staircase, in hall. (Photo Tim Benton)

Thirty-seven drawings, including FLC 19.700, were devoted to this scheme. Three points could be made about it. The *pan de verre* facing the staircase block was very much in Le Corbusier's mind, with the League of Nations scheme behind him and the Centrosoyus still in play. Furthermore, the great window, facing southwest, produced a spectacular effect on the almost windowless northeast side, now the facade you would see on arrival by car. Light striking down through the open staircase hall would have brilliantly illuminated the ground-floor hall window facing northeast, in what would otherwise have been a dark, blocklike silhouette. Second, as already mentioned, the presentation of the *pan de verre* on the southwest facade involved the opening out of 'rhetorical' window facing the end of the ramp on the top floor, which survived as a reminder of the placing of the master bedroom in the first project.

The development of the presentation drawings for the December 17 scheme shows every sign of being rushed through with unseemly haste. It is difficult to be certain which drawings preceded the stencil-numbered set and which were prepared between December 1928 and February 1929, when the tenders for the new project were called in. Few major modifications are involved, apart from a reduction in size of the cellar. It is clear that no real thought was given to the main lines of the design until some time between February 21 and March 9, 1929, when the basement plan FLC 19.436 (LC 2089) was produced in which the staircase has been reoriented to its final direction. But the set of final plans did not emerge until April 12, by which time a second important decision had been taken, to remove the chauffeur's apartment

Figure 15. Villa Savoye, ramp. (Photo Tim Benton)

from the ground-floor plan and place it, with that of the gardener, in a double lodge. Other changes differentiate the March drawings from those of April: modifications to Madame Savoye's bathroom, the arrangement of corridors to the son's room and guest room, the placing of the service doors in the setbacks on the southeast side, and so on.

The history of the design of the lodge is intriguing for two reasons. First, it is quite clear that Le Corbusier conceived of the lodge in terms of the plans he had made in 1928 for the Maisons Loucheur, semi-detached houses to be dry-assembled using steel structure and zinc-lined walls. The first designs for the lodge postdate the final version of the plans for the main villa of April the window over the terrace, always a rather controversial idea. It was this single factor, as much as the projection of the back wall of the garage onto the plane of the southwest facade, that led Le Corbusier to close off the two 'wings' of the first-floor plan on that side. Third, the exploded ground-floor plan allowed Le Corbusier to 'classify' the organs of the circulation and service bedrooms with even more clarity than in the first project. The chauffeur's family and the two maids were given separate *Existenzminimum* cells that are so close in design to the Maison Minimum or indeed the lodge plans that they could be mistaken for each other (see FLC 20.753).

In all these things we can see Le Corbusier's mind working to gather what he can from the wreckage of his scheme and associate it to his general principles. Above all, the space created for the staircase on the first-floor plan led to the solution that resolved the problem of the first project. If the salon, kitchen and pantry could be accommodated on the northwest front, why not move the son's and guest bedrooms around and fit in the master bedroom on the southeast, where Madame Savoye had explicitly wanted it? Furthermore, the thematic introduction of a contrast of vertical with horizontal was not lost. Although the December scheme involved the deployment of a service staircase that would have had little formal impact on the interior, being enclosed by a wall, the April emendation revealed the 'pure vertical organ' that may have made nonsense of the function of a staircase intended to move servants discreetly from bedroom and ironing room to kitchen but nonetheless adds enormously to the drama of the entrance hall. Another dramatic discovery in December was the 12, 1929, and were for a double house, to include both the chauffeur and the gardener.[46] Second, this decision, which would have involved a lodge costing 76,300 francs instead of the 30,000 estimated in February, depended on the decision to remove the chauffeur's apartment from the ground floor of the villa to make room for an additional suite for guests.[47] This guest apartment was actually constructed and had to be re-adapted for use by the chauffeur after June with a new wall and additional plumbing when the lodge proved too expensive.[48] The small single lodge was designed during June, passing through three variants to the final scheme of July 7. The cost is difficult to disentangle from the accounts, but it was around 50,000 francs (including a contract of 32,000 francs for the builder).[49]

The lodge is an emblematic building, forming a visual and conceptual bridge between the forms of the Villa Savoye, with its demonstration *fenêtre en longueur* hovering over *pilotis*, and the mass-housing prototypes that since the Dom-ino and Citrohan schemes had included numerous variations of the Maison Minimum.

At this point we must ask what real effects the circuitous design history of the building had on the Villa Savoye as we see it. First, we can point to the forms that must be read in terms of an accretion and transference of meaning. The bellied curve of the master bedroom in the first project becomes an empty shell, a solarium (Figure 12). The window, which originally lit the bedroom, now serves as a rhetorical gesture, the culmination of the *promenade architecturale*. In many of Le Corbusier's designs, master bedrooms have the curving walls and expansive form connoting both luxury and an anthropomorphic reference. But these forms also worked, in the Villa Savoye, at a purely formal level, as a sensuous response to the purity of the prism below. We saw this in the sketches for an unparticularised building (FLC 24.983). It is typical of Le Corbusier that he tried to put this sensual, fleshy feel back into the master bedroom with the elaborate 'swimming-pool' bathroom fittings and concrete 'chaise longue' posture slab. The long false window screening the terrace on the southwest side is made more paradoxical by the aerofoil shape of the *pilotis* (Figure 13). A similar detail appears in the *pilotis* of the ramp (Figure 15). We have noted the significance of the free-standing spiral staircase (Figure 14). Most of the losses in clarity, the complex variations in grid, the complications of the classification of facade into distinct living functions, the tangle of corridors and toilets on the first floor, have little overriding impact. The basic imagery is almost identical, so much so that plans for the first project are frequently reproduced accompanying the photographs of the completed buildings.[50] And yet much of the impact of the ramp today depends on the contrast with the open vertical staircase (Figure 15), a juxtaposition only added in the final stages of the design.

Sadly, the painting scheme for the house has not survived in the documents, apart from some mention of burnt umber, grey and black for some of the concrete fitments, and blue for the salon walls.[51] An interesting reference is provided by Celio the painter, who charged extra for repainting the ground-floor external walls 'red, then after new instructions, green'.[52] A sheet showing the

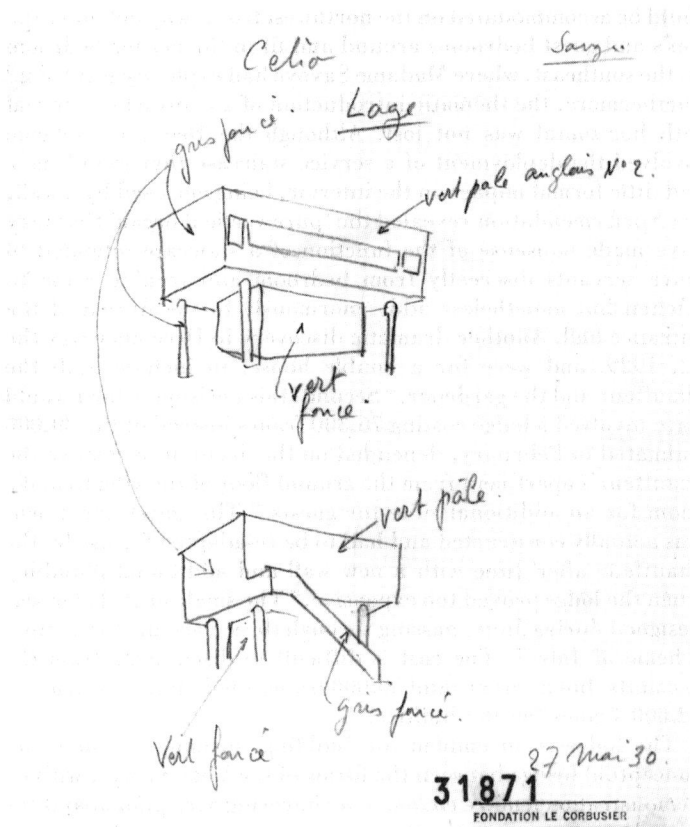

Figure 16. Photocopy of colour indications for lodge, dated 27 May 1930 (FLC Archive, Doc 124).

painting scheme for the lodge confirms the use of dark green for the ground-floor walls, dark grey for the sides, and 'pale English Green no 2' for the main wall on the first floor, facing the entrance (Figure 16).[53] Clearly, lodge and villa shared the rooted colours of vegetation, the colours of the prairie and the orchard, and this idea overcame the more usual use of russet or red for the shaded lower portion of Le Corbusier's domestic buildings (for example, those at the Weissenhof-Siedlung). Finishes in the villa generally were upgraded substantially during construction, as has been mentioned. The first project would have used rubber flooring not only for the ramp but for the bedrooms as well, but Madame Savoye insisted on parquet for the latter. Much money was spent on the exotic turquoise mosaic surfacing of the bath and surround for Madame Savoye's bathroom in *graiblanc*.[54] The light fittings included a trough with twenty-eight light bulbs (15 watts each) running along the joint between wall and ceiling in the master bedroom, and a glass tube with forty light bulbs (25 watts) was designed and introduced spanning the salon.[55] Most of these, along with the windows, were replaced in the 1960s, after damage sustained during and after the war. A surprisingly large bill, contested by the client, was submitted by Le Corbusier's favourite landscape gardener.[56]

Le Corbusier was sensitive about the technical quality of his buildings, but the material history of the Villa Savoye is a sorry one. The total cost, not counting various direct payments by the clients that are not recorded in the Le Corbusier archives, was around 815,000 francs, but the story does not end there. Right up until 1937 the house was providing a catalogue of disastrous technical failings. The first of a litany of pathetic letters from Madame Savoye is dated March 24, 1930;[57] the terrace, garage and cellar were flooded, rain was coming in through the boudoir window, the noise of the rain on the skylight over Madame's bathroom was 'infernal and would stop us sleeping', and so on. On April 30, four months after the builder had claimed that his work was substantially finished, work on the plumbing, central heating and wiring channels was causing severe problems. Cormier included a sketch showing one of the partition walls completely cracked from top to bottom after the attentions of the electrician. The central heating engineers, by bending their pipes between a *pilotis* and the downpipe in the garage, had pried the latter loose at the top, causing more flooding on the terrace above.[58] The installation of the electric cooking apparatus in June 1930 was held up, causing extra expense, due to the lack of sufficiently powerful wiring.[59] Although Le Corbusier wrote claiming his final account of honoraria on September 6, 1930,[60] repairs and finishing continued throughout the winter, and it is not certain that the house was permanently inhabited before the spring of 1931 (painting was still in progress in July), although in a letter of July 13, 1931, Le Corbusier claimed that the house had been lived in for a year. On December 19, 1931, Cormier reported that there were 4-5 cm of water in the cellar after a rainstorm due to the siting of a land drain (needed due to the lack of mains drainage for the servants' rooms) just by the southeast wall.[61] In April 1934, water was still penetrating into the cellar; the central heating system was proving inadequate, requiring a more powerful boiler; the walls were producing saltpetre deposits, and humidity was still a problem. On September 7, 1936, Madame wrote again:

> It's raining in the hall, it's raining in the ramp, and the wall of the garage is absolutely soaked. What's more, it's still raining in my bathroom, which floods every time it rains.[62]

Furthermore, the lodge was uninhabitable because of condensation and humidity, and these problems recurred in September 1937. As Madame Savoye tartly remarked: 'Nevertheless, there always seems to be someone in your office to send me visitors, if not to reply to my letters'.[63] On October 11, 1937 she wrote:

> After numerous demands, you have finally accepted that this house which you built in 1929 is uninhabitable. Your ten-year responsibility is at stake and I have no need to foot the bill. Please render it habitable immediately. I sincerely hope that I will not have to take recourse to legal action.[64]

After agreeing to the measures to be taken, Le Corbusier concluded that correspondence with a letter to M Savoye:

> Anyway, I would like to convince you confidently that we will do our best to satisfy you and that you must consider us as the *friends of your house*. Furthermore, I would like to remain your friend too; our relations have always been trustworthy. I am and will always remain the friend of my clients.[65]

And on an earlier occasion, on June 28, 1931, with parts of the house still unfinished, he had written to thank Madame for dinner:

> You should place on the table of the hall downstairs a book pompously labelled 'Golden Book', and each of your visitors should inscribe their name and address. You'll see how many fine autographs you will collect. This is what La Roche does in Auteuil, and his Golden Book has become a veritable international directory. Having said that, let me thank you once again, yourself and M Savoye, for all the pleasure and real joy it has given me to find your house so perfectly inhabited. It's not that usual. One final word. Perhaps the two planters in the entrance hall would gain by being sown with vivacious, abundant, high, unruly plants.[66]

Art, for Le Corbusier, transcended reality.

Notes

Abbreviations used in the notes for reference to drawings and documents:

FLC: Fondation Le Corbusier rubber stamp numbers, added to the drawings c 1973.
LC: The stencilled numbers placed on presentation drawings by the atelier and logged in a 'Black Book', usually with a precise date and increasingly, after 1929, with the name of the draftsman.

Doc: Pencil numbers used to identify the individual sheets of documents in the boxes of archive material at the Fondation Le Corbusier. These numbers may become redundant as a result of a rationalisation of the archive.

1 Le Corbusier, *Précisions sur un état présent de l'architecture et de l'urbanisme* (Paris: Vincent, Fréal, 1930; 1960 edition), p 134.
2 Published in *Précisions*, p 134.
3 *Précisions*, pp 135-136.
4 *Précisions*, pp 136-138.
5 *Précisions*, pp 136-138.
6 *Précisions*, p 48.
7 *Précisions*, p 42.
8 *Précisions*, p 132.
9 See Bruno Reichlin, 'La Ville de Mandrot à le Pradet (Var) 1929-32', in *Le Corbusier: La Ricerca paziente* (Lugano: 1980). One drawing for this project includes a copy of the Villa Savoye on a neighbouring site (FLC 22.309).
10 *Précisions*, p 54 ff.
11 Seven points are listed in 'The Plan of the Modern House': 'free plan, free facade, independent skeleton, long windows or *pans de verre*, *pilotis*, roof garden, and the interior equipped with *casiers* and stripped of furniture', *Précisions*, p 123.
12 Le Corbusier, *Une Maison – un palais* (Paris: Crès, 1929), p 7.
13 Tim Benton, 'La Matita del Cliente', *Rassegna* 3 (1980): 17-24. The five main stages of the design of the Villa Baizeau in Tunis are recounted in this article.
14 See FLC 24.985. The dates for the five main stages of the Baizeau design are as follows: Project A – February 16-24, 1928; Project B – March 9; Project C – end of June; Project D – 1st variant, August 30, 2nd variant, September 18; Project E – a number of variants extending from November 1928 to May 1929.
15 FLC 24.983, south elevation, Villa Baizeau, Project B. Of thirteen distinguishable marginal sketches on this drawing, only two relate specifically to the Baizeau project.
16 At the scale used for the Baizeau plans on this sheet, the square plan would measure c 22.5 m x 23.25 m.
17 Five drawings for the Ocampo project were completed on September 18, 1928. Only a few other drawings record this scheme, which was a routine reworking of the Villa Meyer project. Of the three sketchbook pages pasted onto the sheet FLC 31.044 (21 cm x 21 cm each), one is clearly for Ocampo, while the other two deal with the Poissy site.
18 A sheet of drawings matching these can also be found among the archives for the Planeix house (Planeix, doc 2).
19 See also the introduction to the house in *L'Oeuvre complète, 1929-1934* (Zurich: Girsberger, 1957), p 24.
20 Edward F Sekler and William Curtis, *Le Corbusier at Work: The Genesis of the Carpenter Center for the Visual Arts*, (Cambridge, Mass: Harvard University Press, 1978).
21 William Curtis, *Modern Architecture since 1900* (New York: Phaidon, 1982), p 192. See also his Unit for the Open University course A305, History of Architecture and Design 1890-1939 (Unit 17) (1975). My own work on the drawings for the Villa Savoye began in connection with a radiovision programme for this course (RV17), which included a fold-out sheet of the main stages of the design. (This sheet was inadvertently included among the Le Corbusier drawings in the Foundation at the numbering stage [FLC 19.479]).
22 Tim Benton, 'Le Corbusier's *Propos Architectural*', *Le Corbusier: La Ricerca paziente*, pp 23-44. I was able to set out the design stages of the Villas La Roche, Stein, Baizeau and Savoye in the Lugano exhibition, 1980. See also my 'Drawings and Clients: Le Corbusier's Atelier Methodology in the 1920s', *AA Files* 3 (1983).
23 Fixed points for dating these projects are given by the stencil numbers on presentation drawings and some dates added to the drawings themselves. For Project A, they are LC 1096-2008 (October 10, 1928) and LC 2011 (October 14). For Project B, five drawings are dated in pencil: FLC 19.635 and 19.636 (November 6, 1928), 19.662, 19.714, 19.661 (November 7, 1928). Project C has a presentation set – LC 2030-2033 (November 26-27, 1928) – as does Project D – LC 2054-2058 (December 17, 1928), LC 2090 (February 9, 1929). Project E includes LC 2089 (February 21, 1929), LC 2104-2105 (April 12, 1929), and onwards. Several other drawings fitting into this scheme are dated on the drawings. To group the variants within the 'projects', I have used the documents in the FLC as well as a logical analysis of the progression of ideas. For dated lodge drawings, see notes 46 and 49.
24 *L'Oeuvre complète, 1910-1929* (Zurich: Girsberger, 1960), pp 186-188.
25 I count seventy-seven drawings for the variants of Project A, not including the 'prefiguring' drawings (such as FLC 8.507, 24.983 and 31.044) or two drawings (FLC 25.044 and 8.522), which may relate to the Savoye scheme. By contrast, the Project E schemes (February 1929 onwards) number only fifty-one drawings, excluding the lodge.
26 FLC doc 285 (Madame Savoye's two-page brief), FLC doc 767 (Pierre Jeanneret's note), FLC doc 762 (Madame Savoye's comments on drawings with LC numbers 1096-1099). None of these are dated.
27 For example, she wanted in the salon 'indirect lighting and lamps over the dining table . . . this room should not be strictly rectangular, but include comfortable corners'. Other references are to separate lodgings for the gardener and chauffeur (the latter to be housed over the garage) and an approving reference to the kitchen of the Villa Church at Ville d'Avray.
28 FLC docs 120, 590 (both dated November 5, 1928) and docs 145, 144, 239. Totals above 785,000 francs reflect errors in addition; those below fail to incorporate some of the subtotals.
29 FLC docs 596 and 119 (copy), dated December 21, 1928: 'We include the blueprints for the third study of your house at Poissy. We have carried out the reductions which we think will allow us to reach the proposed price'.
30 Under Project B, I include FLC 25.036, 25.043, 25.039 (first variant); 19.659, 19.699, 19.698 (second variant); 19.660, 19.635, 19.636 (third variant); 19.663, 19.662, 19.714, 19.523, 19.661 (fourth variant).
31 For the starkest contrast, compare the perspectives from the west for Project A (FLC 19.424, LC 2007, October 10, 1928) with that for Project C (FLC 19.702, c November 26, 1928).
32 FLC 19.523 (the torn fragment from FLC 19.714) includes calculations comparing Project B with the 'other project' (Project A). The latter is costed at 725,000 francs (sic, correct total is 726,750), based on a crude method of multiplying different categories of floor area by different factors. My estimate for Project B duplicates these procedures.
33 In Project C, I include thirty-eight drawings, of which FLC 28.740 and 25.037 have been filed under Baizeau, and 20.753 under Maisons Minimum. FLC 19.710 includes the calculations of areas on which my cost estimate is based.
34 FLC docs 146 (October 26, 1928) and 54 (October 31, 1928).
35 FLC doc 120.
36 FLC doc 760 (undated, in Pierre Jeanneret's hand).
37 In Project D, the first variants include FLC 19.709, 19.701, 19.558, 19.559, 19.560, 19.555, 19.557, 19.712, 19.708, 19.561, 19.556, 19.568, 19.711, 19.528. The remaining sixty-seven drawings that correspond closely with the scheme sent to the client on December 21 include the sheet LC 2054-2058 (dated December 17, 1928), but also a number of drawings that include modifications carried out in the process of supplying details to the tradesmen and builder for their tenders during January and February 1929. At least two of these drawings, LC 2090-2091 (March 9, 1929), overlap with the first drawings for Project E.
38 FLC doc 593 (February 15, 1929).
39 For example, FLC docs 757-758 (Cormier's tender of February 7, 1929) specifically offered an alternative exterior treatment in *ciment pierre grésé* that would have involved a supplement of 22,000 francs. Cormier also included alternative estimates for more expensive floor tiles and a cavity wall treatment of the partition wall between master and son's bedrooms. All three were ignored in the calculations of cost by Pierre Jeanneret, but all were rapidly adopted (FLC doc 678-679, April 18, 1929). Similarly, the painter and glazier Celio offered plate glass as an alternative to cheap glass for the windows at the price of 9,000 francs, and Pierre Jeanneret noted that this sum had been 'agreed', although, once again, it was left out of the calculations for submitting to the client (FLC doc 325-330, February 7, 1929).
40 FLC 19.436, LC 2089 (dated February 21, 1929), indicates a basement plan with the staircase orientation changed. It seems that work on the new scheme was going on during March, but no drawings were sent to the client or builder until the final set, which dates from April 12, 1929 onwards (eg FLC 19.439, LC 2104).
41 Cormier's detailed accounts, including extras, were submitted in five *mémoires* and summarised in a letter of December 30, 1930 (FLC doc 886-887). Cormier's total bill came to 414,884.60 francs (compared to the original contract of 276,000 based on the tender of February 7 and the contract of March 5, 1929 (FLC doc 759). For the ensuing haggling, see FLC docs 259-263, 871-878.
42 FLC docs 713-714 and 680. On April 20, 1929, Cormier was already able to charge 38,925 francs for work on the foundations and cellar. By the time the last details were being drawn (eg FLC 19.469, LC 2172, June 19, 1929), Cormier's bills had reached 156,200 francs (FLC doc 708-711, June 24, 1929) for work on the first and second storeys.
43 FLC doc 307 (August 2, 1934).
44 His name appears frequently in the 'Black Book' which logged the LC number drawings. In a letter to the author, he wrote (August 28, 1976): 'Yes, I was in the atelier, rue de Sèvres during the period you mention, from September 1928 to July 1929 . . . Looking through the *Oeuvre complète* . . . Verlag Girsberger, 1930, I remember working on some of the plans pages 190 and 191. I also worked on detail sections of walls, floors and parapets that I do not find published. In connection with the Villa Savoye, I drew the typical details on page 174 of the above publication for use on this and other jobs for DOORS, WINDOWS, CABINETS AND ROOFS . . . Le Corbusier normally concentrated on the design part of the projects, coming to the atelier more in the late afternoon, evening or night'.
45 *Précisions*, p 230.
46 For the double lodge, there are twenty-two drawings, including FLC 18.273. Apart from two rather tentative drawings, FLC 19.720 and 19.612, all relate very directly to the dated drawings: FLC 19.610 (April 27, 1929), 19.449 (LC 2124, May 6, 1929), 19.450 (LC 2125, May 7, 1929), 19.457 (LC 2160, June 5, 1929), 18.273 (June 9, 1929). There is no evidence for any serious design for the lodge at an earlier date, confirmed by the lack of tenders by the builder, but some apparently early site plans (FLC 19.544, 19.545, 19.718, 23.276) do include some indications of a lodge.
47 FLC doc 131 includes rough calculations by Pierre Jeanneret for a 'large lodge' (76,300 francs) compared to a medium lodge (64,000 francs). The former sum included one estimate that can be dated to May 17, 1929 (FLC doc 251-252).
48 FLC doc 893-895, Cormier's letter, August 3, 1929.
49 For the single lodge there are only nine drawings, including FLC 18.312 (filed under Loi Loucheur) and 8.681 (filed under Guiette). The dated drawings are FLC 19.470 and 19.471 (LC 2189, July 7, 1929). In addition, there are details of the dog kennel and siting, mostly from January and February 1930.
50 See, for example, *L'Oeuvre complète, 1929-1934*, p 25, where the wrong section is illustrated, a mistake that has been faithfully copied in countless later publications.
51 FLC doc 279-284, Celio's bill, July 10, 1931.
52 FLC doc 317-320, Celio, December 1930.
53 FLC doc 124, sketch by Pierre Jeanneret dated May 27, 1930.
54 See Cormier's sketch, FLC doc 134 (January 8, 1930).
55 Perfecla's bill, FLC doc 277 (March 24, 1930).
56 FLC docs 628, 638 (March 31, 1930), 640 (May 13, 1930) and 639, 637 (May 31, 1930) included in Crépin's list of plants and layout of planting. A letter by Le Corbusier to Crépin (FLC doc 265, July 17, 1930) appeals to the latter's loyalty, claiming that Le Corbusier had insisted to Madame Savoye that Crépin be chosen for the job. Crépin was also the gardener for the Stein house and had a reputation as an artistic landscape-artist. Site drawings by Pierre Jeanneret in January 1930 (eg FLC 19.539, LC 2282) show a deviation from the rectilinear arrangement of drives with flanking flower beds, introducing a proposed picturesque treatment of curving drives and informal beds of plants.
57 FLC doc 764.
58 FLC docs 776-777.
59 FLC docs 139-140 (July 17, 1930).
60 FLC doc 768.
61 FLC docs 220-223.
62 FLC doc 313. See also FLC doc 8 (July 17, 1930), a letter from Louis Notté, an expert called in by the Savoyes to advise on the central heating, who recommended a larger boiler.
63 FLC doc 34 (September 7, 1937).
64 FLC doc 712.
65 FLC doc 581 (October 31, 1937).
66 FLC doc 599.

Maison La Roche-Jeanneret

Paris, France 1923

15.205
Plans, ground floor, gardens, basement and entrances, and detailed section, spot heights, keys and interior layout. There is also a print from tracing paper with the same number. Indian ink and pencil on medium paper, 54cm x 101cm.

15.111
Perspective of the building, sketch of the facade, elevation. Pencil, green pencil and black ink on sketching paper, 42cm x 56cm.

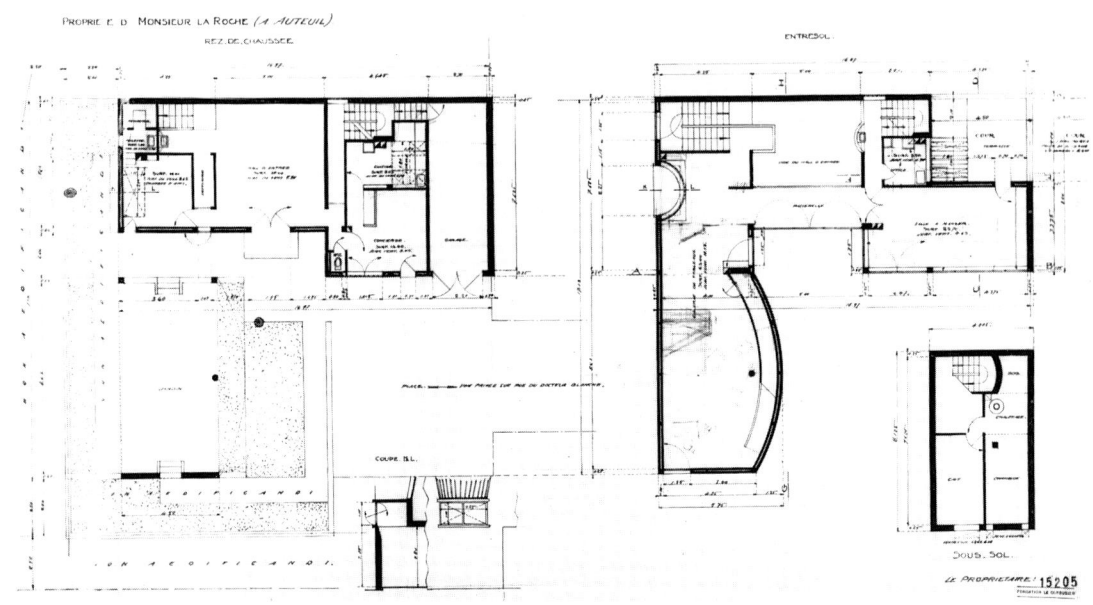

Villa Meyer

Neuilly-sur-Seine, France 1925

31.514
Mme Meyer, Study sketch, seven interior perspectives with titles. April 18, 1926. Indian ink on tracing paper stuck on thick white paper, 111cm x 75cm.

31.538 *Overleaf*:
Mme Meyer, Axonometric, dated 21 April 1926. Indian ink on sketching paper backed on white paper, 110 cm x 75 cm

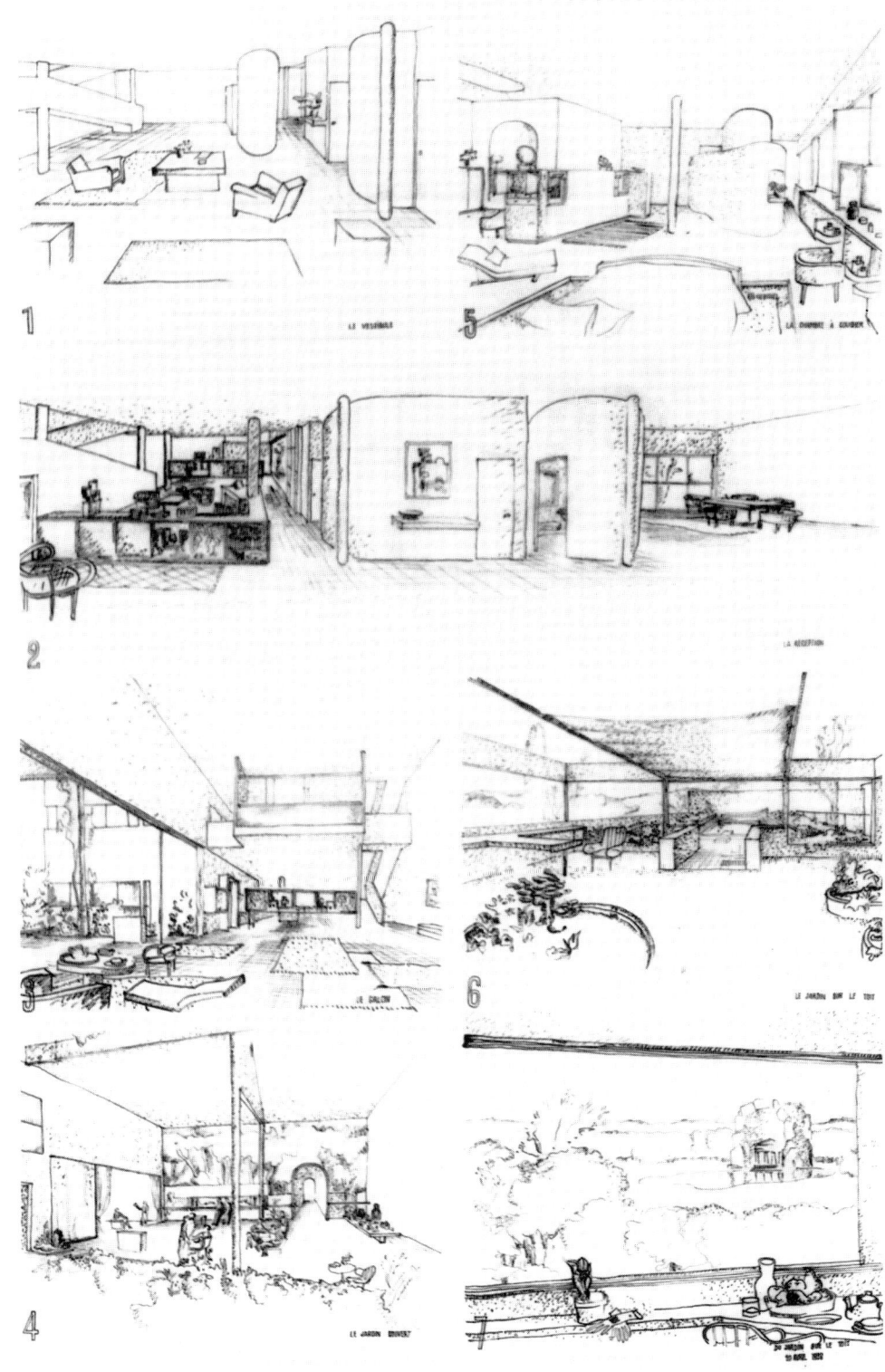

MME MEYER
663
21 AVRIL 1926

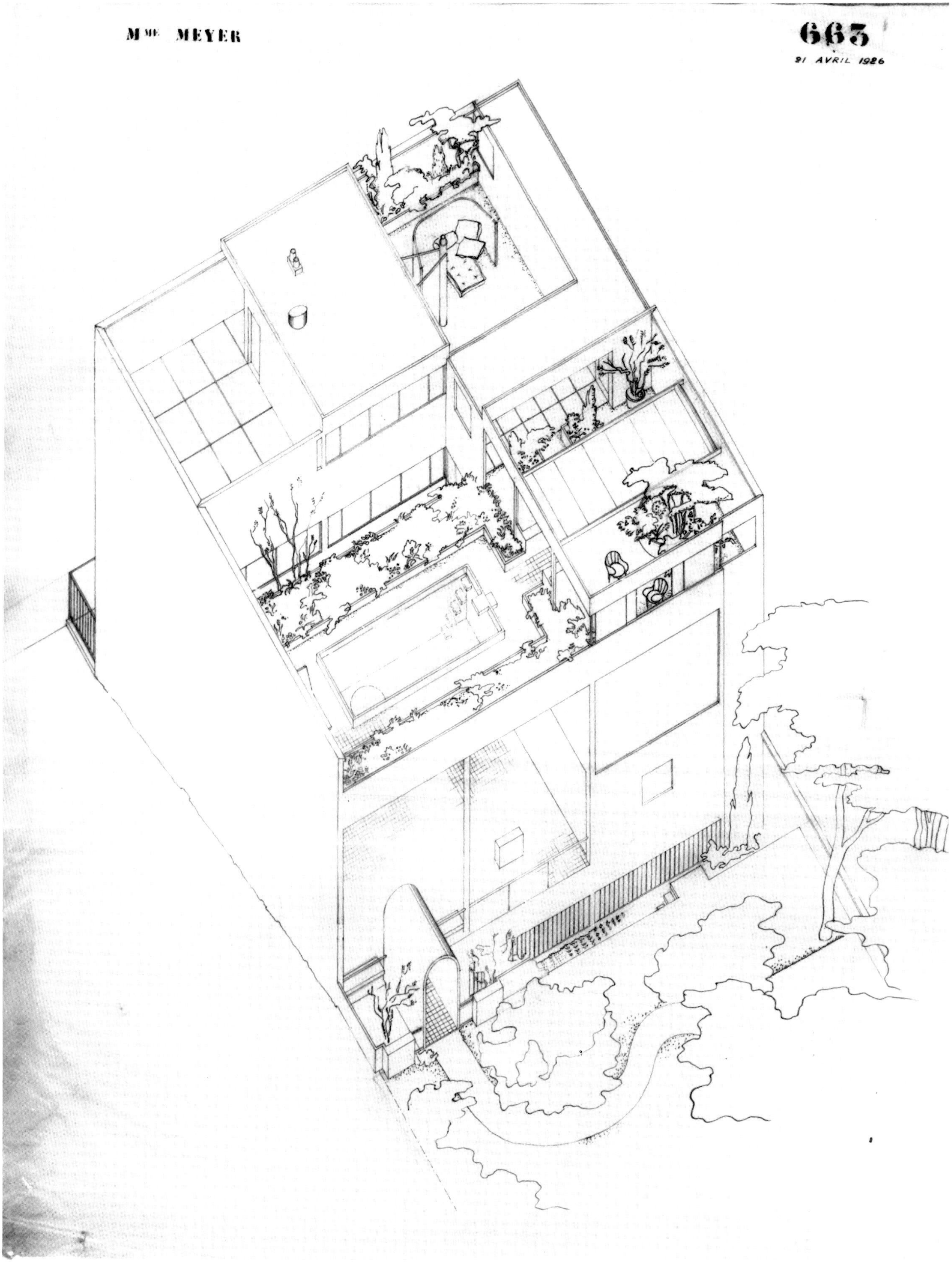

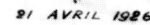

Villa Cook
Boulogne-sur-Seine, France 1926

8.308
Axonometric of the interior (the roof does not appear in the drawing). There are four gelatine prints of this plan with the same number. Indian ink on tracing paper, 53cm x 87cm.

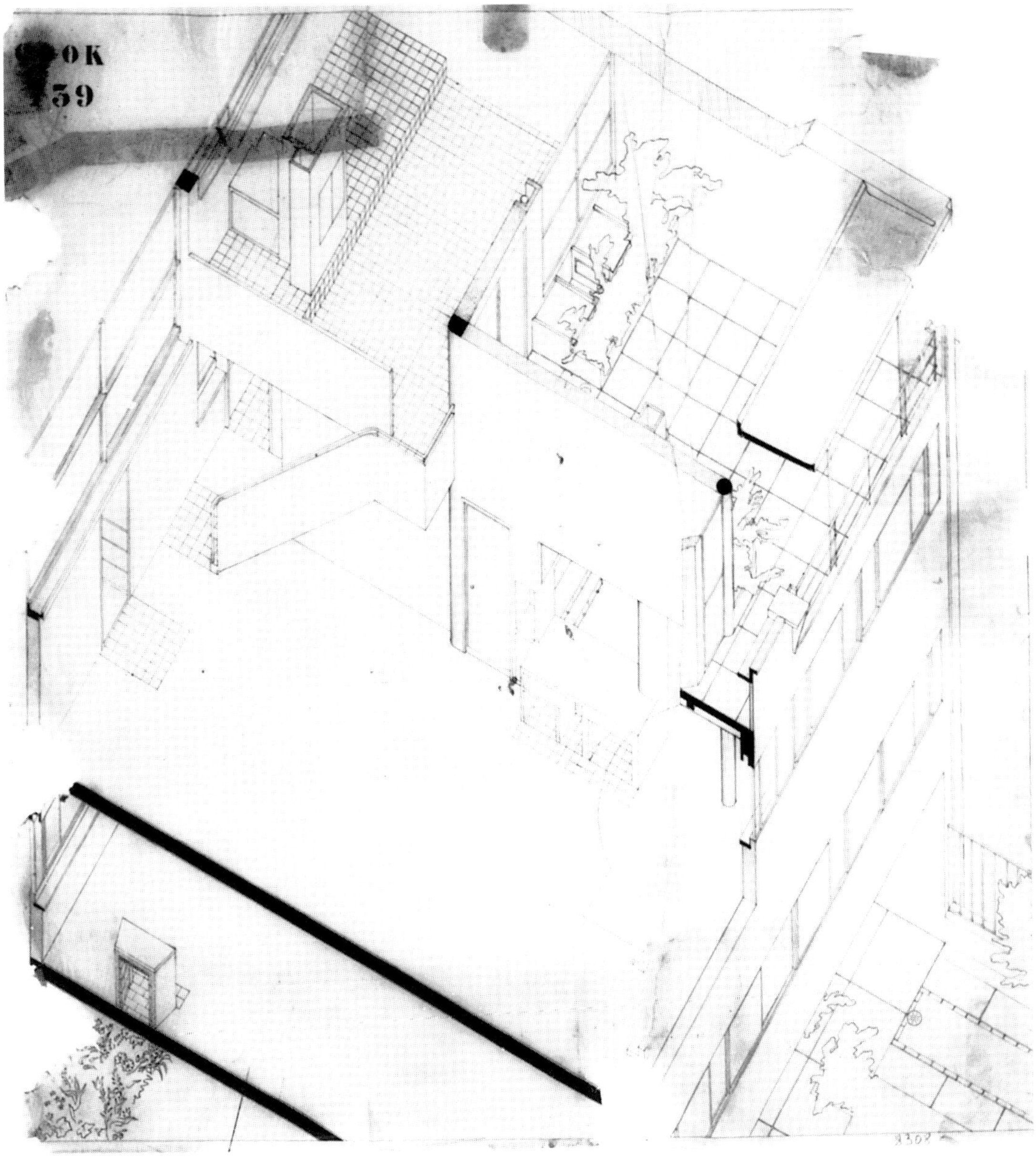

Maison Ternisien
Boulogne-sur-Seine, France 1926

7.891
Axonometric of the house, small sketches towards the left-hand side. At the bottom left, the number 15. There are three gelatine prints on drawing paper classified under the same number, of which one is in colour. Pencil and Indian ink on sketching paper, 53cm x 87cm.

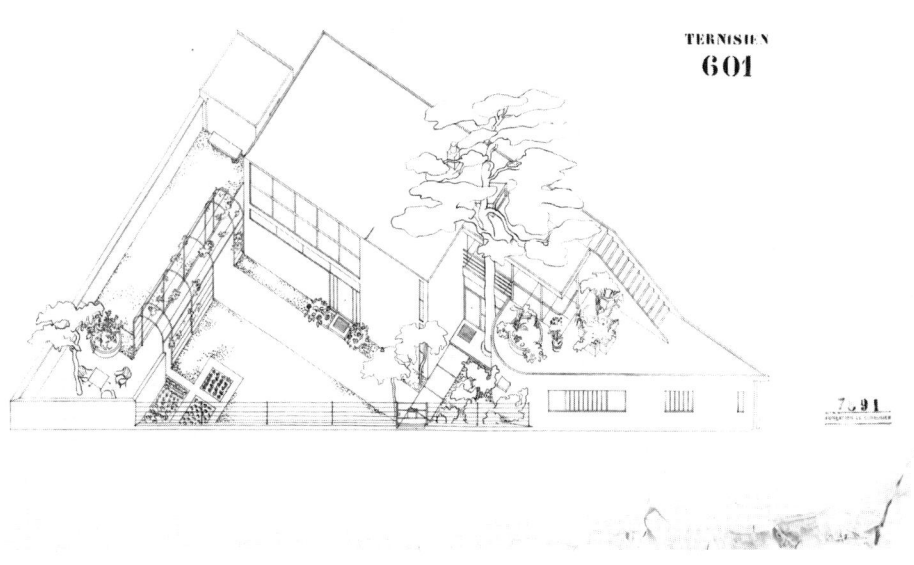

Villa les Terasses

Garches, France 1927

31.513
Two axonometric views studying the exterior polychromy, stencilled No 25. Two documents on tracing paper (19cm x 25cm) stuck on white drawing paper, pencil and gouache, 31cm x 65cm.

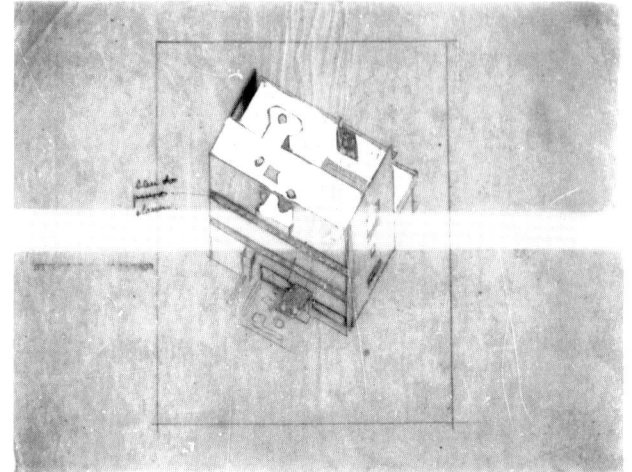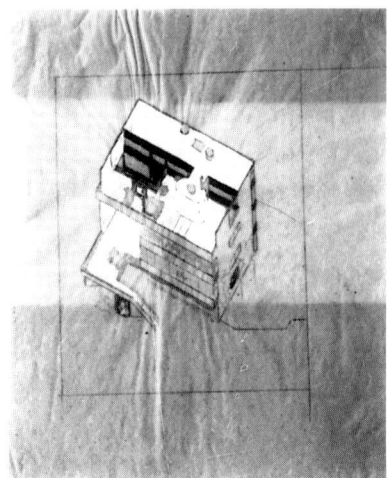

31.480
Five perspective sketches, three of the exterior (a general view, a north view and a south view), and two of the interior (showing the hall and raised garden in pencil). At the bottom of the text, in Le Corbusier's hand: 'This document (this drawing is the original) expresses the first flowering of the effort (modest but impassioned) from 1918-1925. First cycle of a manifest new architecture. I say . . .' Le Corbusier, July 26, 1926. Indian ink and pencil on tracing paper on card, 83cm x 65cm.

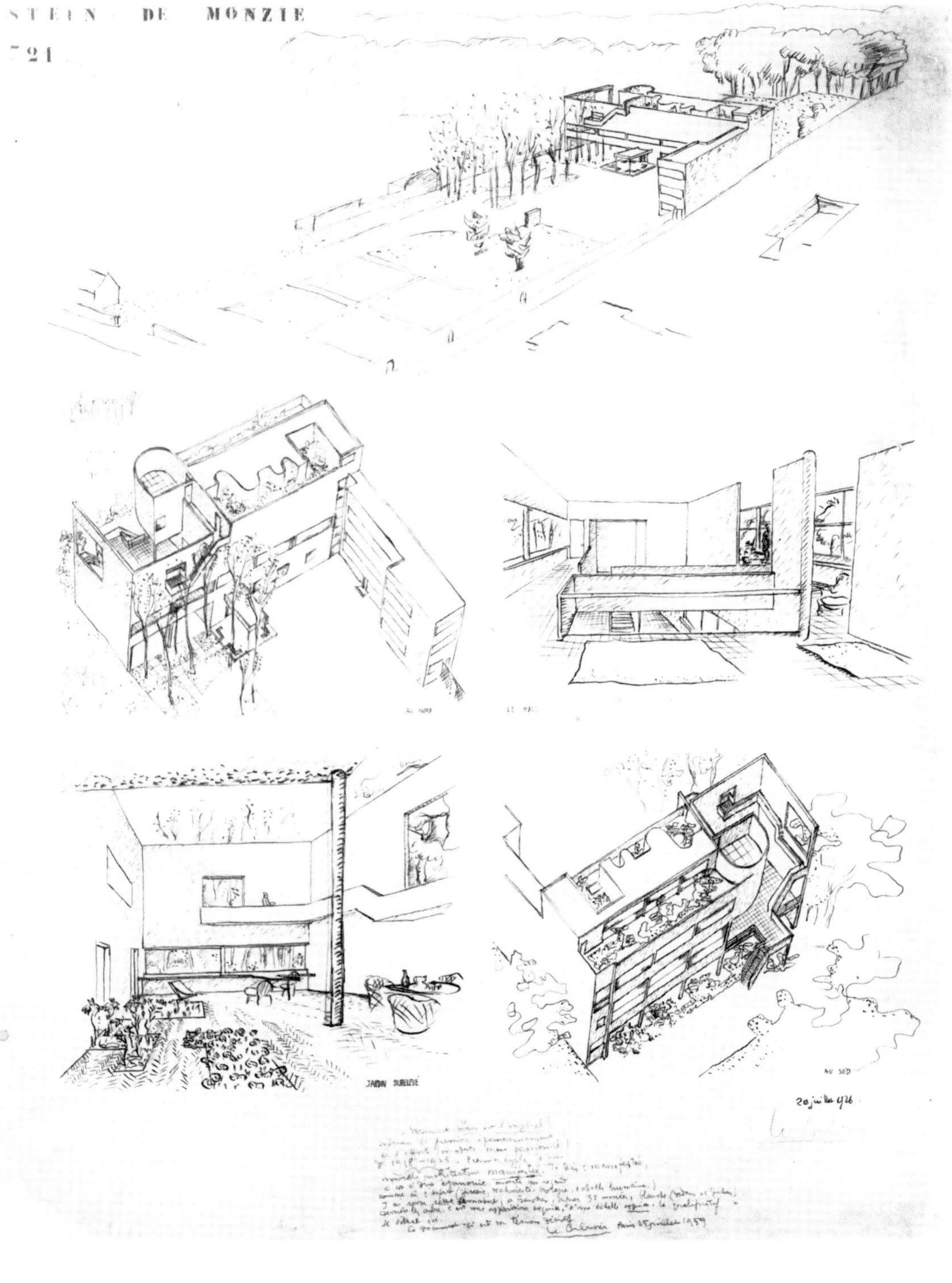

10.572
Study drawing in axonometric perspective with section showing the structure on the first level, sketches around the drawing. Pencil on sketching paper, 90 cm x 110cm.

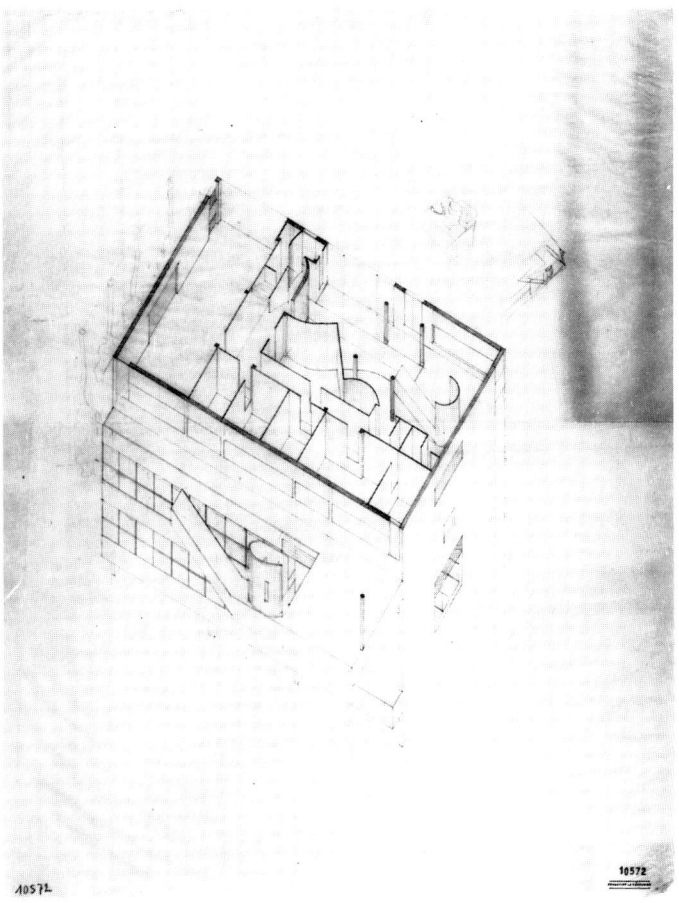

Villa Planeix
Paris, France 1927

8.908
Axonometric, bird's-eye view of the building. Pencil and colouring pencil on sketching paper, 33cm x 37cm.

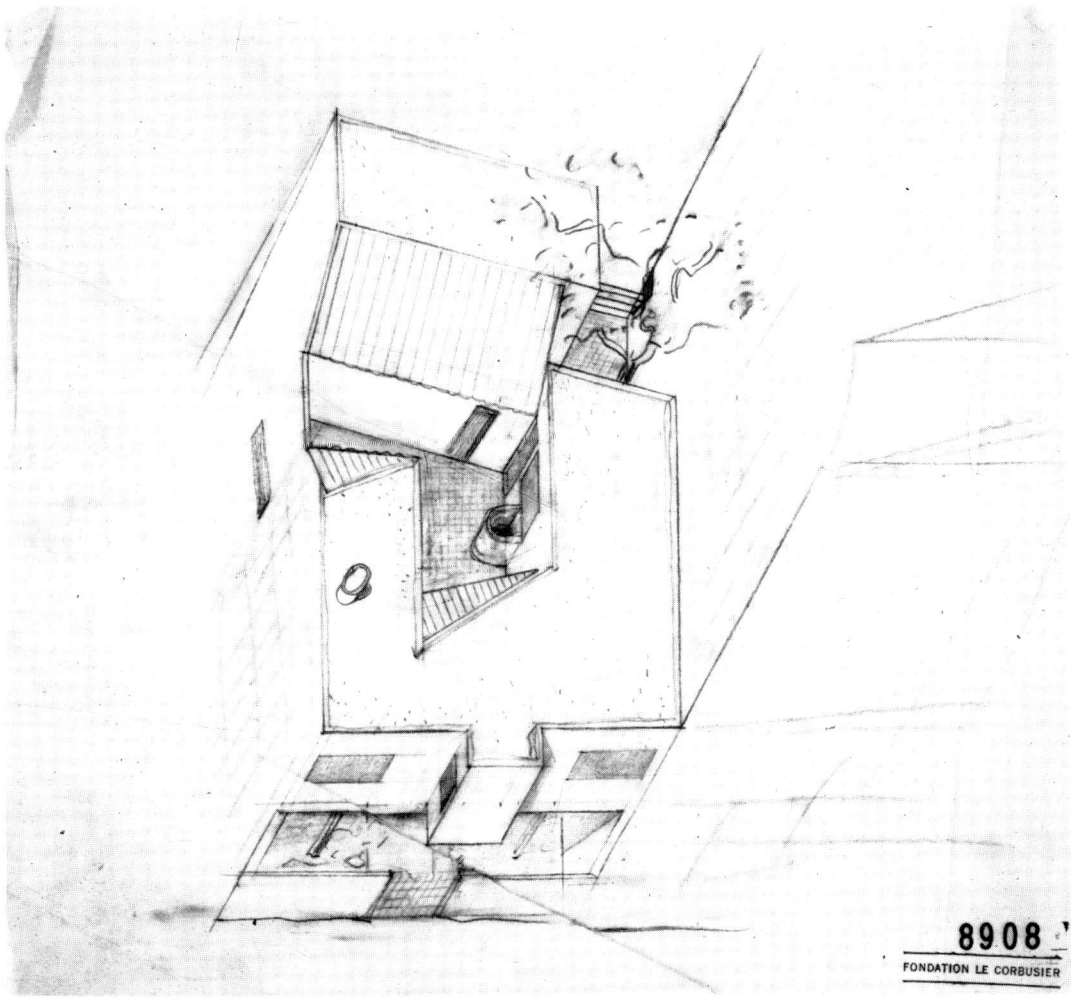

Villa Ocampo

Buenos Aires, Argentina 1928

24.235
Study sketches, floor plan and elevation with keys. Pencil on fine translucent paper, 50 cm x 65 cm

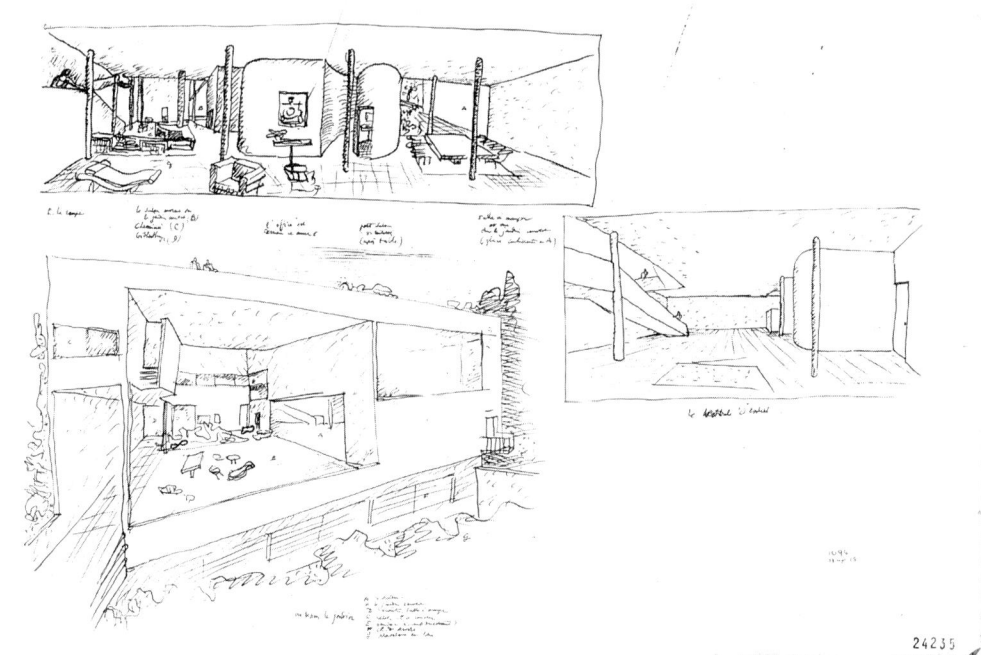

Villa Baizeau

Carthage, Tunisia 1928

24.983
Study drawing of a façade elevation with other sketches around it. Pencil on sketching paper, 52 cm x 110 cm

31.014
Three study sketches, perspective of the villa with a study of the polychromy, numbering acording to the colours of the facades, and comments. Pencil and colouring crayons on medium paper, 35cm x 95cm.

25.031
Three sketches, perspectives from different viewpoints with colour notations. Pencil on sketching paper, 35 cm x 93 cm

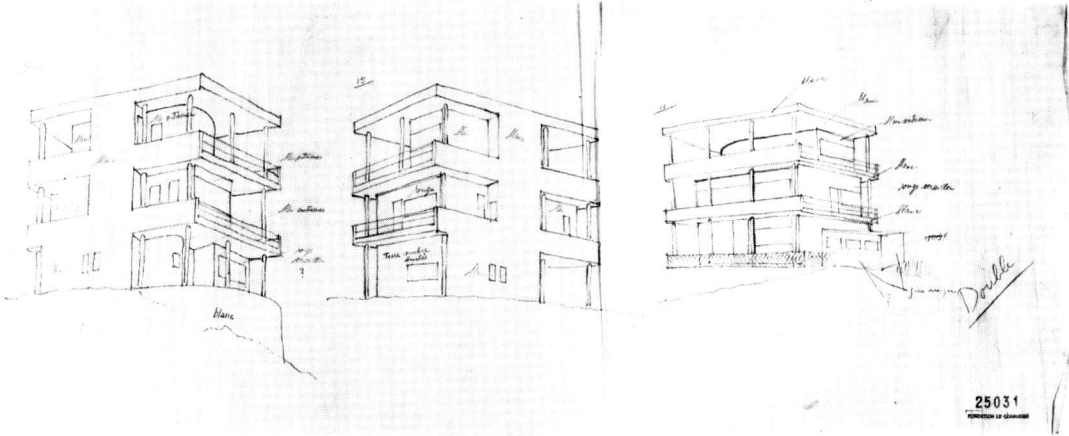

Villa Savoye
Poissy-sur-Seine, France 1929

19.423
Perspective study sketch of the house. Indian ink and pencil on tracing paper, 64cm x 101cm.

19.583
Numerous study sketches, plan of one level, interior perspective and bird's-eye view of the house with notes, spot heights and calculations and the number 28 at the bottom right. Pencil, colouring pencil and white chalk on sketching paper, 51cm x 110cm.

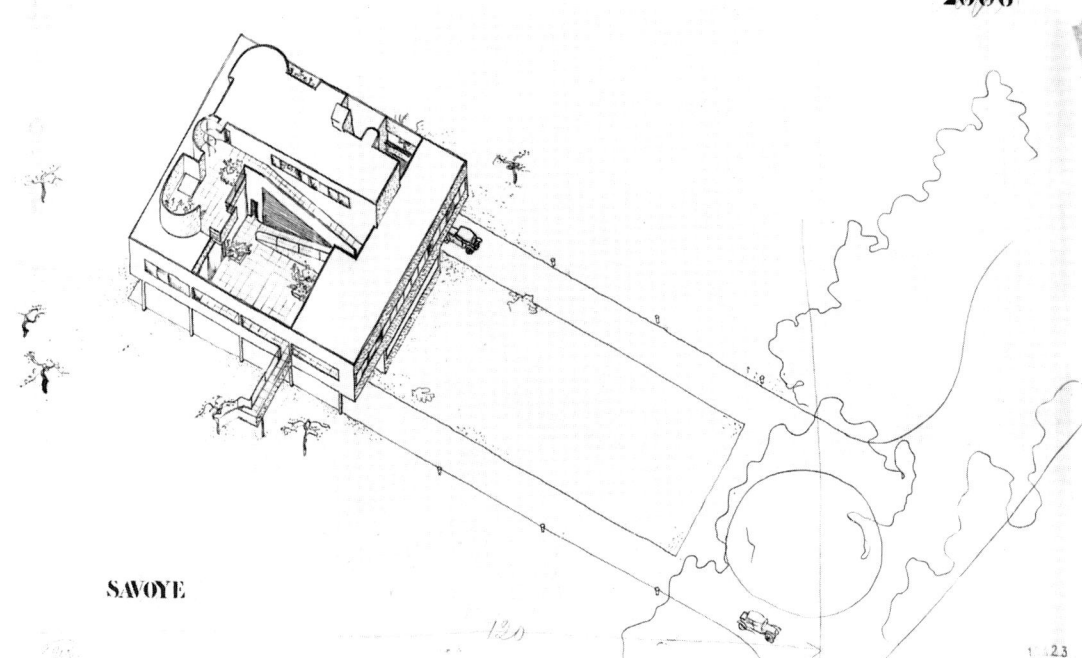

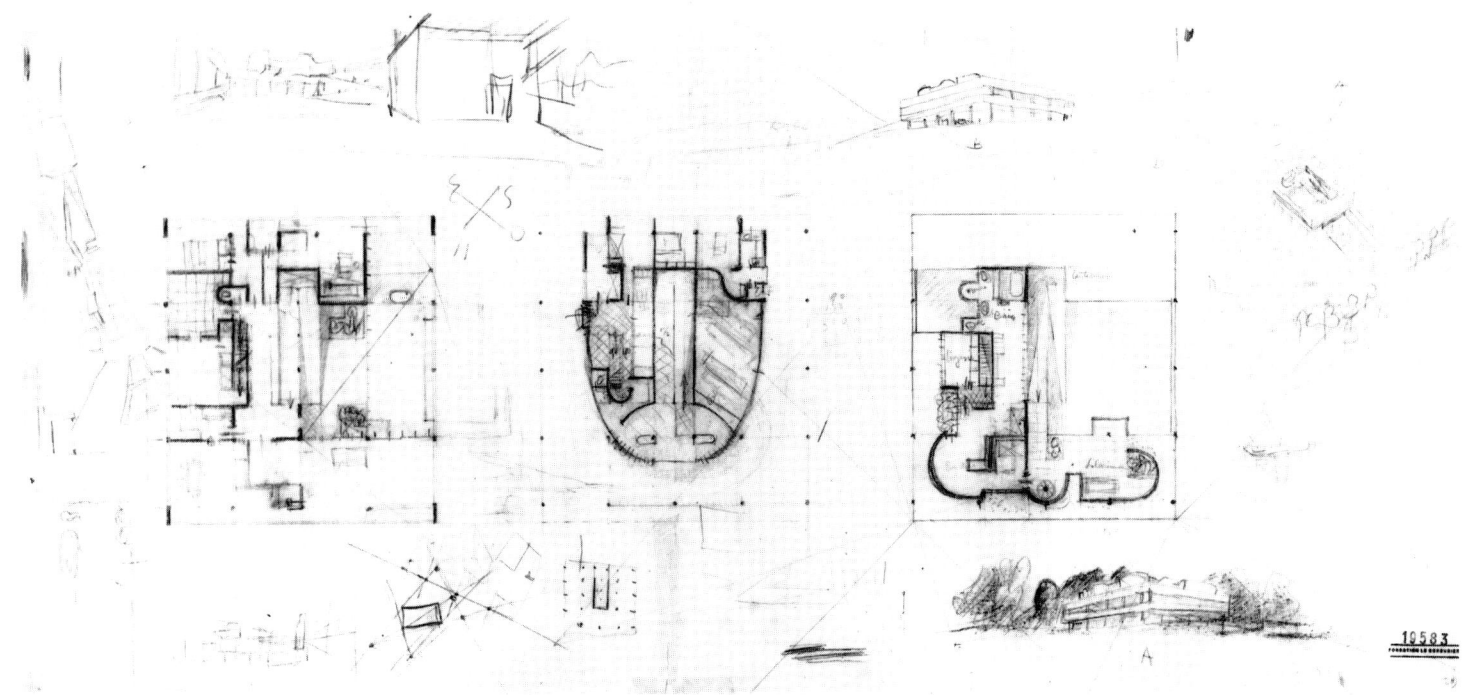

19.556
Study drawing, plan of a level, spot heights, various sketches. Pencil and colouring pencil on sketching paper, 55cm x 63cm.

19.561
Sketch, plan of a level and perspective of the villa, keys. Pencil and colouring pencil on sketching paper, 50cm x 80cm.

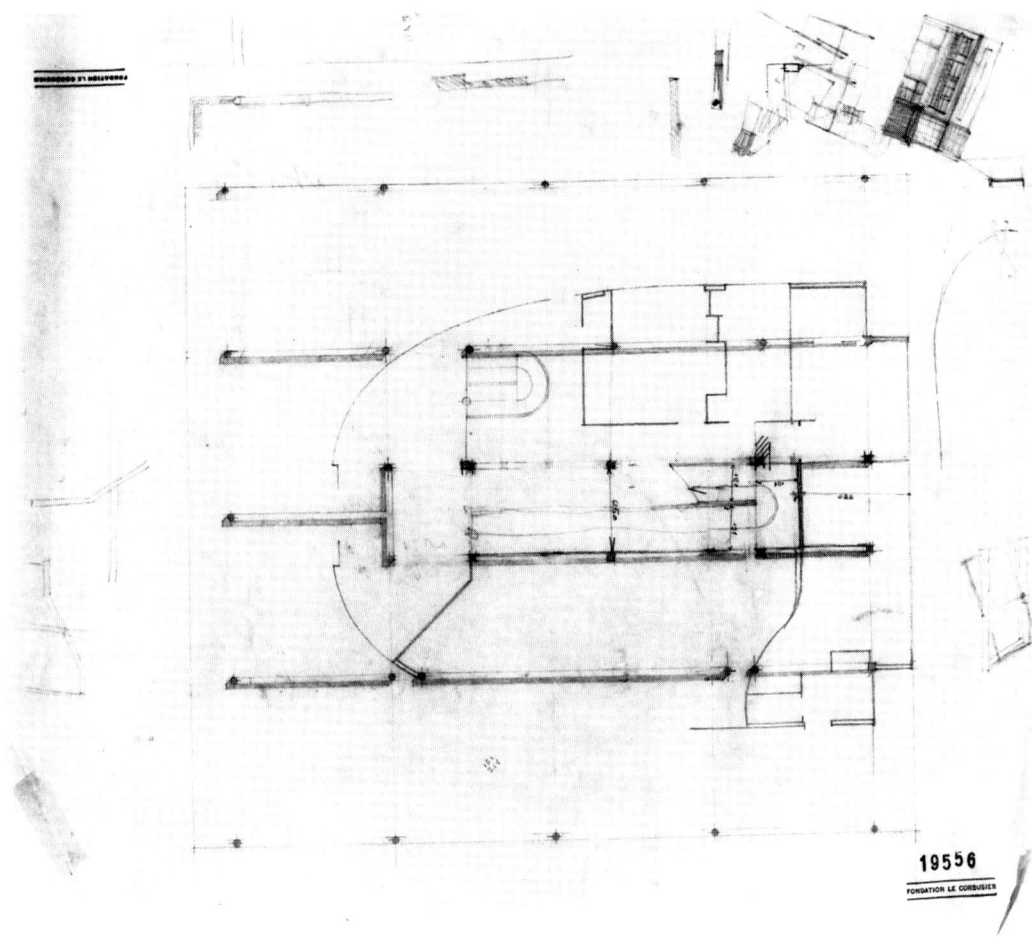

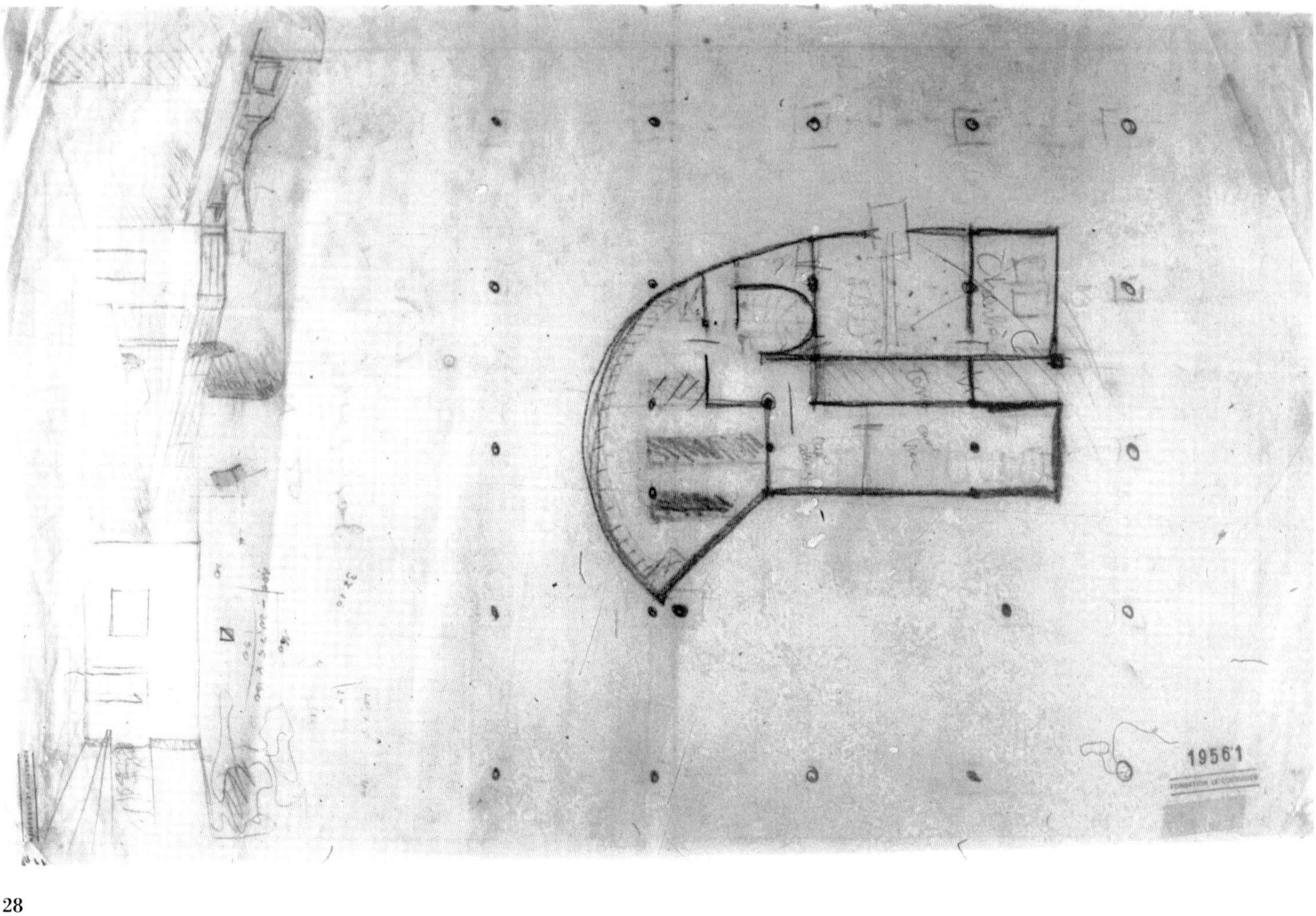

19.698
Sketch, plan of the terrace level, with keys. Charcoal on sketching paper, 52cm x 61cm.

19.699
Sketch, plan of one level with keys. Charcoal on sketching paper, 54cm x 58cm.

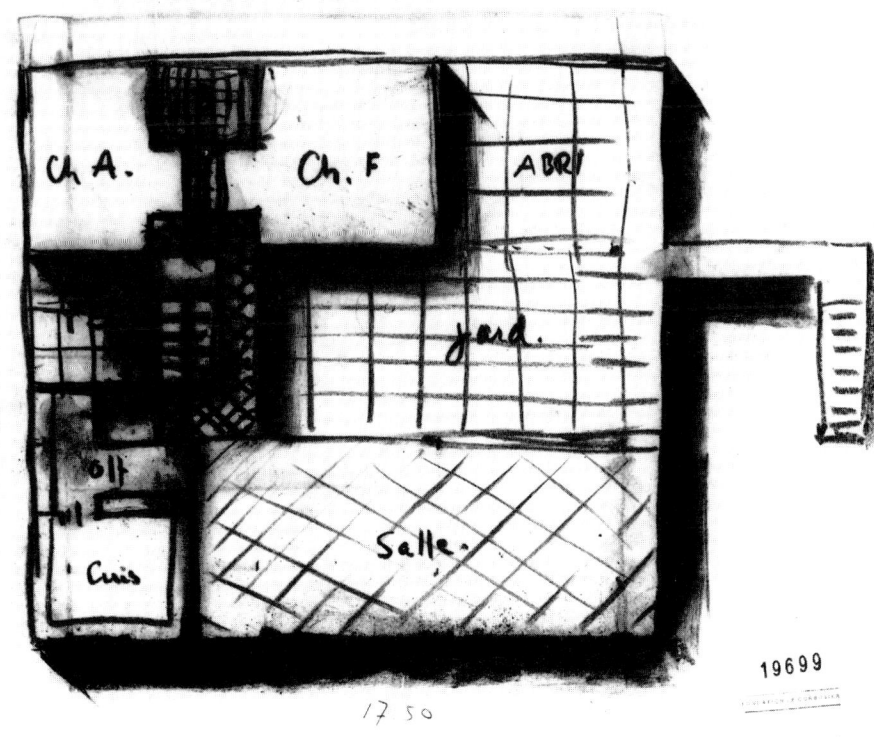

19.700
Four sketches, plan of one level with keys. Pencil on sketching paper, 57cm x 56cm.

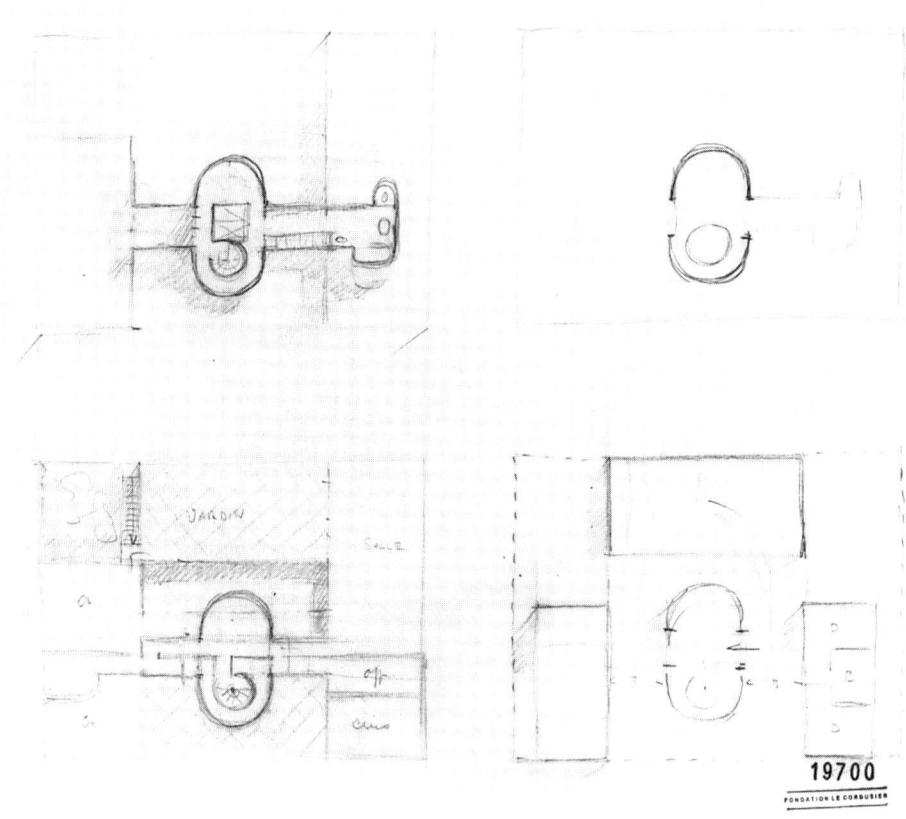

19.660
Study sketch, plan of one level showing interior layout. Charcoal on sketching paper, 44cm x 52cm.

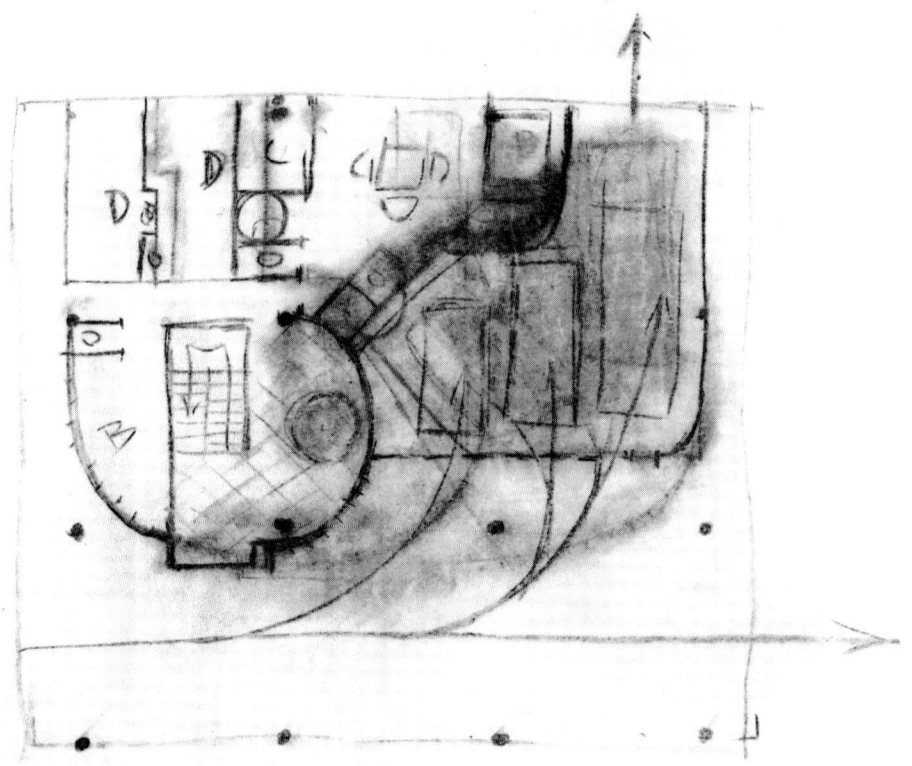

The Chapel of Ronchamp

DANIÈLE PAULY

AT THE OUTSET OF MY RESEARCH ON THE CHAPEL of Ronchamp, when first exploring the archives and the large corpus of architectural drawings kept at the Fondation Le Corbusier, I found myself face to face with the documents in their rough stages, and it was probably this that most aroused my interest. The relevant documents were all in the state in which they had been left by Le Corbusier or his close collaborators. Thus the first task was to sort, analyse and classify the material.[1]

To shed some light on the work of exploration I undertook into the written archives, it should be noted that some of the archives which directly concerned the commissioning and realisation of the project had already been gathered together by the staff of Le Corbusier's studio at the time of the project's execution. Meanwhile, in the course of my research, other documents were found by chance in the various files assembled by Le Corbusier himself. It was most important to respect their order (or apparent disorder), since on numerous occasions we found a seminal idea, the first outline of a form, among these scattered documents. Therefore, at the beginning, a considerable amount of detailed analysis was necessary; it was carried out with the same sense of precaution necessary for a fragile assemblage that must not be disturbed in any way. Indeed, it was mainly this initial approach to virgin material that later made it possible to reconstruct the different phases of the process of architectural creation and to retrace the genesis of the project.

An analogous method was necessary for the corpus of architectural drawings. Analysing the project for the chapel of Ronchamp proved particularly revealing; unlike most of Le Corbusier's other projects, for which only a small number of preparatory drawings have been found, it was possible in this case to retrieve almost all of the study sketches, notebook sketches and studio drawings; they give the project's essential characteristics in a few strokes and make it possible to grasp the birth of the architectural object. At the time I began my work the earliest notebook drawings, the tracing paper sketches and Le Corbusier's drawings, as well as the studies and plans executed by the rue de Sèvres studio, had been neither catalogued nor analysed.[2] Here, too, it was above all a matter of undertaking to identify them and establish their chronology; I was thus able to distinguish the two stages in the genesis of this work and, by establishing the genealogy of the project, it became possible to situate within it most of the studio drawings and studies.[3]

It should also be mentioned that in the inventory of sources judged essential to my research, Le Corbusier's texts represented a precious help. It is well known that Le Corbusier was an astute observer of his own work; in this case, he made abundant commentaries on Ronchamp, and his discussions of the work and the origin of his references, as well as his own commentary on the architectural object,[4] exercised a significant, determining influence on my research. This discussion authoritatively enriches the ways in which one reads the architectural work.

Finally, it should also be mentioned how essential, as a complement to my investigations of the archive documents and the corpus of architectural drawings, the testimony of individuals – clergymen, public figures, collaborators of Le Corbusier, etc – was. They took part in the commission or participated in the 'architectural adventure'. I had the chance to meet some of them.[5] It is also essential to point out that for my research on Ronchamp, I decided to go back only to those sources that, in my opinion, authorised the 'reading of an architecture'.

But what is meant by the 'reading of an architecture'? It is a matter of retracing the project's genealogy, finding and analysing the architect's references, and attempting to 'decipher' the architectural object. This deciphering consists of considering the architectural object in relation to its site, studying it first as a whole and then in each of its separate elements, and describing and interpreting its forms and its spaces.[6] This reading is both easy and complex: easy because of the real importance of the documents that we found and the abundance of commentaries by the architect; complex because this architecture is truly imbued with the 'phenomenon of the unutterable' as a result of its inventive richness and poetic dimension. Le Corbusier, on returning to the hill of Bourlémont several years after the project, asked himself: 'But where did I get all of that from?'

In writing this essay devoted to the publication of the drawings and plans for Ronchamp which were made in the studio, I intend to present several of the elements that authorise this 'reading of architecture'. This said, I should add that it is the preparatory sketches tracing the genesis of the idea, rather than the more elaborated studies, that have held my interest; in a real sense, they 'tell the story' of the project's birth. That is why I have chosen to present several of the first sketches which illustrate the research undertaken: it makes it possible to uncover those references that figure in the project's elaboration and to grasp the architect's creative process. Le Corbusier published a portion of these sketches in a pamphlet entitled *Textes et dessins pour Ronchamp*[7] and explained himself in the following manner:

> Publishing the sketches of an architectural work's genesis may be interesting.
>
> When assigned a task, I am in the habit of storing it in my memory, that is, of not allowing myself to make any sketches for months.
>
> The human brain is made in such a way that it has a certain independence: it is a box into which one can pour in bulk the elements of a problem and then let them float, simmer, ferment.
>
> Then, one day, a spontaneous initiative of one's inner being takes shape, something clicks; you pick up a pencil, a stick of charcoal, some colouring pencils (colour is the key to the process), and give birth onto the paper: out comes the idea . . .

If the first notebook sketches show an already synthesised idea of the project, it is because a fairly long period of time passes between the commission and the architect's first contact with the site. This corresponds to the incubation phase alluded to by Le Corbusier; the gestation during which the idea reaches its maturity is clearly of prime importance. As I have shown in my monograph on Ronchamp,[5] Le Corbusier, as early as his first visit to the hill where the chapel was to be built, immediately traced the building's plan in four lines and gave its essential volumes. These sketches express a kind of immediate intuition; a response to the site which indicates the building's entry into the landscape. Le Corbusier noted: 'Ronchamp? Contact with a site, situation in a place, eloquence of the place, word addressed to the place'.[8]

Figure 1. Early plan of building (FLC 7.470)

Figure 2. Eastern elevation and calotte of tower, Sketchbook D17, p 15. (Reproduced by permission of the Architectural Historical Foundation and the Fondation Le Corbusier)

Elsewhere, in a work that he devoted solely to Ronchamp, he explained: 'On the hill, I had carefully drawn the four horizons . . . [These] drawings have been misplaced or lost; it was they which architecturally triggered the acoustic response – acoustics in the realm of forms'.[9] The plan's four lines are indeed a response to the site; they are two curves opening up onto a vast landscape and designed to receive the pilgrims; two straight lines that rejoin them and close the figure (Figure 1).[10]

The building's volumes were also defined in the earliest sketches. One of the first notebook pages [11] shows two sketches: one for the elevation of the eastern side, the other suggesting the form given to towers (Figure 2). This elevation is characterised by the bulging mass of the roof, which acts as a hood over the exterior choir. This covering's appearance reminds one of a shell, the crab shell Le Corbusier spoke of when describing the birth of the project. He told how, after finding it on a Long Island beach during a trip to New York in 1947, he noticed with surprise how strong it was when he put the entire weight of his body on it; he decided to keep it among the *objets à réaction poètique* that he liked to collect. This shell inspired in him the idea for the form of the chapel's roof – an organic form corresponding to an organic plan – as well as its structure; and just as the hollow, very resistant shell was composed of two fine membranes, the roof was made up of two thin veils of reinforced concrete:

> Give me some charcoal and some paper; it all begins with a response to the site. The thick walls, a crab shell to round out the plan, which is so static. I bring in the crab shell; the shell will be placed on the stupidly but usefully thick walls; to the south, the light will be made to enter. There won't be any windows – the light will enter everywhere, like a stream.[12]

Thus, from the outset, Le Corbusier had a very precise idea of the appearance that the building's roof would take . But he did not merely transpose this form into the architectural space; he elaborated the very particular aspect of this shell and transformed its initial appearance by imagining two parallel casings, creating a structure similar to that of an aeroplane wing (Figure 3).

In the same way, Le Corbusier almost spontaneously came up with the idea for the form of the towers that would overlook and illuminate the secondary chapels. On the same notebook page there is an outline of one of these towers; in this case also the source is to be found in Le Corbusier's own store of references. Thus the form and the principle of lighting adopted here derive from one of the many references that the architect accumulated over the course of his travels. In this particular instance, he visited the Villa Adriana at Tivoli, near Rome, in 1911; in the serapeum cut out of the rock, the recess of the apse is lighted by a chimney emerging from the rock to catch the light like a kind of periscope. Le Corbusier retained, in a few drawings, this principle of lighting; several decades later, he considered using it for the underground basilica at La Sainte-Baume, a project which was never realised. He used the sketches he made at Tivoli to develop this principle and later published a few of them in his *L'Oeuvre complète* (Figure 4) to help explain the genesis of the idea.[13] This idea would reach its fulfilment in the 'wells of light' that are the towers of Ronchamp. A note on a small sketch found in the file 'création Ronchamp' points to the source of this idea: 'Some light! In 1911, I had noticed something like that in a Roman grotto in Tivoli – no grotto, here at Ronchamp, but the hump of a hill'.

The Tivoli example eloquently reveals the role played by references in Le Corbusier's process of architectural creation. My purpose here is not to dig up and describe all the references, conscious or unconscious, that lie at the origins of Ronchamp: for this, the reader should refer to my book on Ronchamp.[5] Rather, in order to attempt to grasp the architect's method, it seems to me essential, with the few examples that I have chosen to present, to understand the manner in which these references figure in the process of creation. And it is essentially through the drawing – the writing down of 'sight' – that they are retained and take their

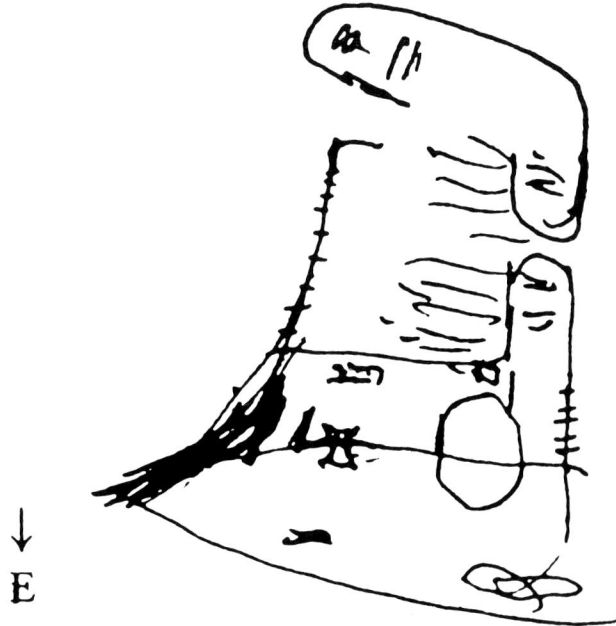

Figure 6. Plan, Sketchbook E18, p 8. (Reproduced by permission of the Architectural History Foundation and the Fondation Le Corbusier)

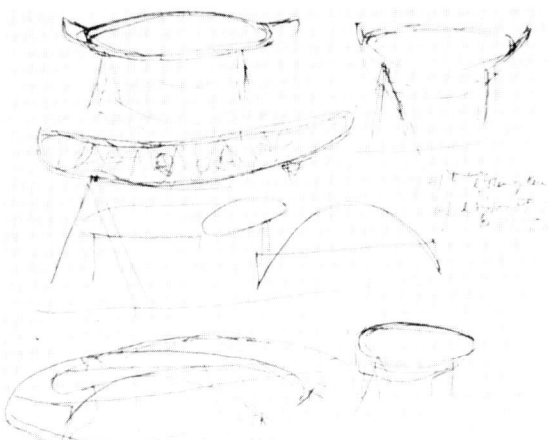
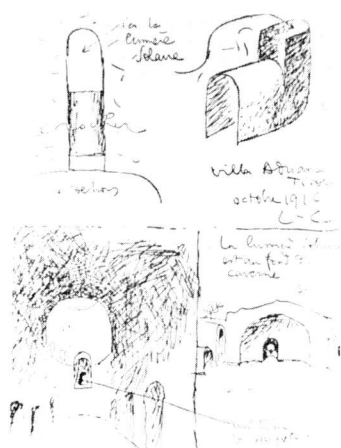
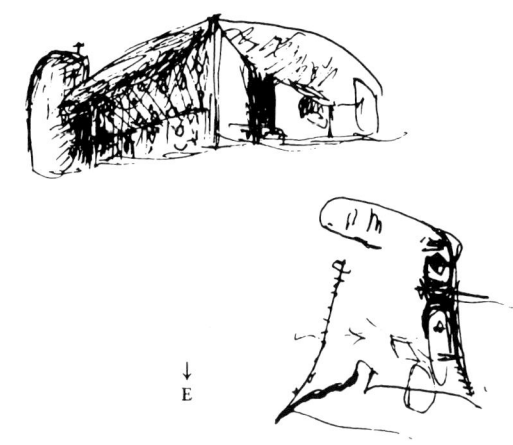

Figure 3. Sketches for roof

Figure 4. Sketches of lighting in serapeum Villa Adriana, Tivoli

Figure 5. Southeastern elevation and plan, Sketchbook E18, p 7. (Reproduced by permission of the Architectural Historical Foundation and the Fondation Le Corbusier)

place in the architect's own history; it is also through the drawing that they re-emerge at the moment of 'invention'. Thus, if the memory of the Villa Adriana came back to the architect's mind almost immediately, it was not only because Le Corbusier went to Tivoli and visited at length the impressive site but, above all, because he chose to draw what struck him and what he wanted to remember most. This example shows that drawing served in a real sense as a 'memory' for the architect.

We have just established that the essential course to follow had already been adopted in the earliest sketches. Some of these sketches, made in a notebook and dated June 1950, show quite clearly how the initial idea for the plan evolved and became explicit in a few strokes (Figures 5, 6). The four lines that initially outlined the plan became more accurate, and in two sketches the quasi-final plan was realised: the southern and eastern sides came together at an acute angle, and the northern and western sides curled at their extremities, forming three loops designed to contain the secondary chapels. The locations of the window openings and the interior arrangement with the location of the furniture were indicated in a few lines. This plan shows a clear favouring of asymmetry; later studies in the studio by Le Corbusier and Maisonnier only confirm the overall course adopted.[14]

Figure 7. Southeastern elevation, Sketchbook E18, p 9. (Reproduced by permission of the Architectural History Foundation and the Fondation Le Corbusier)

The same notebook pages show how the elevations were jointed with the organic plan and roof and how the masses were organised among themselves (Figures 5, 7).[15]

Le Corbusier described his architectural process in the following terms: 'Three phases to this adventure: 1. identifying with the site; 2. spontaneous birth (after incubation) of the whole work, all at once, and all of a sudden; 3. the slow execution of the drawings, the purpose, the plans and the construction itself'.[16] After this 'spontaneous birth' following the fundamental phase of gestation – during which the ideas began to take shape and the references came into play – the workshop studies were made. These carried out on a larger scale the process of creation introduced in the notebooks and the tracing paper sketches. I shall give only one example here, but it is a significant one because it presents an overall vision of the architectural object: it is a study in pencil by Le Corbusier,[17] giving the four elevations of the building. I shall not describe it in detail, but I should nevertheless point out that it clearly expresses the major contrast embodied in the overall form of the chapel. Indeed, one can read in the forms the dual function that the architect wanted to give the building: the small chapel providing a shelter for prayer and meditation, and the place of worship capable of receiving a vast crowd of pilgrims. On the one hand, there is the idea of the 'deep grotto', rendered by the effects of soft, round masses that surround the observer and give a sense of reassurance. On the other, there is the intention of creating a welcoming place, as expressed by the concave form of the walls opening up towards the horizons and by the dynamic character of the roof's mass, which acts as a covering over the south entrance and the exterior choir. In this way, the chapel's forms conflict with each other and balance each other at the same time: the bold projection of the southeastern corner responds to the solid, squat masses of the towers; the bulging, sail-like form of the roof's shell is balanced by the verticality of the large southwestern tower and this tower, solidly anchored in the ground and overlooking the site, acts as a beacon. The walls, which seem to turn their backs on the landscape in order to contain and protect an enclosed space, respond to the walls 'opening up' towards the horizons: the building is at once an open-air cathedral and a place for Christian mystery.

Thus the studies executed in accordance with the first sketches contained the essentials of the architect's intentions. By starting with these notebook sketches, dated May and June 1950, it was possible to find the sketches and workshop studies corresponding to the first phase of the work and to establish their chronology;[18] these studies, drawn up between June and November 1950, constitute the preliminary project and make the course to be followed for the whole explicit.

Next, I singled out the second phase of the project, which was elaborated in the sketches and drawings made after January 1951 (at which time the preliminary project was presented to the Commission of Holy Art). The modifications made were in response to opinions expressed by the clients; they were the product of the final perfecting of the idea by the architect and his studio staff.[19] They did not alter the overall conception of the building but were concerned mostly with fine details. This is not the place to describe these changes, but we should note that in the sketches[20] and outlines for the definitive project[21] the overall dimensions were reduced in response to the desire to create a more powerful play of volumes and a denser interior space: to this end, the lines of the building are hypertense, 'like bowstrings' as the architect explained.

In this second phase of the project, it is interesting to examine a few examples that provide an understanding of the manner in which the work of research that began with an idea or a form was refined. Therefore let us consider an example already cited: the form and structure of the roof. We have indicated the primary sources for Le Corbusier's conception of the chapel's roof: the crab shell of which he spoke and the aeroplane-wing structure that one finds in his drawings. He further developed the initial idea, and in his desire to tighten the lines of the building to the utmost degree, he made the east side and the large southeast corner fit together with the west side 'like a growing wave'.[22] It is interesting to discover how he created this 'growing wave' profile for the slope of the roof. During my research, I found in an archive chest a review on which was written, in Le Corbusier's hand, 'Ronchamp preparation documents'; these show that he had noticed an illustration representing the cross-section of a hydraulic dam (Figure 8). The similarity between this cross-section and the curve given to the slope of the roof is quite evident; we should bear in mind that the plan required that it be possible to collect rainwater, since this was in short supply on the hill. The architect therefore imagined the roof's incline – starting with its highest point at the southeastern corner and going down to its lowest point to the west – with a profile analogous to that of a dam's outfall. He used a form that evokes and corresponds to a very specific function.

The dam motif evident in the building's overall form reappears in certain details. It inspired, for example, the ski-jump look that the architect gave to the scupper carrying the rainwater to the west, towards the water tank. The dam cross-section (Figure 8) bears a note by Le Corbusier: 'See *Propos d'urbanisme*'. In the *Propos*, there is a sketch made by the architect in 1945 depicting a dam (Figure 9). I have, moreover, discovered other sketches of this same dam,[23] one of which (dated May 14, 1945) bears the following note by Le Corbusier: 'A simple straightforward perspective – the outfalls are a hydraulic form that must be determined through experiments'. In this instance, he tested the form by applying it to the rainscupper of Ronchamp several years later (we should note that the earliest sketches for the gutter date from February 20, 1951, and clearly belong to the second phase of research sketches).[24]

These two examples are representative of the work carried out during this phase of research, which followed the work of giving shape to the original idea. Of course, this research was continued throughout the project and not just during this second series of sketches; this second series only completed and refined the research done by Le Corbusier in his studio.

The example of the dams sheds light on the architect's creative method: starting with an initial idea – in this case, creating an organic form corresponding to an organic plan – and with an intuition – to use the crab shell – he 'invented' an original form that characterised the chapel of Ronchamp in a decisive way. The initial form of the shell was developed, revised, and took on the structure of an aeroplane wing; and the necessity of collecting water led to the architect's adoption of the profile of a hydraulic outfall for the mass of the roof. From this synthesis of ideas and forms was born the 'prow', the 'full sail' of Ronchamp.

Thus in order to find the sources of inspiration that would complement his work, Le Corbusier drew on a very diverse store of references which was as much the product of travel reminiscences (such as Tivoli) and personal memories (such as the crab shell found on Long Island), as it was borrowings from the language of contemporary technology (the aeroplane wing, hyd-

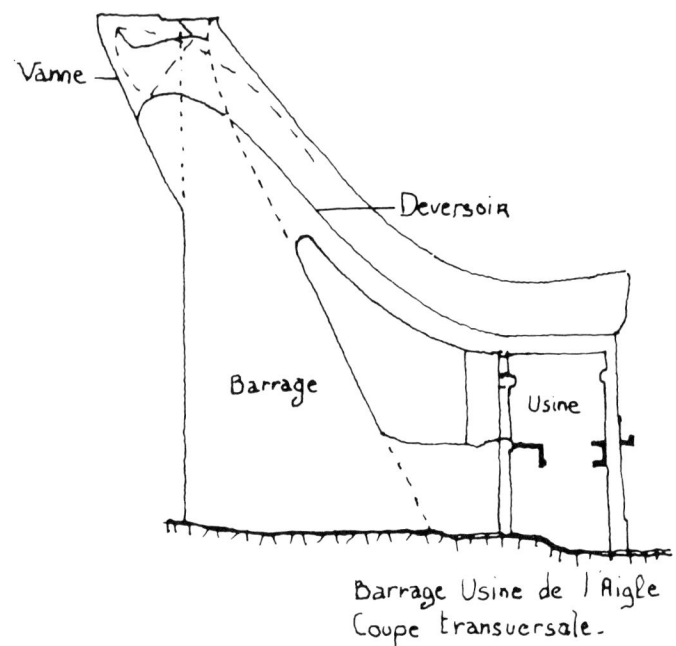

Figure 8. Hydraulic dam, cross-section. From *Reconstruction*, October 1948, p 12.

raulic dams, etc). It was obviously not a question of compiling a kind of catalogue of forms or models to be directly transposed into a project but rather one of retaining ideas and solutions, of noticing analogies of forms attributable to analogies of function. This is the case with some of the sources that I should like to mention now. Unlike the direct influences that I have just described and to which Le Corbusier explicitly referred, these sources reveal instead, to my mind, the workings of an unconscious process.

Indeed, parallel to the explicit references that come into play in the process of the creation of the architectural work, there are a number of unconscious influences that enter into the process either during the gestation of the work or during the elaboration of the project. But before discussing these influences, it would be useful to dwell for a moment on this incubation phase, which is to my mind of the utmost importance in Le Corbusier's creative process. It seems, moreover, to be one of the constants of his work method, as much in painting as in architecure. He explained, as we remember: 'When assigned a task, I am in the habit of storing it in my memory, that is, of not allowing myself to make any sketches for months'; he added that the human brain is like a 'box' in which one lets the 'elements of a problem simmer'. During this phase, even if indeed he did not draw, some of the work of research and documentation necessary to master the elements of a given problem was nevertheless carried out. In our particular instance, that of Ronchamp, the architect informed himself about the site, the tradition of pilgrimage associated with the place, and its devotion to the Holy Virgin; he looked into the rituals of the Catholic religion and spoke with ecclesiastics; he studied and annotated a monograph devoted to the site of Ronchamp, consulted reviews of religious art, etc. Thus, before anything else, he gathered information, accumulated documents, took notes. Then these various elements were sorted out, analysed, assimilated, perhaps reused, sometimes forgotten. Only then did the idea become precise. Enriched by sources emanating from his unconscious, the idea emerged, clearly formulated by the drawing: only then did Le Corbusier 'invent'.

Among the implicit sources that I was able to discover,[25] and for which I was able to establish a clear relation with the Ronchamp project, one seems to be particularly revealing; it is found, like a number of others, among the architect's travel souvenirs. During a 1931 trip to Northern Africa, Le Corbusier visited the valley of

Figure 9. Dam at Chastang, pen and ink sketch.

the M'zab in the Algerian desert.[26] I found several drawing notebooks[27] marking out the whole itinerary of this journey and showing in particular the fascination that Mozabite architecture held for the architect: he paid attention to urban sights, street scenes, the effects of volumes, plays of light and shadow, as well as to relationships of proportions, details of the organisation of dwellings, the layout of patios and indoor spaces, and principles of light admission. He noted in particular how the openings were distributed parsimoniously in the thick walls and remarked that this sort of loophole with deep splays preserved an indispensable freshness inside the building and diffused the light in a very precise and restrained manner. The similarity between this kind of opening and those in the southern wall of Ronchamp is certainly remarkable (Figure 10); here, too, this principle allowed a very exact control of the amount of light inside the chapel, creating that atmosphere of semi-darkness so conducive to meditation. Le Corbusier noted that some of these loopholes also acted as placement niches. Later we see this same idea at work at Ronchamp, in the thickness of the southern wall, to the east, where there are hollows designed to hold objects of worship during open-air services. At Ronchamp, as at M'zab, we find the same whiteness of the material, a whiteness of lime serving to catch the light and exalt the purity of the forms: '. . . there, the volume of things appears clearly; the colour of things is explicit. The whitewash is absolute: everything stands out, everything is absolutely etched in, black on white: it is honest and direct'.[28] In both places, we find walls of the same thickness: in the one case, this serves to protect from heat and retain shade; in the other, the deep splays permit the calculated and attenuated diffusion of the light, and the thickness of the southern wall serves to buttress the mass of the roof.

We cannot claim that the Mozabite architecture analysed by Le Corbusier directly and consciously influenced the chapel of Ronchamp. Here instead we are dealing with that kind of reference that he retained through the drawing, over the course of his travels and throughout his experiences and his research. There is another example that seems sufficiently demonstrative to be mentioned here. Over the course of my research I found by chance, among the vast mass of documents amassed by the architect,[29] a review from 1930 with a photograph of the funerary steles of a Jewish cemetery in the Middle East:[30] the form of these steles disturbingly evokes that of the chapel's towers. There is nothing that really allows us to see a relation, even an unconscious one, between the two; let us say that it is an image, among so many others, that he saw and perhaps preserved in his memory. These references are far from being purely formal. They involve a multitude of observed and assimilated facts, 'spatial facts' and 'architectural facts': these are plays of volumes, ideas for arrangement, approaches to the site, proportional relationships, lights and shadows, colours, effects of building materials, *modenaturas*; they are also solutions that respond ingeniously to a particular problem, forms of know-how, of 'ways to make'. Didn't Le Corbusier take pleasure in repeating that 'art is the way to make'?

For Le Corbusier this constant enrichment of what constitutes the architect's knowledge came about as much through his travels and his visits to buildings as through his visits to museums and libraries, particularly in his formative years. And all of the information that he gathered along the way and that became his own sometimes re-emerged, without becoming really visible or conscious, at the moment in which he 'invented', in which he created his own architectural language.

This process was marked with hundreds, even thousands, of sketches, innumerable annotated notebook pages that constituted, throughout his life, his 'long, patient search', for – and I must insist on this point – it was fundamentally through the constant practice of drawing that Le Corbusier was able to retain all those references representing possible sources for the architectural project. And here, to my mind, lies the key to his creative process.

In a work published during the last years of his life, *L'Atelier de la recherche patiente*,[31] Le Corbusier explained the importance of the drawing as 'memory':

> When one travels and is a practitioner of visual things, architecture, painting, or sculpture, *one sees with one's eyes, and one draws in order to take inside, into one's own history, the things that one sees.*[32]
>
> Once things have been interiorised through the work of the pencil, they remain within for the rest of one's life; they are written there, inscribed.
>
> To draw oneself, to follow outlines, to fill up spaces, to explore volumes, etc, is first of all to see; it is being perhaps qualified to observe, perhaps qualified to discover . . . at this moment the phenomenon of invention may arise. One invents, and one even creates; one's whole being is brought into the action; this action is the central issue.

Thus the drawing enables one to see better, to glean the essentials of a form or an idea, to establish relationships, to take note of details; it is a way of making observations, of registering information, of singling out a problem or a solution; it is a way of 'understanding things', as the architect gives us to understand. The numerous drawings that are not part of the corpus of architectural drawings published here constitute in themselves an exceptionally rich collection. I undertook the study of these drawings a number of years ago[33] because they seemed to me of essential importance in understanding the artist's method. These drawings, including those from the period of his youth and formative years – life-studies, building surveys, portraits, landscapes, sketches made in museums, etc – as well as those that mark all of his production – still-lifes, studies for paintings or sculptures, drawings of women, sketches made during his travels – give us a glimpse of the architect's vast curiosity, his powers of observation, his understanding of the world and his powers of invention. It is by starting with this 'sedimentation', with a plurality of things seen and retained through drawing, that the phenomenon of invention can occur. It was with this knowledge that Le Corbusier sustained the work of creation. And the drawing thus serves to concretise this invention, to express the idea.

Figure 10. Mosque of Sidi Brahim at El Atteuf, M'zab. (Photo Danièle Pauly)

Indeed, if the drawing is 'memory' for the architect, it is also, during the project, the instrument of research and creation. We quoted earlier these comments of Le Corbusier's: 'Then, one day, a spontaneous initiative of one's inner being takes shape, something clicks; you pick up a pencil . . .' The drawing is thus the immediate transcription of the idea that is taking shape: 'To see first of all the project in one's mind'. He went on to explain, 'The drawing is useful only in contributing towards the synthesis of ideas already thought out'.[34] In the same way, the notebook sketches that we mentioned above make plain how, in a few strokes, the essentials of the idea are given. The drawing, made in ink, is linear, concise, synthetic; at the same time it is a research tool that, in the detail studies, for example, helps the idea to become manifest, to formulate itself definitively. Although ink permitted the lively and rapid writing in the notebook sketches, it was with charcoal that the architect gave forth, in the studio, the first expression and traced in broad strokes the first outlines ('Give me some charcoal and some paper; it all begins with a response to the site . . .') Colour helped to determine choices; it was the 'key to the process', as the architect indicated. Finally, he sketched out the more advanced studies in pencil; the pencil allowed for a more precise rendering and made it possible to present details and to represent the density of the masses, the plays of light and shadow, the 'life of the forms'. As Le Corbusier himself explained, the overall conception of the project was always, for him, defined at the start, and one may assert that for him the drawing was in a real sense *cosa mentale*.

The vast production of drawings existing alongside the architectural drawings is, to my mind, the most eloquent possible illustration of Le Corbusier's relationship with history. We have seen how the multitude of remembered images and ideas comprising the architect's personal history and experience nourished his creativity and enriched his architectural vocabulary and how he fed the project with the study and knowledge of history, even though this is not immediately discernable. If I have been able to cite some of the sources that seemed essential to an understanding of the genesis of the project, it is because I made the effort to seek them out or because the architect chose to reveal them in explaining his procedure and commenting on his work. It is also in order to demonstrate that creation, far from being the fruit of inspirational genius, depends much more on a long and minute work process, a 'long, patient search', as the architect liked to repeat. This said, the manner in which his relationship with history was registered in the work of architectural creation lay rather in the realm of the inexplicable, the 'unutterable'. In a work entitled *Territorio dell'architettura*, Vittorio Gregotti explained:

> It is, however, necessary to know that the whole experience, as history, tends towards becoming presence and signification at the moment of the project, that is, becoming action for the subject; and then, anew, becoming historical experience.[35]

I believe that, for Le Corbusier, history intervened in a real sense as a dynamic element in the creative process. And in the project that I have chosen to analyse, I have been able to ascertain to what degree this was confirmed at various stages and levels. I have dealt at length with the role of references in the gestation and research phases. I have also mentioned the importance that the architect attributed to knowing the history of the site, which entailed the devotion to the Virgin Mary and the tradition of pilgrimage associated with the place. Finally, through the forms he imagined and the spaces he created, he firmly established the chapel in architectural tradition. In fact, as surprising as this work may have appeared to his contemporaries, its users find that it has certain affinities, and even a certain intimate resemblance with, Roman churches, for example: the same sacred atmosphere, the same bulky volumes, the same thick walls, the same deep splays, the same semi-darkness conducive to meditation. In this way, the building expresses a kind of intimacy, an implicit bond with the past.

Le Corbusier's architectural language had the basis of its originality in a 'creative' and dynamic vision of history; he spoke of the links existing between 'architectural invention' and knowledge of the past in the following terms:

> ... Carried away by the defence of the rights to invention, I used the past as a witness, this past which was my only master and which continues to be my permanent counsel.
>
> Every level-headed man, once cast into the unknown of architectural invention, can really only sustain his impetus by looking to the lessons provided over the centuries. The testimonies provided by the ages have a permanent human value. One may consider them folklores – a notion expressing the flower of the creative spirit in folk traditions – by extending their realm beyond man's home to that of the gods.
>
> Flower of the creative spirit, chain of traditions which embody it and each link of which is and can only be a work that is innovative, and often revolutionary, within its working; a contribution.
>
> The history that bases itself on reference points preserves only these faithful testimonies; the imitations, plagiarisms and compromises fall behind them, abandoned, even destroyed.
>
> Respect for the past is a filial attitude natural to every creator.[36]

This text seems particularly to reveal an 'intimate and profound harmony with the past' that determined Le Corbusier's attitude. For him, history was truly 'the mark of human presence',[37] and architecture was the 'memory of peoples', to use Ruskin's terms. In a profound sense, it is a relationship of 'sympathy' towards history that most authoritatively characterises this development. He said, 'But we who intensely experience the current epoch of modern times . . . we have extended our sympathy to the entire earth and to all the ages . . . '[38] It is essentially through the constant, unfailing practice of drawing that this fundamental relationship to history is expressed.

Translated by Stephen Sartarelli

Notes

1 I was associated with the Fondation Le Corbusier from 1973 to 1977, and after having worked on the archives, I was assigned the research work on drawings.
2 That is, about ten years ago. I was able at the time to distinguish the studies executed or revised by Le Corbusier from those made by his collaborators, especially Maisonnier.
3 I was able to establish the chronology of the studies and drawings, but this chronology does not figure in this publication.
4 Le Corbusier, *Ronchamp, les carnets de la recherche patiente*, notebook 2 (Zurich: Girsberger, 1957); and *Textes et dessins pour Ronchamp* (place not given: Forces Vives, 1965).
5 See Danièle Pauly, *Ronchamp, lecture d'une architecture* (Strasbourg: APPU/Paris: Ophrys, 1980), p 24 ff.
6 We shall not treat this matter here; see above-cited work.
7 Unpaginated.
8 Le Corbusier, *Textes et dessins pour Ronchamp*, unpaginated.
9 Le Corbusier, *Ronchamp, les carnets de la recherche patiente*, p 89.
10 Outline of the plan made from the first notebook sketches: Fondation Le Corbusier (FLC) no 7.470 (charcoal and red pencil on tracing paper, signed 'LC' and dated June 6, 1950; 75 cm x 118.5 cm).
11 Sketchbook D 17, p 15.
12 Le Corbusier, in the file 'Création Ronchamp' (FLC archives).
13 Le Corbusier, *L'Oeuvre complète, 1946-1952* (Zurich: Girsberger, 1967), pp 28-31.
14 For example, FLC nos 7.435, 7.369, 7.415, among others.
15 Sketchbook E 18, pp 7 and 9.
16 Le Corbusier, *Textes et dessins pour Ronchamp*, unpaginated.
17 FLC no 7.433, black pencil and coloured pencil on tracing paper, 110 cm x 75 cm.
18 For example, FLC nos 7.470, 7.417, 7.433, or 7.412 and 7.414.
19 Le Corbusier's studies were taken up again in the workshop by Maisonnier above all; I was easily able to distinguish Le Corbusier's studies from the rest (see Pauly, p 40).
20 Sketchbook E 18, sketches dated February 1951.
21 For example, FLC no 7.324.
22 See Pauly, Figure 20, p 49.
23 Investigations into various archive chests.
24 Sketchbook E 18, pp 18 and 19.
25 See Pauly, pp 132 ff.
26 I was able to take the 'M'zab voyage' and retrace part of Le Corbusier's itinerary. I did the same for the Villa Adriana at Tivoli.
27 These notebooks of drawings are distinguished from the sketchbooks by their format; they are larger than the latter and consist of drawing paper; they are spiral notebooks whose pages we have numbered according to the drawings of Le Corbusier (cf Notebook C 12).
28 Le Corbusier, cited in Maurice Besset, *Qui était Le Corbusier?* (Geneva: Skira, 1968), p 17.
29 An analysis of the contents of the numerous portfolios of Le Corbusier enabled me to uncover the richness and diversity of the material gathered to stimulate his creativity. In addition to drawings and sketches, these portfolios contained many magazine clippings, photos, reviews, and documents of a great variety.
30 In VU, no 137, December 1930 (FLC archives).
31 Le Corbusier, *L'Atelier de la recherche patiente* (Paris: Vincent, Fréal, 1960), p 37.
32 My emphasis.
33 To this end I am preparing a descriptive catalogue of some of these drawings.
34 Le Corbusier, cited in Jean Petit, *Le Corbusier lui-même* (Geneva: Editions Rousseau, 1970), p 30.
35 Vittorio Gregotti, *Territorio dell'architettura* (Milan, 1966). See also 'The Territory of Architecture' (*Architectural Design* vol 56 5/6-1985).
36 Le Corbusier, *Entretiens avec les étudiants des écoles d'architecture*. (Paris: Editions Minuit, 1957).
37 See Manfredo Tafuri, *Teorie e storia dell'architettura* (Roma:Laterza, 1968), pp 62-63.
38 Le Corbusier, *Quand les cathédrales étaient blanches* (Paris: Plon, 1937), p 16.

Ronchamp Chapel
Ronchamp, France 1951

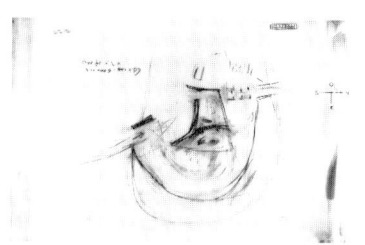

7.470
Study sketch, siting of the chapel, calculation of surface areas, orientation. Le Corbusier, June 6, 1950. Charcoal and red pencil on thick paper, 75cm x 1,185cm.

7.307
View in plan, study sketch of the situation, No 2 on the left-hand side. Le Corbusier, June 6, 1950. Pencil on thick paper, 56cm x 64cm.

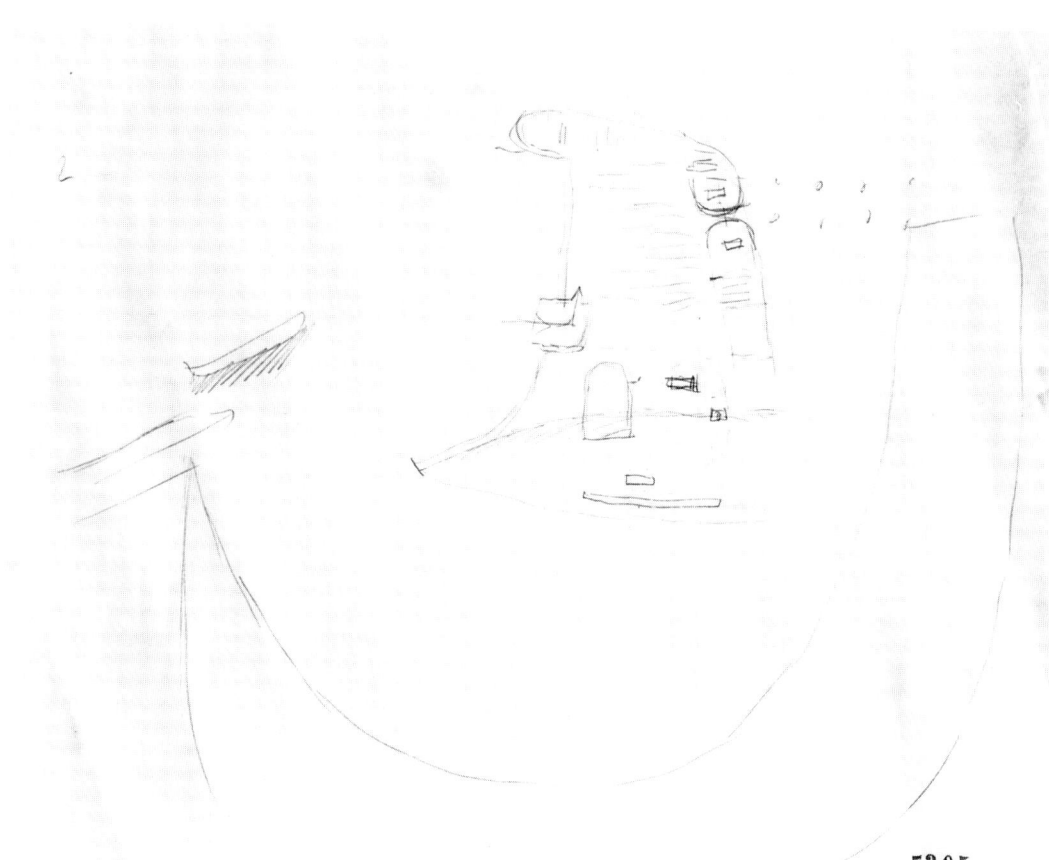

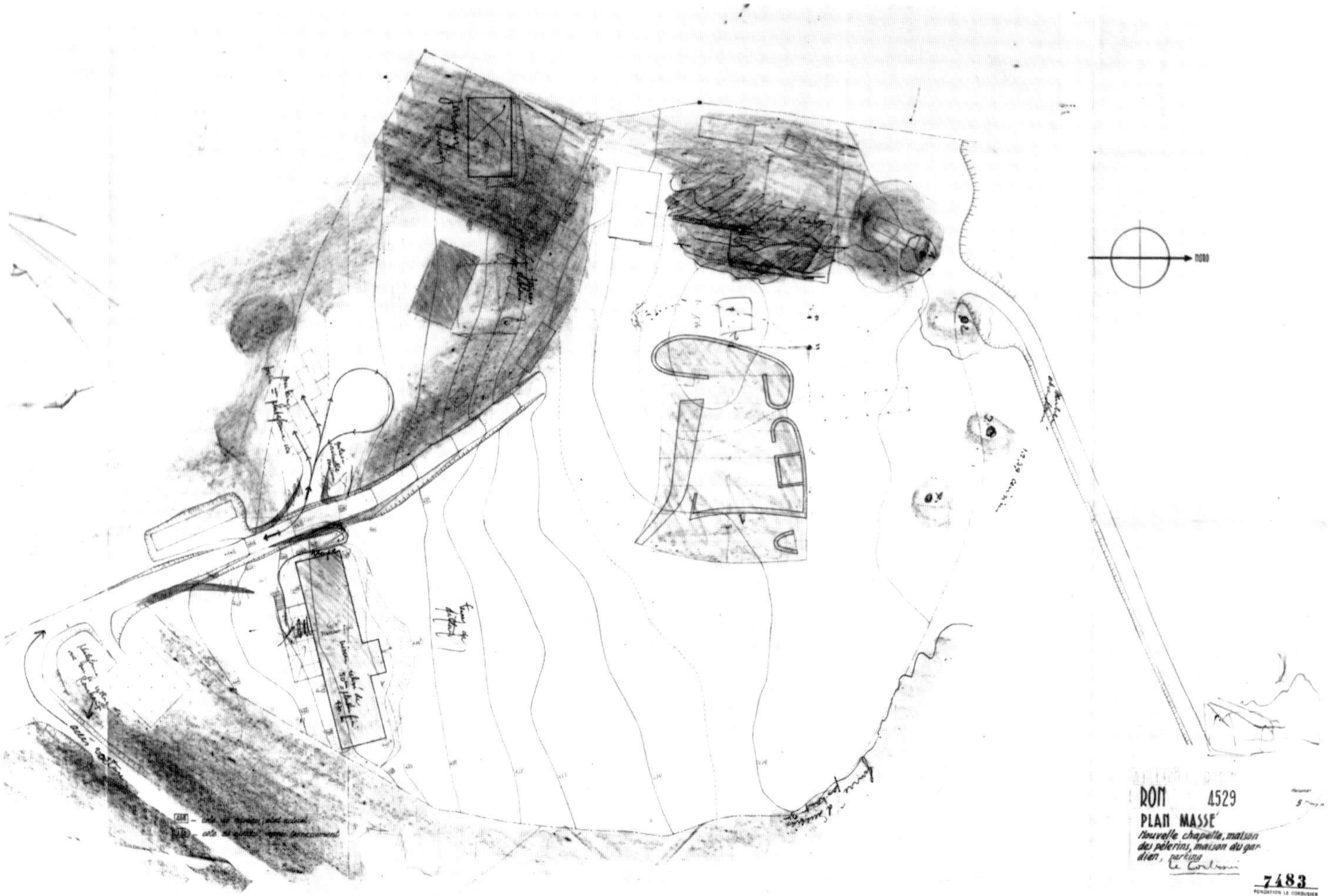

7.311
Plan of the chapel showing stair, sacrysty, etc, notes on the drawing. Le Corbusier, June 6, 1950. Pencil and colouring pencil on thick paper, 54 x 66cm.

7.481, 7.483
Mass plans of the chapel, pilgrimage house, porter's lodge, parking and pyramid: colouring, sketches, notes added to one print. Mass plan of the layout of the site. Contour lines, spot heights, calculations on the prints. Both drawn by Maisonnier, stamped by the atelier. There are prints of the same plan classified under the numbers 7.126, 7.480, 7.482, and 7.484. Scale 1:200. Pencil, colouring pencil and blue ink on heliotype. Paper prints, 72cm x 108cm (7.481), 72cm x 118cm (7.483).

7.407
Perspective sketch of the chapel and surroundings. Pencil on sketching paper, 71cm x 106cm.

7.412
Elevation of the east and west facades and north/south section, silhouettes, shadowing, colouring. Pencil and colouring pencil on thick paper, 59cm x 55cm.

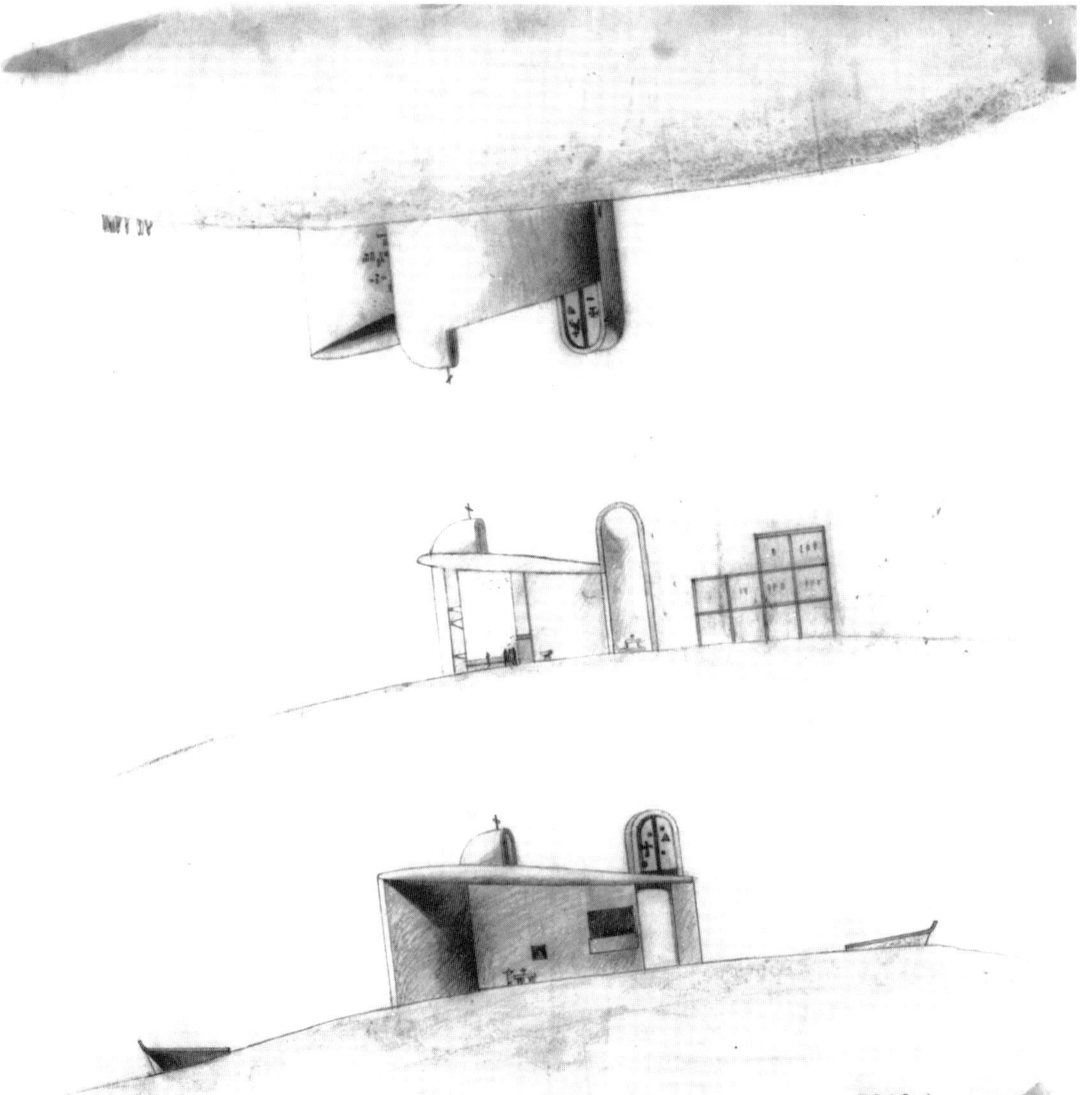

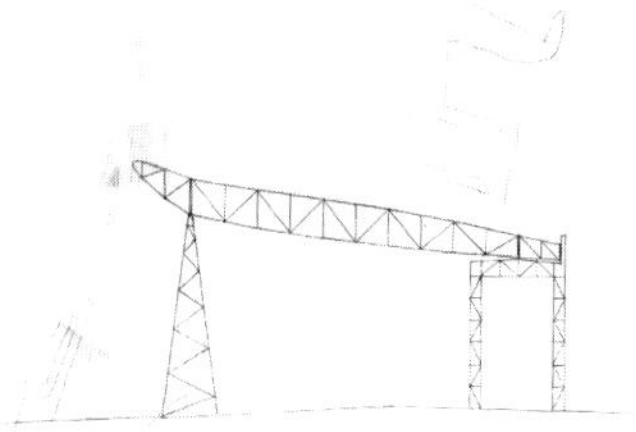

7.314
Study drawing with sketch showing structure, and various other sketches. Part of one sketch at the bottom left of the page is missing. Pencil on tracing paper, 32cm x 53cm.

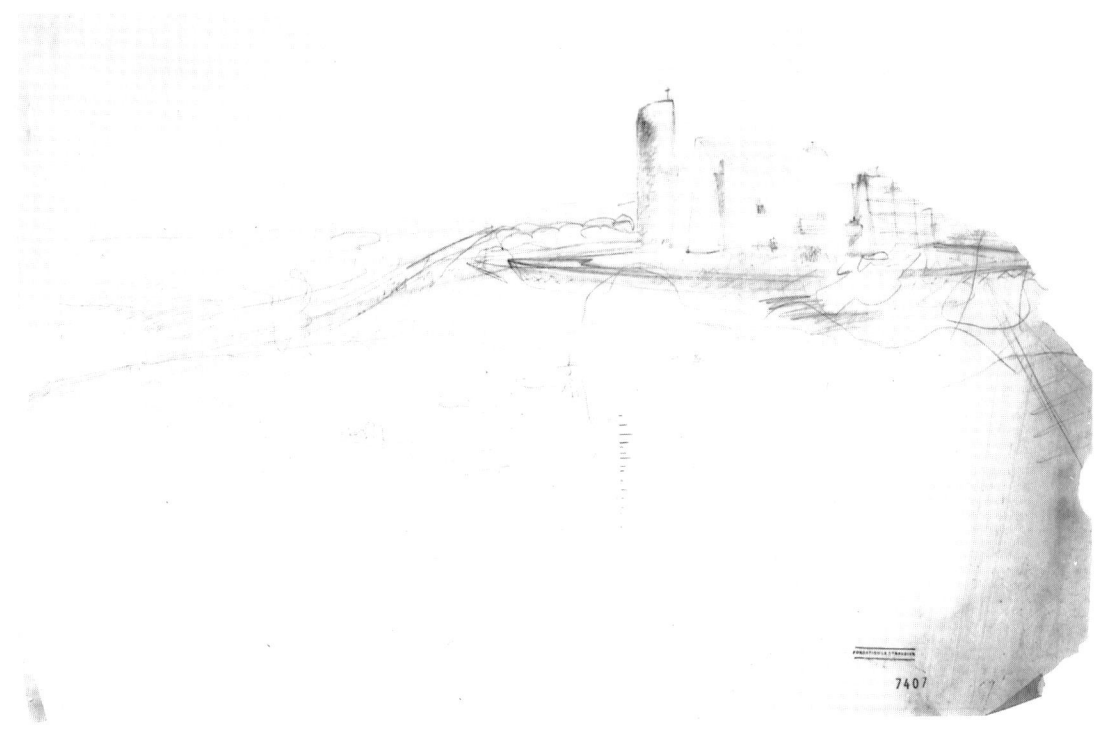

The League of Nations, the Centrosoyus and the Palace of the Soviets, 1926-31
KENNETH FRAMPTON

THE THREE PALATIAL PUBLIC STRUCTURES designed by Le Corbusier and Pierre Jeanneret between 1926 and 1931 are effectively the apotheosis of their first career, coming as they do at the end of an ecstatically enthusiastic period during which they still subscribed to the manifest destiny of the machine age. And yet, while these works seem to have been conceived as large mechanisms, they were, nonetheless, just as decidedly organised and inflected by monumental systems of order and control deriving directly from the French rational classical tradition. This literal dichotomy between an engineer's aesthetic and architecture, to coin the duality around which Le Corbusier's *Vers une architecture* of 1923 had been structured, was first given an overtly mechanical-classical formulation in the Le Corbusier and Pierre Jeanneret entry for the Société des Nations (SdN) competition on which they started to work in April 1926.

Société des Nations (League of Nations), Geneva
First Project on the Mon Repos Site, 1926-1927
It is obvious that the vast programme for the SdN complex compelled Le Corbusier to think out his Purist architectural format at a new scale, and in so doing, he tackled for the first time the problem of evolving an appropriate modern form for the accommodation of a representative structure. The culture of Purism, as elaborated by this time, hardly embraced the issue of monumentality within its purview. Thus, in March 1926, the brief for the Société des Nations was enough to overwhelm a young and ambitious architect, not only because of the spectacular beauty of the lakefront site – the parkscape bordering Lac Leman outside Geneva – but also because of the utopian and international scope of the organisation and the enormous scale of the programme. The basic accommodation required was as follows: a 2,500-seat auditorium, together with foyers and ancillary suites for the general secretary, and for the press, together with the usual telephone and telegraph services and six large commission rooms; and a library. The building had to be laid out on a 66,406 m² site, bordered on the west by the Geneva-Lausanne road and on the east by Lake Geneva (Lac Léman) itself.

While the general axial, classical structure of Le Corbusier's Société des Nations is fairly well known from the published drawings, the subtle way in which a sense of ordinance and propriety was achieved, together with the specificity of certain references, is perhaps not so immediately evident. And yet, for those who were privileged to examine the drawings closely (above all, one must assume, the jurors themselves), Le Corbusier's SdN drawings are inscribed with intertextual references which not only insist on a Neo-classical reading, but also make pointed asides as to the specific roots of Le Corbusier's architectural culture. One assumes that H P Berlage, John Burnet, Josef Hoffmann, Victor Horta, Charles Lemaresquier, Karl Moser and Ivar Tengbom, to mention the most worldly members of the jury, could hardly have missed the intention of the two protagonists caricatured under the section of the peristyle to the Assembly Hall; for the seated figure with his high-heeled boots and boater is patently Auguste Perret, while the standing silhouette with homburg and walking stick is Le Corbusier himself (23.168). The ironic inference is clear enough; the old and the new representatives of rational classicism are here, for a moment, situated side by side on the threshold of a new era. A reference of an equally cryptic nature, and one which has only become evident through the publication of this archive material, is the sculptural group over the general secretary's suite at the apex of the Assembly Hall, facing over the lake. Four figures are depicted on the high pedestal above this presidential pavilion (23.174), and these are as follows: a lion on the left, a horse and a man standing together in the centre and, on the right, a crow. The strange iconography of this sculptural group requires some explanation. The central figures are apparently derived from the Dioscuri, transposed by Behrens (after Schinkel's Altes Museum) into a symbol for the German State and used by him on top of his St Petersburg Embassy of 1912 and again in the Festhalle erected for the Werkbund Exhibition of 1914. Le Corbusier's free interpretation of this icon is not without certain implications, for the horse, instead of being restrained by a man, is now running free – surely a sign of Dionysian energy – while the remaining male figure, instead of being rigidly frontalised, as in Behrens' version, adopts a graceful asymmetrical posture, evocative of Apollonian calm. The attendant beasts left and right comment at a more intimate level on the generic meaning of the inner dialectical pair, for the lion seemingly stands for Jeanneret, while the crow, poised as if on the verge of flight, is clearly meant to signify as the image of a pun, the 'crow-like' one, that is, the volatile personality of Le Corbusier himself. Le Corbusier's awareness of being technically dependent upon the expertise of his more technocratic cousin is confirmed by the compensatory statement which he made late in life: 'I am the sea and he is the mountain and as everyone knows these two can never meet'.[1]

Aside from these idiosyncratic, yet significant references, rational classicism is present as a legacy in Le Corbusier's SdN Assembly Hall in ways which are more overt (23.181 and 23.183): first of all in the Palladian structuring of the assembly head building about an ABABA rhythm, then in the provision of a peristyle, labelled as such, and finally in the elaborate hierarchical sequence of entry comprising a *scala regia* followed by a *pas perdus*. This sequence continues under the belly of the auditorium itself as a *promenade architecturale* (23.229) and is perhaps comparable to that long corridor which, with more sinister intent, is featured in Albert Speer's New State Chancellery of 1937. In this instance, however, the long and impressive promenade terminates in the general secretary's suite facing out over the lake (23.288).

Rational classicism is evident in the proposed cladding of the polished granite veneer, in the paving and intercolumniation of the principal lobbies (23.181, 23.183 and 23.179) – surely indebted to Perret's Théâtre des Champs Elysées foyer of 1912 (23.173) – and even in the organisation of the Secretariat library which seems to make an explicit reference to Henri Labrouste's Bibliothèque Nationale, above all in the organisation of the reading room and in the placement of the bookstack to the rear (23.190, 23.253). Classicism is also evident in the studies for the placement of sculptural enrichment, in the low relief sculptures

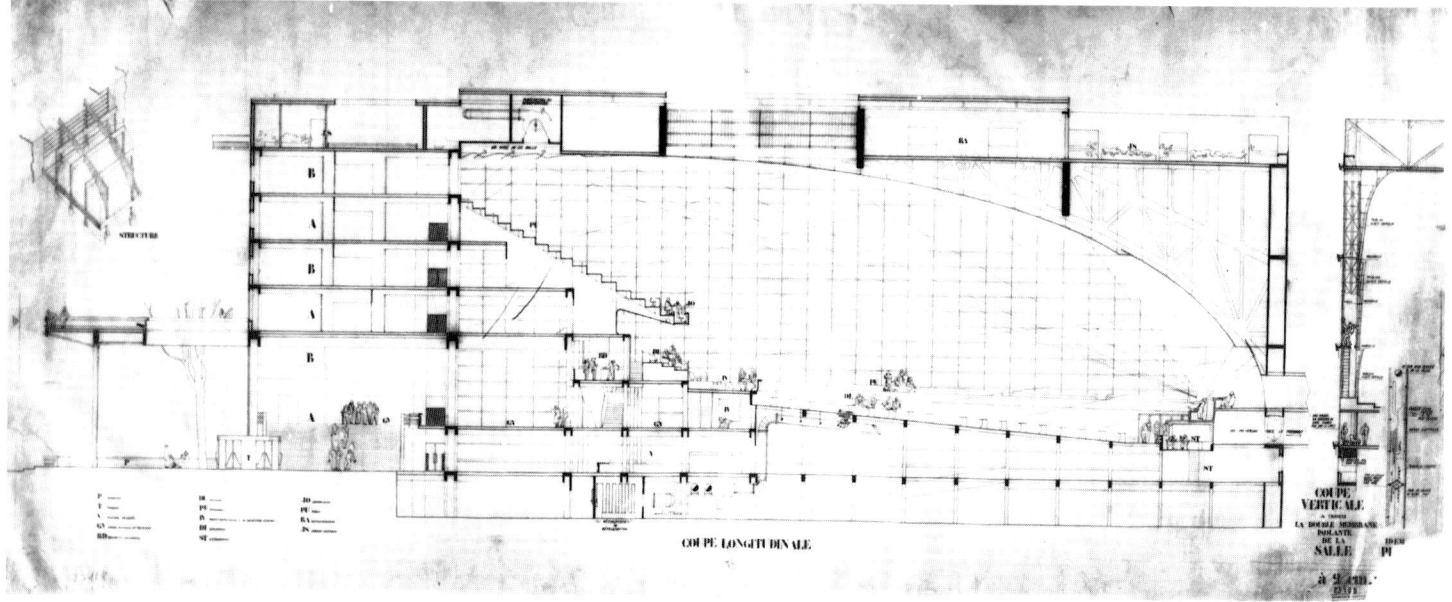

Figure 1. Assembly Hall, longitudinal section (FLC 23.168).

shown under the *porte cochère* fronting the Assembly Hall (see 23.194 versus 23.246). Apart from this, Julien Gaudet's classical 'elementarism' is directly utilised by Le Corbusier as a compositional method in the alternative layout which he was to append to the main site plan bearing the caption: 'An alternative proposal employing the same compositional elements'.[2]

Neo-classical again, or in any event within the architectural tradition of the Enlightenment, was the dramatic proposal made for illuminating the assembly chamber. This large volume was dialectically conceived as being lit through translucent glazed surfaces, on which the light would play in more or less the same way irrespective of whether the source was natural or artificial. It is characteristic that Le Corbusier referred to this manner of illumination as though it were some kind of patent device or technological breakthrough, comparable to the ducted air-conditioning system which he adopted for the main chamber. Next to his diagrams illustrating the system of *chauffage par le procédé d'aération ponctuelle*, he provided a parallel plate demonstrating the precepts of *éclairage étincelant* – sparkling light – which showed how the Assembly Hall would be illuminated throughout the day by diffused light coming through three top lanterns and through translucent double-glazed curtain walls flanking the auditorium (23.178). It may be claimed that through this arrangement, he was able to combine classical Enlightenment symbolism with modern technology. Thus while permanently and evenly illuminated during the day, the hall would literally glow with light at night, thereby symbolically suggesting the wisdom and diligence with which the nocturnal deliberations of the SdN would assure security to the world at large. A notion of transcendental technology is also implicit in those plates which compare *les salles de format favorable à l'acoustique* to more traditional circular or semi-circular shapes classified as *anti-acoustique* (23.216). The care with which the acoustics of the hall were worked out in consultation with Gustave Lyon is indicated in 23.187 and again in 23.216, where the adopted scheme bears the caption: 'All the reflected sound waves are parallel to the walls, there are no secondary reflexions'.

The transcendence of modern technique is also evident in the steel framing to the main hall where the primary longitudinal trusses take their roller-bearing support off two sets of twin reinforced concrete pylons (Palladian format) which are also used to bracket the main elevator shafts. This hierarchical structural order is complemented by the integration of these trusses with the transverse frames and with the lantern roof lighting as sketched out in drawing 23.262 and finally incorporated into the actual framing layout developed by the Zurich engineers Terner and Chopard in January 1927 (23.396). It is interesting to note how this framing was simplified by the architects for the final presentation, the number of bracing members being reduced (Figure 1) and the curtain wall being greatly simplified (23.170). The Terner and Chopard design also makes Le Corbusier's debt to Behrens' AEG Turbine Factory of 1910 explicit, above all in the exposed hinged joints flanking the outer perimeter of the hall, where each truss takes its hinged bearing off a stubb concrete column.

It is convenient to mention at this juncture Le Corbusier's habit of transposing a given typological solution to another context, whereby a kind of internal code is established, displacing the attributes of one situation to another. Thus, the twin reinforced concrete pylons of the SdN Assembly Hall reappear as the intermediate attached *pilotis* to the Pavillon Suisse of 1932, thereby bestowing upon a fragmentary *redent* slab drawn from the typology of La Ville Radieuse the connotation of being a 'monumental' front, comparable to the frontal presence such a form as this first had in the SdN building! This apparent 'transposition' is also supported by the partially radial configuration given to the plan of the foyer situated to the rear of the Pavillon Suisse. Are we justified in seeing this ancillary block as though it were the vestigial remains of the SdN auditorium?

The 'machinism' which permeates Le Corbusier's SdN proposal makes itself most manifest in the complex circulation system adopted for the Assembly Hall. That this system was privately conceived as some kind of biological metaphor is dramatically indicated in the sketch plan of the hall depicting three superimposed levels (23.381). This drawing includes a brief sketch of an aorta conceived as a kind of Klein bottle or bivalve where the public passes through one half and the journalists through the other. This scissors stair system which alternatively delivers its users to the A or B floors (clearly annotated as A and B in the large section of the hall shown on Figure 1) is first sketched out in two alternative forms on drawing 23.263, the journalists and visitors entering into the A section of the stair and the general public entering into the B. The transverse section drafted out in drawing 23.173 shows how the B floors only give access to public galleries while the A floors feed the two-storey committee rooms, *les salles des grandes commissions*. The overall system for

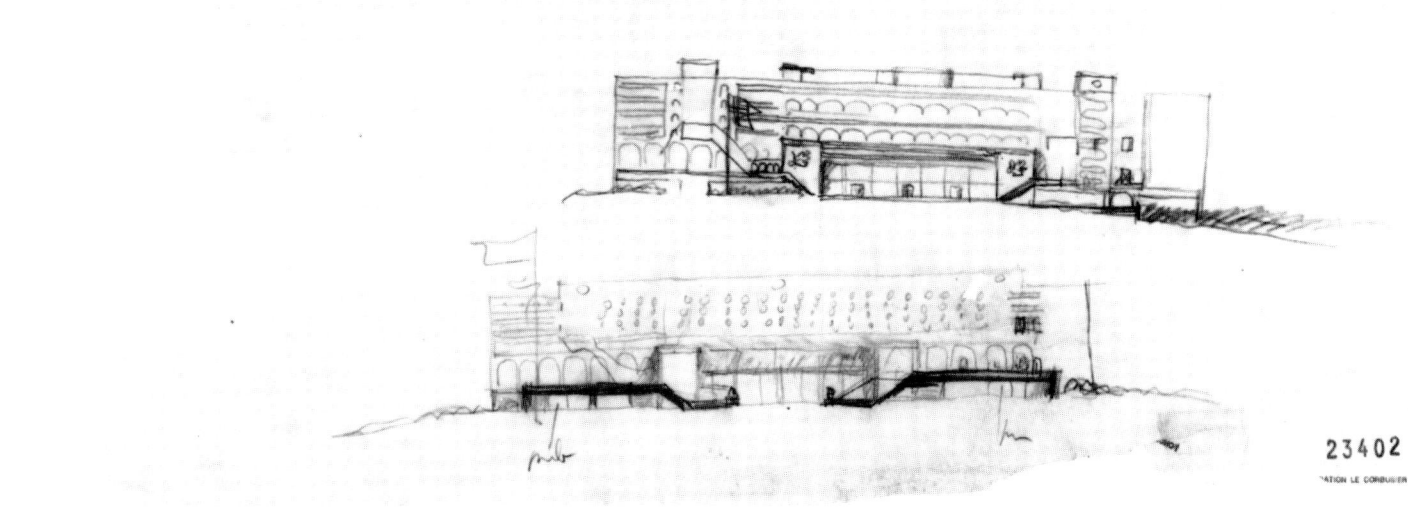

Figure 2. Assembly Hall, sketch for facade (FLC 23.402)

classifying the users of the hall is first shown clearly in the plan 23.237, which also gives indications as to the separate system of service access and shows the twin elevators serving the main body of the hall.

Machinism of a more mechanical order is evident in the fenestration to the Secretariat, which is fitted throughout with sliding steel sashes, that is, the *fenêtre en longueur* which Le Corbusier had characterised in his Five Points of a New Architecture of 1926 as the typical mechanical element of the house. The Secretariat fenestration complements this mechanism with a sliding, lightweight tubular steel cleaning cradle – the so-called *passerelle bicyclette* – which was designed to be suspended from the reinforced concrete cornice running around the top of the curtain wall facade. This cornice was also envisaged as having roller shutters fitted to its underside, while a comparable inner slot afforded a pelmet for the curtains on the line of the internal sill below. It is typical of Le Corbusier's technological romanticism that this integrated facade, complete with built-in radiators, should be accorded a certain metaphorical status in his account of the SdN debacle published under the title *Une Maison – un palais* in 1928. 'I have one master', he wrote, 'It is the past'. And elsewhere in this book, opposite an axonometric of the Villa Garches which he regarded as a prototype for his Palais des Nations, he wrote, '. . . We are strengthened by the past because the past has proven to us that under conditions of clarity and lasting equilibrium, the house becomes typified, and that when the type is pure, it possesses an architectural potential . . . it is able to elevate itself to the dignity of a Palace'. Conversely, he referred to his Palais des Nations as 'the administration house of the nations; it is an organism, a mechanism of precise ends. It is a machine for living in'.[4] Elsewhere in *Une Maison – un palais*, under the elevation of his SdN Secretariat block, he displayed a diagram of the garden facade at Garches, drawn to the same scale and accompanied by the caption: 'The disposition of the windows is the same as those on the Villa Garches'.[5]

This transposition of a house into a palace and vice-versa is a key notion underlying Le Corbusier's output, and the elaborate metaphorical substance of his entire endeavour is incomprehensible if we do not understand that it is grounded in this fundamental notion of a transposable hierarchy. The house/palace syndrome was conceived by Le Corbusier as the archetypal double. On this dialectical base, compounded of both classicism and utopian socialism, he established his metaphorical fulcrum: a Purist mythology derived in part from the antique and in part from the technology of the nineteenth century. To this end he combined, in his book *Précisions* of 1930, a sequence of telling images: A J Gabriel's Palais de la Concorde, an ocean-going liner, the SdN Secretariat block, and his own version of what he thought of as an American skyscraper. Not only was the house now transposed into the palace, but the liner, in its turn, was read as a classical structure, thus permitting the SdN Secretariat to be seen as a transcendental integration of the two. This particular identification of the baroque palace with the ocean liner may well have had its origins in the utopian socialist theories of Victor Considérant, particularly his *Considérations sociales sur l'architectonique* of 1834.

Despite this assumption of classical attributes, the early sketches for the Assembly Hall indicate the difficulty Le Corbusier experienced in bringing himself to project a totally monumental facade, evident, for example, in the sheets 23.227, 23.402 (Figure 2), and 23.317, this last being dated November 16, 1926. As these drawings make clear, Le Corbusier had first thought of handling the principal elevation in much the same way as he had treated the entry facade of the Villa Garches, that is to say, he considered relieving the sobriety of a basically symmetrical Palladian *parti* with asymmetrical secondary elements. Similar asymmetrical inflections are evident in the placement of massed flags in early sketches for the SdN, as shown in drawing 23.246. Once again, as Figure 2 indicates, the twin monumental stair to the foyer was originally placed on the exterior, in a manner not dissimilar to the projecting garden stair at Garches.

Le Corbusier regarded his SdN site layout as a *conception paysagiste* (23.249), a phrase evoking both English picturesque and German romantic classicism, and this hybrid intent seems to be confirmed by his use of both the *allée classique* and the *bosquet anglais*. However, the principles according to which the building and its landscape would have been integrated into the existing site went well beyond the scope of the nineteenth-century eclectic landscape tradition, for as Colin Rowe and Robert Slutzky have pointed out, Le Corbusier's SdN project introduces a series of parallel longitudinal planes and spatial slots running perpendicular to the main east/west axial approach. A visitor approaching via the *cour d'honneur* would have had to pass through a series of guillotine planes which,

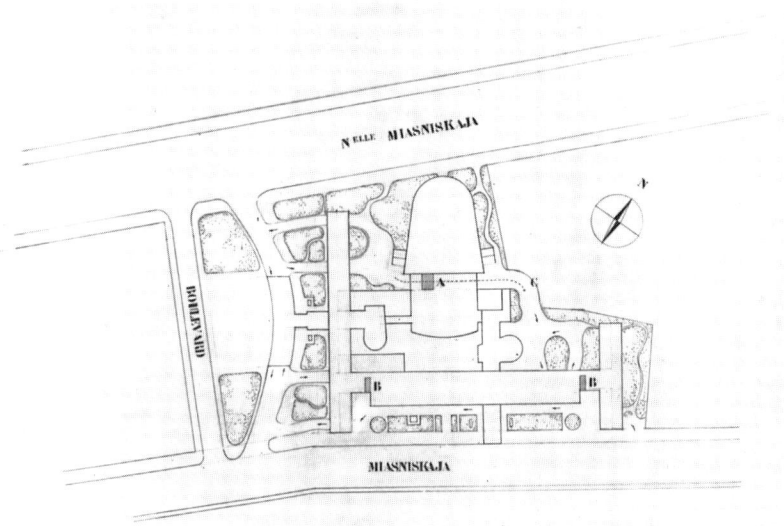
Figure 3. Centrosoyus, site plan (FLC 15.864).

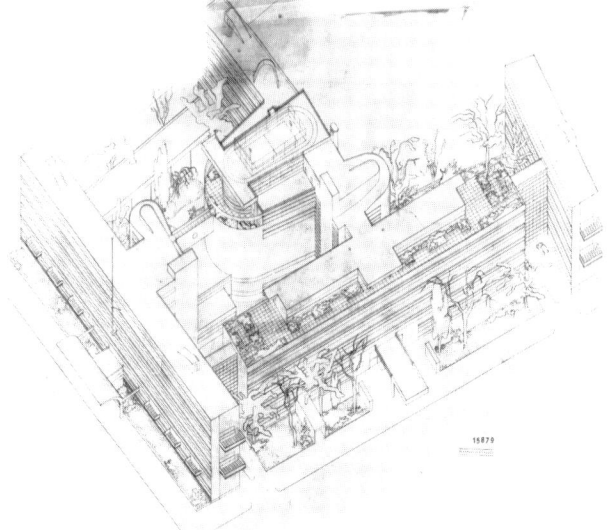
Figure 4. Centrosoyus (FLC 15.879).

either built or planted, granite or green, would have had the effect of deflecting the eye to lateral views of the lake and its attendant foliage. The centre of axial vision would alternately compress frontally and expand diagonally, thereby creating a perceptual ambiguity as to the size and scale of the spatial slots suspended in front of the Assembly Hall.[6]

Centrosoyus – Central Union of Consumer Co-operatives, Moscow, 1928-1929

The Soviet Central Union of Consumer Co-operatives expanded very rapidly under the auspices of the New Economic Policy of the Soviet Union, and in January 1928 it organised, in conjunction with the Society of Civil Engineers, an initial competition for new premises on an 11,000 m² site bordered by the old radial axis of Myasnitskaya Prospect – renamed Kirov Street in 1935 – and cut by two new routes, the new Myasnitskaya Prospect and a boulevard linking the old and the new streets (cf plans 15.684 (Figure 3)-15.692 and perspectives 16.114, 15.689, 16.246). Out of the thirty-two competitors who entered the initial competition, B M Velikovsky and V M Vionov received the first prize. Two further competitions were staged for the same project on exactly the same site; the first of these was an international competition involving a number of foreign competitors, including Max Taut and Sir John Burnet as well as Le Corbusier, and the second, with predominantly Russian competitors, was staged in October 1928.

It is somewhat paradoxical that Le Corbusier was to emerge as the winner from this, the third and last competition, travelling to Moscow in early October and presenting his second project there on October 22. As Jean Louis Cohen has informed us in his essay, 'Cette Mystique: l'URSS':

> On October 27th, the majority of the Soviet participants in the third competition declared that it was indispensable for the future of the new architecture to entrust full control to Le Corbusier and Pierre Jeanneret, and this was done on the 30th. (During this period, Le Corbusier had been running around town: he held a conference presided over by Lunacharsky at the Polytechnic Museum: Alexander Vesnin presented him with 150 architectural projects drafted by his students; he met with Ginzburg, Eisenstein, Meyerhold, etc.) In this address, the competition participants pointed out that 'the conservative traditions continue to remain in command', therefore, 'Le Corbusier's project will be a clear and effective representation of the architectural ideas of today'.[7]

In his four successive schemes for the Centrosoyus (the first dating from October 1928, and the last finished in Paris in January 1929 and accepted by the Soviet authorities in the following March, see Figure 4), Le Corbusier was able to re-use some of the typological components which he had first developed in his design for the Société des Nations, although it has to be admitted that in this transposition a number of modifications took place; above all, there was the initial appearance of the typical Radiant City slab block, first built out in the Pavillon Suisse of 1932. In fact, it is possible to claim that the *parti* adopted for the Centrosoyus anticipated in certain aspects the layout of the Pavillon Suisse – namely the frontal slab with the primary public element to the rear (see sketch layouts 15.923). That Le Corbusier tried out many *redent* variations is evident from drawing number 16.248. The initial scheme seems to have been worked out in a very naive way. Early preliminary sketches show that he even considered a tower (16.238, 16.222 and 16.223) and quite different means of access. For example, elliptical ramps are shown inside on drawing 16.066.

The evolution of the Centrosoyus passed through four separate stages of which the first was a series of sketches in which Le Corbusier evolved the Centrosoyus in the forms of a perimeter block (16.245, 16.238, 16.222, 16.223 and 16.239). One of these early drawings (16.111) also shows the Centrosoyus complex surrounded by other ministries, projected in *redent* formation on the adjacent sites. The second stage and the first definitive *parti* (see sketches 16.246 and 15.671) was published in Le Corbusier's *L'Oeuvre complète 1910-29* and in *L'Architecture vivante* (see drawings 15.879 and 15.687). In this version the assembly hall is oriented on a northeast/southwest axis with the frontal seven-storey slab blocks ranging exactly parallel to the new 'boulevard' and to the Myasnitskaya Prospect respectively. This composition has a schematic quality absent from the penultimate project which was also published in *L'Oeuvre complète 1910-29*. In this third and almost final version the assembly hall has been rotated ninety degrees so that it aligns on a northwest/southeast axis, while the layout of the frontal blocks has been orthogonally rearranged. The result is that only the slab along Myasnitskaya Prospect is now parallel to the street frontage. The other principal block facing the new boulevard is no longer parallel to its frontage (15.692, Figure 3, Figure 5, 15.917 and 15.918). It appears that in the fourth and final version an alignment with the street frontages was insisted upon by the Soviet authorities (16.113, 15.836, 15.871 and 16.114). This much is hinted at in drawing number 15.932 dated March 1929, in which Le Corbusier distinguishes between *notre project*

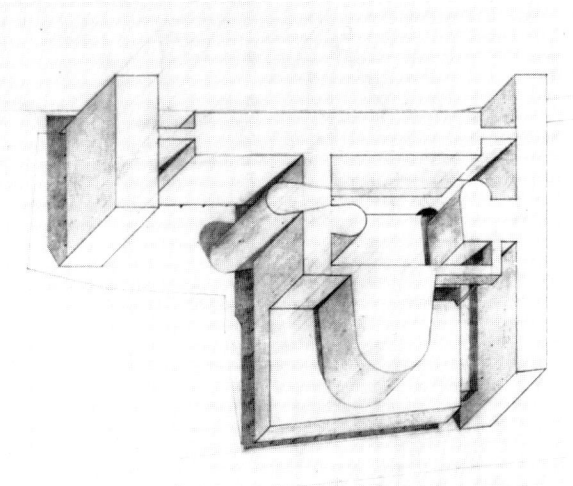

Figure 5. Centrosoyus (FLC 16.052).

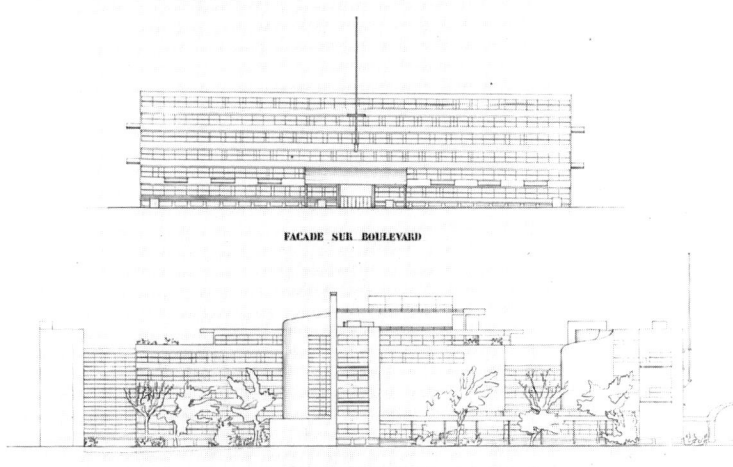

Figure 6. Facades to new boulevard and Myasnitskaya Prospect (FLC 15.685).

décembre and *leur project mars 1929*.

In the earliest Centrosoyus scheme, the main elements of Le Corbusier's initial SdN scheme are reproposed for the Moscow situation. Like pieces of the Cubist collage, the original SdN Secretariat wing is apparently dismembered and redistributed about the perimeter of the Myasnitskaya site, while an assembly hall of reduced size is reconstituted in the centre of the block. This is particularly evident in the boulevard elevation of the first scheme where the SdN elevation is replicated, including projecting balconies at either end (Figure 6). These balconies are eliminated in the later schemes. Le Corbusier also made an equally classical, ie axial, use of sculpture in the Centrosoyus, as in the axial placement of Soviet industrial and agricultural symbols in the boulevard facade (see 15.707, 16.689, 23.194 and 23.246). In the second scheme for Centrosoyus the whole complex is elevated above the ground on *pilotis*, creating an extensive and freely planned foyer underneath. This move, consistent with the precepts of the Five Points, is seminal since it introduces a more fluid concept of circulation into Le Corbusier's general repertoire; above all, in this case, it brings about an elaborate sequence of ramps which are initially combined to provide alternative summer and winter routes to the 1,000-seat auditorium, elevated at the first floor. As this extremely elaborate provision would indicate, Le Corbusier became obsessed with circulation at this time, a fixation which assumed for him the status of a biological metaphor. Of his final project for the Centrosoyus, in which, ironically enough, the circulation had been simplified, he wrote:

> It is obligatory to classify this vast crowd entering and leaving at the same time. It is necessary to make a kind of forum for such occasions; for people whose overshoes and furs will be covered with snow in winter, one must provide well-organised check rooms and systems of circulation . . . A system of *pilotis* almost entirely covers the ground. These raise the offices into the air which do not begin until the first floor. Underneath one is able to circulate freely in the open or in a forum of enormous size served by two principal entrances. Within this forum are to be found elevators, paternosters (continuous elevators arranged in a chain), and immense helicoidal ramps which, replacing stairs, allow for rapid movement. It has been appropriate to set up such a classification in a building which knows two moments: the first, a period of disorderly flux on a vast horizontal ground plane like a lake, the second a period of stable, immobile work, sheltered from noise and comings and goings, the offices where each one is in his place and controllable . . . *Circulation* is a word that I used incessantly in Moscow, in order to explain myself, to the point that several delegates from the various Soviets ended up getting nervous about it . . . I stuck to my position . . . *Architecture is circulation*. If you weigh this point, you will find that it condemns academic methods and consecrates the principle of the *pilotis*.[8]

The circulation of the fourth and definitive Centrosoyus project is, in fact, extraordinarily ingenious and elegant. It consists fundamentally of two separate sequences. The first of these is a pair of free-standing helicoidal ramps which, together with the elevators, serve the office accommodation; the second is an elaborately ramped *promenade architecturale* linking the two separate entrances, situated on the old and new Myasnitskaya streets, respectively. The point of this bipartite system was to provide independent access to the auditorium from both the city and the Centrosoyus foyer. The Centrosoyus is thus the occasion for a totally new concept of interior space in Le Corbusier's work, that is to say, for the invention of the warped floor plane as a distributory surface extending through a forest of *pilotis*. This lake-like space, which departs radically from any Beaux-Arts concept of distribution, re-emerges as a tour de force in the free-flowing *plans inclinés* of Le Corbusier's Palais des Soviets of 1931.

In the Centrosoyus Le Corbusier paid great attention to the elevations flanking the principal streets at the expense of the other facades which, while they are developed in elevation, are left unconsidered from a three-dimensional or plastic point of view. It seems as if the main street facades were thought of as the only representative fronts worthy of elaboration. That the mythically 'aeronautical' detailing proposed for the Centrosoyus was the same as in, say, the Villa Garches and the SdN project, is borne out by use of *tube d'avion* as an elliptical section for the balustrading of the Centrosoyus (16.156).

Société des Nations, Second Project, Parc de l'Ariana Site, 1929

The exact conditions under which Le Corbusier and Pierre Jeanneret came to work on a second project for the SdN in February 1929 remains shrouded in mystery (23.278). The official selection of a new site seems to have provoked Le Corbusier into making one last effort to gain the commission by producing an alternative proposal for the site, which he submitted in April 1929. Although this initiative was ill received, Le Corbusier used the occasion to lodge a formal complaint, pointing out that their first project had been plagiarised by the academic architects who had been selected to work on the final building; Messrs Nenot, Vago, Lefevbre and Broggi. Le Corbusier constructed comparative analyses of the individual Beaux-Arts schemes submitted by each of these competitors, in order to prove that these men had infringed the budget restrictions of the original competition conditions (23.204, 23.218). This was to be of little avail, however, for the Nenot design was officially approved by the SdN in June 1929.

The main interest of this second proposal resides in the light it throws on Le Corbusier's working method, for here once again, as in the Centrosoyus, he adopted an elementarist approach to recombining the components of his original SdN entry (23.296, 23.278). Taking a similar tack as in their Centrosoyus design, Le Corbusier and Pierre Jeanneret rendered the Secretariat as a loosely connected sequence of *redent* slabs (23.265, 23.269). Against these linear *redent* formations, they placed helicoidal ramp forms taken directly from the Centrosoyus, and these elements were to remain in the final version of the second project, where the Secretariat block is finally resolved as a U-shaped complex (23.201, 23.202, 23.306). The Secretariat court shown at the position A, on drawing 23.202, is thus served by a vehicular access which passes in and out of the court, through bridged entrances, the movement taking the form of a continuous system of one-way circulation (23.272, 23.328, 23.329). Behind this court was situated the forecourt to the Assembly Hall (B on 23.202). The Assembly Hall is virtually identical to that used in the original SdN scheme except for straightening out the *pavillon du président*. In an early sketch for the Ariana site, the Secretariat and the Assembly Hall face each other to form a single *cour d'honneur*. Other variations include the initial integration of the library with the Secretariat (23.275, 23.269). The library was soon to be detached, however, and thereafter located parallel to the Assembly Hall, to the southeast of the existing *allée* (23.278). In this position it was also partially aligned with the Musée de l'Ariana on the opposite side of the *allée*.

The design of this free-standing library form is of particular interest, for it introduces a new type into the Corbusian repertoire (23.306). Organised about a top-lit bookstack and foyer, an elongated version of this plan was subsequently adopted for the library in the Cité mondiale, designed in the same year for the philanthropist Paul Otlet, on a site situated to the northwest of the Ariana Park. As far as detailed expression is concerned, provisional sketches indicate that the main facade of the library would have been based on the entry elevation to the Villa Garches (23.306).

The Parc de L'Ariana site was situated inland to the west of

Figure 7. Palace of the Soviets, perspective (FLC 27.249).

the Geneva-Lausanne road. Thus, where the layout of the first project had been determined largely by the configuration of a lakeside site, the second was predicated upon the notion of running a main axis parallel to an existing line of trees, entitled in the proposal the *avenue de la Bibliothèque* (23.202). Thereafter, as in the first SdN proposal, the *parti* came to be structured about a series of layered planes cutting up the lateral space between the front elevation of the Assembly Hall and the rear of the Secretariat complex (23.329).

Palace of the Soviets Competition, Moscow, 1931
After the abortive Palace of Labour competition staged in 1923, the competition for the Palace of the Soviets started in earnest with two interrelated contests: the first, an international trial run, staged in June 1931 and limited to invited participants – a competition in which the foreign architects included Le Corbusier, Perret, Gropius, Mendelsohn, Poelzig, Brazini, Lamb and Urban – and second, an open international competition which was publicly announced on July 18, 1931, with a closing date set for October 30. This second competition, which was, in fact, extended for an extra month, generated a hundred and sixty entries, of which twenty-four were by foreign architects. It is characteristic of the context and the revolutionary spirit of the time that a hundred and twelve additional proposals were also received from non-professionals.

The Palace Construction Council, chaired by no less a figure than V M Molotov himself, selected a number of individual Soviet architects and architectural teams to 'work out a plan for the Palace in order to define what further designing was required and to make the competition requirements more precise'. Individual entries were duly received from such disting-

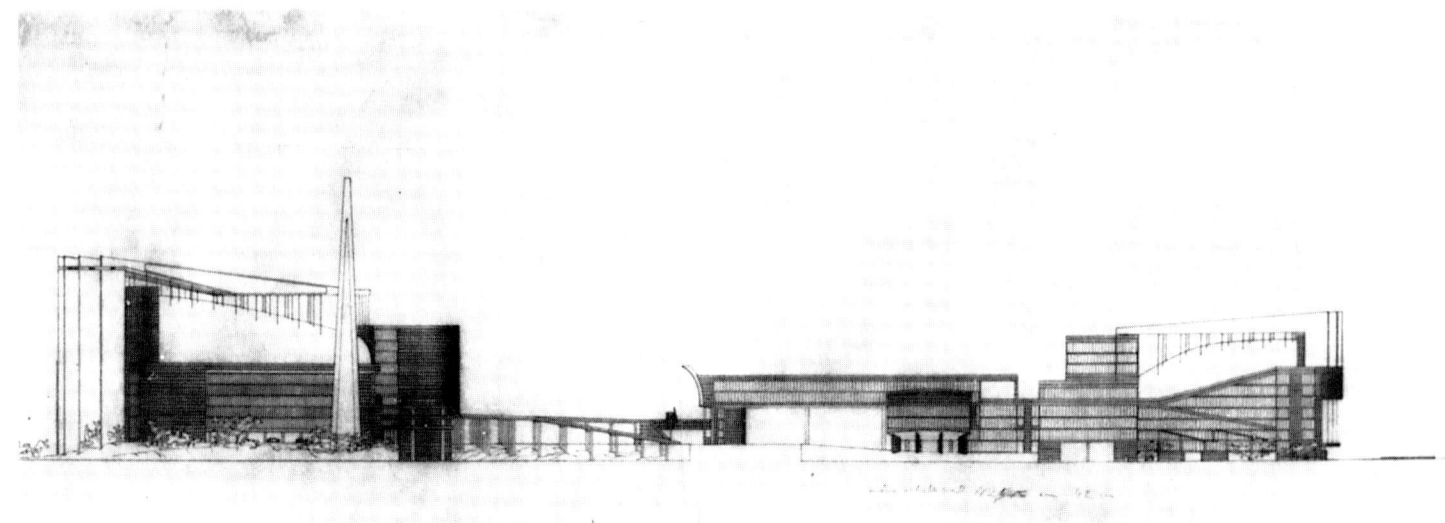

Figure 8. Palace of the Soviets (FLC 27.242).

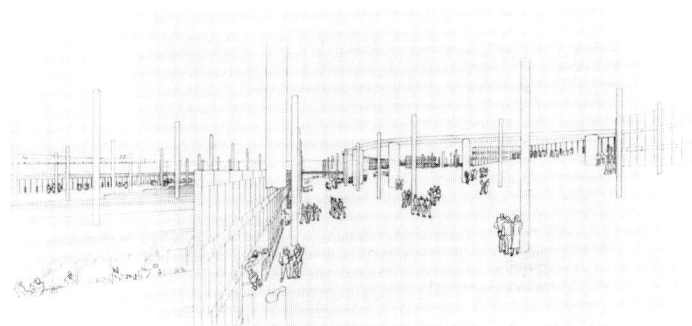

Figure 9. Palace of the Soviets, entrance to Salle A (FLC 27.251).

uished members of the Soviet avant-garde as Konstantin Melnikov, N Ladowsky, and Moisei Ginzburg (who submitted a scheme in collaboration with G Hassenpflug), while group submissions were made by most of the established Russian architectural factions, such as ASNOVA, ARU, SASS, and the recently formed political groups such as VOPRA.

None of these entries, however, irrespective of whether they were Russian or foreign, finally met the hypersensitive standards of the Palace Construction Council, on whose board sat such Party luminaries as Kaganovich and Marshall Voroshilov, the then Commissar for Defence. As far as the Bolshevik establishment was concerned, almost all the entries could be faulted for either excessive formalism or excessive functionalism. Alternatively they were simply deemed as lacking in sufficiently accessible references of a suitably socialist and historical character. Thus the evidently divided Palace Construction Council rebuked the ARU entry for exceeding the site boundary with the following rather naive but nonetheless caustic commentary: '. . . if it was the comrades' intention to point out the inadequacy of the proposed site, there was no need to design a whole project at all'.

These and other such damning judgments were handed down as part of the Resolution of the Palace Construction Council which, on February 28, 1932, announced three premiated awards, one to an unknown American, Hector Hamilton, and two others, which were the invited schemes submitted by Ivan Zholtovsky and Boris Iofan. The initially commissioned foreign architects were all unplaced, although some received special mentions. Likewise, the representatives of the Soviet architectural avant-garde largely failed to win the approval of the Council. Not even the premiated designs of Hamilton and Iofan escaped stricture, with the result that a veil of critical censorship was drawn over the entire affair. In retrospect this may be regarded as anticipating the Central Committee Resolution of April 23, 1932, which called upon all the arts to support Soviet power and in so doing paved the way for the universal adoption of the so-called socialist realist style some five years later.

Like many of the competitors, Le Corbusier was quick to realise that the programme for the Palace of the Soviets was of megastructural proportions. It was this which he had in mind when he wrote retrospectively in *Prélude* in March 1932:

> Bolshevism means everything at its biggest. The biggest proposition. The biggest undertaking. The maximum. Going to the root of the question. Seeing the question through to the end. Envisioning the whole. Breadth.[9]

The scope of the initial programme required no less than two separate large auditoria – the one seating 15,000, the other seating 6,500 – plus four separate smaller auditoria arranged in pairs, the first pair accommodating 500 and the second 200 people. The two larger halls were to have been served by a large amount of ancillary accommodation. The whole brief divided operationally into three groups whose specific accommodation broke down as follows: Group A, comprising a 16,500-seat auditorium together with a restaurant, stage ancillaries, and a certain amount of bureaucratic space given over to diplomats, press, etc (27.593, 27.477); Group B, consisting of a 6,500-seat hall with a similar range of ancillaries, plus an exhibition hall, two large reading rooms, each with a capacity of 200, and a library capable of holding 500,000 volumes (27.722, 27.490); Group C, consisting of the twin 500- and 200-seat halls plus additional restaurant space, etc (27.676). The total area pro-posed for this entire accommodation was 38,810 m².[10]

This programme made it clear that the whole Palace should be capable, when used to its capacity, of accommodating the mass pageantry of the Soviet State, that is to say, it should form a fitting setting for a whole series of events ranging from spontaneous public manifestations to the circus-like performances of V Meyerhold's 'bio-mechanical stage', or it should be able to accommodate such tattoo-like spectacles as Nikolai Evreinov's 'theatricalisation of everyday life!' Le Corbusier was obviously very aware of these demands when he described his project in the following terms:

> The programme called for an immense complex of halls, offices, libraries, restaurants, etc; massive productions with a stage capable of accommodating 1,500 actors and a considerable amount of

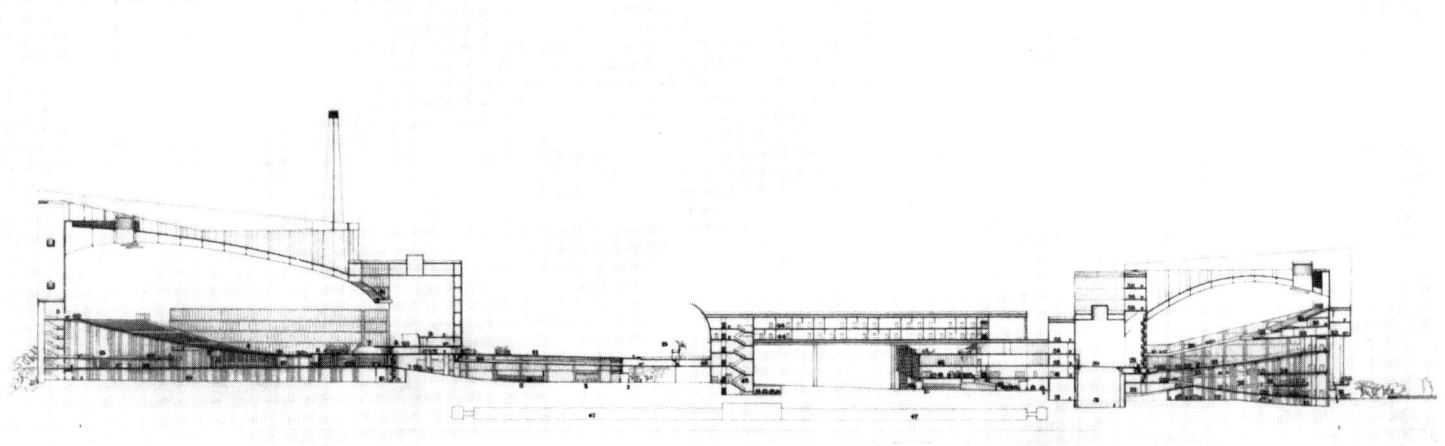

Figure 10. Palace of the Soviets, longitudinal section (FLC 27.243).

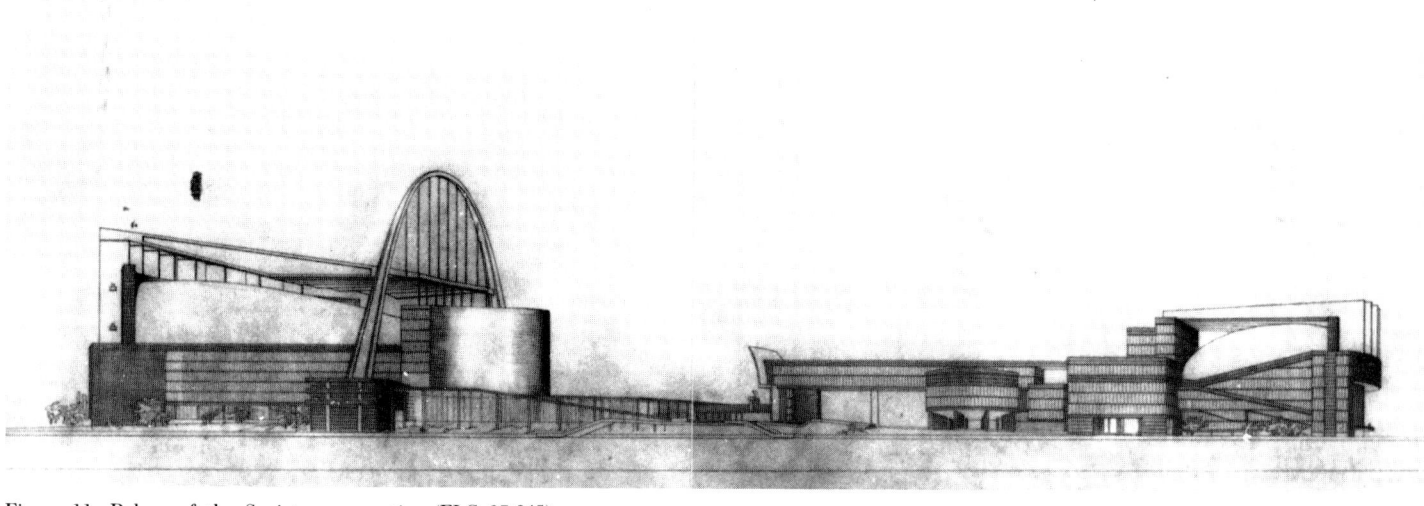

Figure 11. Palace of the Soviets, perspective (FLC 27.245)

scenery. The annexes of such a hall are quite extensive; first, the cloakrooms (it snows in Moscow!) and the vestibules, all sorts of lounges and restaurants. These last-named elements were called 'The Forum' by the authors; a very exact network of circulation permitting the various categories of spectators access to their respective locations; ambassadors, foreign press, Soviet press. Extensive accommodation for actors.

In addition there had to be a way for parades coming from the outside to cross stage and then to go out after making an appearance.[11]

That large-scale manifestations were given the utmost priority in the design of Le Corbusier's Palais des Soviets is borne out by the elaborate system of 'mass circulation' (27.272), and by the visionary May Day perspective rendering, included as part of the final presentation (Figure 7).

Le Corbusier's *parti* took the strategy of the 'continuously inclined plane', implicit in the extensive foyers and ramps of the Centrosoyus, to its ultimate conclusion, the primary aim being to facilitate uninterrupted mass movement in three different areas: on the ground-level concourse between the two large halls and their ancillaries, on the elevated open-air agora with its capacity for accommodating mass demonstrations of up to 50,000 people, and in the partially elevated *plans inclinés* or foyers of the large auditoria, rising upwards over basement parking to terminate in switch-back ramps giving access to the auditoria *parterres* above. At only one point in this whole complex, namely, at the entrance to the 6,500-seat Salle B, were the pedestrians permitted to approach a building, at grade level, under normal conditions. Thereafter the 'warped' foyer ascended towards a datum, which was about a storey's height below the lowest level of the raked 6,500-seat auditorium. From this threshold, ramps doubled back into the vomitories above. Two mezzanine restaurants were to have been suspended between these large *plans inclinés*, one for the public (+15.00) and one for delegates (+19.00). Access to these restaurants was to be via the same switch-back ramps mentioned above, which were rhetorically expressed as glazed 'tubes' on the exterior flanks of the small hall (Figure 8, 27.266). Beneath an interior perspective showing this circulation system Le Corbusier wrote:

... Veritable 'classification machines'; the various classes of visitors, while mutually seeing each other, follow these precise routes which lead them automatically to their destination. (The routes, inclined planes, constitute a kind of *routes de montagne*).[12]

A similar switch-back system was developed for the 16,500-seat hall, otherwise known as Salle A, where pedestrians entered from the centre of the site through a complex filter of coat-checking counters (Figure 9). Alternatively, they could gain direct access from the basement (which provided for automobile circulation and storage) via various elevator/stair cores arranged around the perimeter of the large hall (27.272, Figure 10). Once again, Le Corbusier developed the notion of the building as a 'classificatory device', only now, as in the Meyer/Wittwer design for the Société des Nations of 1927, the process of classification was to be largely effected through the combined interaction of automobile movement and restricted elevator access. The archive is replete with sketches examining different ways for combining vehicular flow with the isolation of various classes of users (27.401, 27.839, 27.787 and 27.688). Again, a mezzanine restaurant for delegates plus a kitchen, etc was to have been inserted between *les deux plans inclinés* of the foyer and the raked shell of the auditorium. The effort expended in trying to resolve all this complex movement through a series of sloping floor planes and coordinated ramp landings, together with the provision of food service to the suspended restaurants, is shown in a sequence of study sketches – including drawings 27.784, 27.791, 27.233, and 27.280 – the last of these being dated November 24, 1931.

One of the most ingenious parts of the whole composition is the heterogeneous mixture of accommodation which would have literally encased the stage, fly-tower and scenery dock of the 6,500-seat auditorium. This galleried complex was integrated with the 500- and 200-seat twin auditoria which made up the bulk of the Group C accommodation. Level by level, this ancillary accommodation of the 6,500-seat hall seems to have been organised as follows. The lower level (+19.00) accommodated the stage, the scenery dock, changing rooms, and the grade-level library entrance and elevator/stair core, all of which had direct corridor access to the twin auditoria to the rear. The next two levels (+23.00 and +27.00) were largely devoted to the library, the card catalogue, a collection of various reading rooms, offices and a small lecture space. The subsequent floor (+31.00) was given over entirely to exhibition purposes. It was also the point at which an elevated two-storey slab of offices projected out from the auditorium 'bustle' to link the fly-tower to the acoustical shell behind the open-air tribune (27.249). The remaining floors, asymmetrically added to the mass, were devoted to further reading rooms and bookstacks.

This archive material testifies to the effort expended in designing this extraordinary machine; above all, to the tremendous energy involved in attempting to manipulate *les plans inclinés* so as to

Figure 12. Palace of the Soviets, perspective (FLC 27.247)

coincide with the level of the suspended restaurants and the vomitories to the elevated auditoria. The 6,500-seat hall clearly presented as many difficulties in this respect as the larger volume, even if its actual section was derived directly from the auditorium of the Centrosoyus. Among the numerous study sketches devoted to resolving the multiple systems of access to this particular hall, the sheets numbered 27.603, 27.879, 27.401, 27.557 and 27.493 give an indication of the range of difficulties encountered.

The other critical problem was the invention of a structural system which would be appropriate to both the colossal mass and the irregular roof sections of the larger auditoria. As late as November 1, Le Corbusier remained uncertain as to how to render the roof structure of these outsized volumes. This section (27.583) also reveals that he had yet to arrive at the absolutely spinal organisation of the composition: witness the eight variations published in *L'Architecture vivante* (Fall and Winter 1932), p 30, entitled *les diverses étapes du project*, of which the last is dated November 22.

The unstructured elevation of the largest auditorium, as seen from the elevated podium/plaza, already shows the compositional problems imposed by such a large mass (27.933) and at the same time indicates the possibility of using an exposed suspension structure as a way of breaking down its scale. To engage in structural expressionism at such a colossal scale was, of course, to break decisively with the *classical* principle of integrating the structure with the auditorium roof, which was indeed the policy adhered to in the SdN entry and the Centrosoyus. The intent here, however, as evidenced in the earliest sketches (27.497, 27.381), was to create an enormous sky-sign construction capable of playing a role comparable to that assumed by the Eiffel Tower in Paris (see left-hand sketches on sheet 27.494).

The hyperbolic arch solution finally adopted also relates to Le Corbusier's Purist habit of transposing a plan configuration into a section and vice-versa, so that the arch trajectory reflects almost directly the hyperbolic plan of the auditorium. We have to assume that the decision to use such a rhetorical structure – namely, the cable suspension of eight radial steel girders from a parabolic concrete arch, together with the secondary cable suspension of an auditorium shell from the girders themselves – was, at least in part, motivated by designing for a 'constructivist' culture. One senses that after the international debacle over the monumentality of his Cité mondiale, Le Corbusier was determined to prove himself to be more constructivist than the constructivists themselves. On the other hand, as the partially oblique elevation of this structure would indicate (Figure 11), the arch was also intended to function as a surrogate 'dome' and as such to respond both formally and symbolically not only to the other subordinate dome or crown-like element of the small hall, but, above all, to the towers and spires of the Kremlin (Figure 12). The monumental iconic power of this invention has been confirmed by history; it has been appropriated by other designers since, above all by Adalberto Libera in his project for a gateway-arch to the entrance of the EUR' 42 site in Rome and in Eero Saarinen's final realisation of the idea in the Gateway to the West erected at St Louis in 1967.

An appropriate system of structural suspension for the smaller hall was no less easy to devise, as the drawings 27.582, 27.596, 27.849 and 27.870 readily display. Once again the initial impulse was to adopt a steel framing system similar to that used in the SdN Assembly Hall, complete with roller joints which take their bearing from pylons located to either side of the proscenium arch (27.418). As it is, this structure was never fully worked out, no provision being made for the fly-tower structure to receive the load of the six radial girders spanning the depth of the hall.

As one would expect, great effort was also invested in evolving the most effective acoustical shells for each of the auditoria, as is shown by the profile developed for the 6,500-seat hall by Gustave Lyon on November 17 (27.284), and by all the subsequent efforts at refining and integrating this profile with the exterior mass of the hall and its suspended roof system (see drawings 27.382, 27.380, 27.379, 27.285 and 27.286). Equal care was expended on the 16,500-seat hall, which naturally posed greater problems from the point of view of acoustics. The more or less insuperable problem of projecting the human voice in a volume which was over 100 m-deep was met in this way:

> The voice of the actors and the figures on the stage is separated from the audience by an 11 m-wide 'abîme' (note the Wagnerian term). All the sound from the stage is collected at a height of 30 m by a microphone (above the stage) which then relays the sound to a loudspeaker situated at a mathematically determined position in front of the stage. This source projects the sound waves on the acoustical shell of the ceiling, which distributes the sound evenly throughout the auditorium (with a loss of no more than ten per cent in the last row).[13]

It is interesting to note that the difficulty of arriving at an appropriate solution for the hall of such unprecedented dimensions caused Gustave Lyon to collaborate with two scientific specialists, namely, a certain Morin of the Ecole polytechnique and a Dr Marty of the Ecole normale (see drawing 27.239 for the details of the acoustical system adopted).

As in the SdN and the Centrosoyus, Le Corbusier employed the elementarist method of French rational classical composition in resolving the final mass and axial order of the Palais des Soviets. This accounts for the eight variant layouts, ostensibly arrived at between October 6 and November 22, 1931, and for other variations shown on some of the sheets in the archive (27.937, 27.560). (The above dates, incidentally, raise an unsolved historical problem: given that Le Corbusier worked for three months on the second competition, the nature of his first submission at the end of June remains a mystery.) These variations often implied not only different modes of urban composition, but also different approaches to the problem of site access; thus the variation shown on drawing number 27.560 quite clearly presupposes that the bulk of the mass movement would come from the banks of the Moskva River. An equally elemental approach was also taken towards the integration of the so-called Group C with the stage, fly-tower and ancillary accommodation located to the rear of the small auditorium (see drawings 27.341-27.343, etc).

Needless to say, as in their Société des Nations and Centrosoyus, Le Corbusier and Pierre Jeanneret attempted to equip their Palais des Soviets project with an overall plenum airconditioning system which was intended to distribute the conditioned air in the continuous interspace separating the outer and inner membranes of the major auditoria. This, their so-called *respiration exacte*, was never made successfully operative either in the Centrosoyus or in the Armeé du Salut headquarters, built in Paris in 1933, although whether this failure was due to fundamental misconceptions or to the backwardness of technology at the time has yet to be established. In any event, it is another example of the biological myth which was to be integral to Le Corbusier's conception of the machine: the idea of a transcendent technology whose most refined application would manifest itself in organic form. A comparable organisation is also implicit in the double-layered (concrete and plaster) shell roofs to the respective auditoria and in the warped planes that permeate the entire body of the building. This much is also hinted at in the concept of the circulation itself, where the apparent 'absence' of the mass user is compensated for by the various ramps which announce its future presence. This seems to be linked to the metaphorical significance which Le Corbusier ascribed to the concept of a *régime fluvial* where the mass is conceived as flowing in much the same way as water up and down the 10 m-wide ramps serving the public podium.

Although many factors undoubtedly contributed to Le Corbusier's growing disillusion with the manifest destiny of the machine age, none could have had such an impact on his morale as the total rejection of his Palace of the Soviets at the hands of the Russian authorities. This refusal, comparable to the rebuff he had suffered in the SdN competition, was all the more bitter, given the encouragement he had just received from the Soviet State, through the commissioning of the Centrosoyus, the largest structure he was to build until the completion of the Unité d'Habitation at Marseilles, in 1952. As a man committed to the idea of progress and to a broadly conceived notion of the Enlightenment, he simply could not comprehend the Soviet decision. Whether he was a bourgeois architect or not seemed to him to be an irrelevant issue. What was at stake, as far as he was concerned, as the letter that he sent to Anatole Lunacharsky on May 13, 1932, makes clear, was whether or not the Soviets would continue to advance under the symbolic sign of a rising machinist culture.

The Russian dismissal of the work as inappropriately industrial seems to be insensitive when one observes the delicacy with which the project was finally rendered. Once again, as in his Société des Nations design, he was to treat the continuous glazing and the stone veneer (in this instance, Caucasian tuffa 45 cm-thick) as though they were generically the same material. Thus the 'machinism' of the exposed suspension construction was deliberately mediated by the classical symmetry of the overall composition, by numerous peristylar episodes, effected by the *pilotis* and by the equally classical syntax of the skin revetment, be it stone or glass; that is to say, by the general horizontal coursing capped by string courses, etc. And while the relation of the complex to the existing urban fabric of Moscow is possibly the most questionable aspect of the scheme, when looked at in retrospect, the Palace, despite its evident constructivism, was also patently hierarchic and monumental, cradling within its body 'a space of public appearance' which was hardly less classical and political in its overall appointment than the Athenian agora.

Notes

1 See *Aujourd'hui, art et architecture* 51 (November 1965): 110. Special number dedicated to Le Corbusier. Cited in a reportage by Jacqueline Vauthier-Jeanneret and Christian Hunziker.

Such a dualistic formulation is typical of Le Corbusier, and the whole of his life and work is shot through with this Manichean vision which almost certainly derives, in the last analysis, from his Cathar background. The imagery of the Dioscuri is patently dualistic, for in numerous versions of the Greek myth the twin 'brothers' are opposite and complementary. As the offspring of Zeus, Pollux is immortal, while the other, Castor, was originally destined to age and die. The former is associated with the sun, the latter with the moon. They were often represented in Ancient Greece as cavaliers, the former being pugilistic, the latter being a horse trainer. As P V Turner points out in his thesis *The Education of Le Corbusier* (New York: Garland Publishing, 1977), C-E Jeanneret would have first become familiar with Greek mythology at the age of sixteen when he was given Maxime Collignon's *Mythologie figurée de la Grèce* (1912). While this work mentions the Dioscuri, it does not comment at length on their attributes. However, it does mention that they were often depicted as two men standing side by side and leading their respective charges by their bridles.

An account of C-E Jeanneret's adoption of his pseudonym in October 1920 is given by Amédée Ozenfant in his *Mémoires 1886-1962* (Paris: Seghers, 1968), wherein he informs us that Jeanneret's cousin had been named Lecorbésier, which was then modified by Le Corbusier. As for the crow metaphor, this appears to have been derived from the figure known in the Middle Ages as *Corbusier*, who was assigned by the church to kill crows that happened to perch on the spires of churches, thereby preventing them from befouling the cross. The fact that the *corbeau*, or the raven, is the alchemical symbol of change from material to spiritual, from black to white, etc, only returns us to the dualism in which Le Corbusier shrouded his persona. I am indebted to Beatriz Colomina for her help with this material.

2 Le Corbusier, *Une Maison – un palais* (Paris: Crès, 1928), pp 96-97.

3 Le Corbusier, *Une Maison – un palais*, p 68.

4 Le Corbusier, *Une Maison – un palais*, p 78. The mechanised nature of the facade to the SdN is alluded to on p 103, in a text which reads: 'La "passerelle-bicyclette" de nettoyage des fenêtres (ossature de beton, fenêtres coulissantes, caisson exterieur des volets roulants) est une situation technique pure'. Elle apporte une solution esthétique pure'.

5 Le Corbusier, *Une Maison – un palais*, p 103.

6 See Colin Rowe and Robert Slutzky, 'Transparency: Literal and Phenomenal', *Perspecta* 8 (1963): 45-54.

7 J L Cohen, 'Cette Mystique: l'URSS', *Architecture, Mouvement et Continuité* 49 (September 1979): 75. A slightly different and expanded version of the same article was published in English; see *Oppositions* 23 (Winter 1981): 88.

8 Le Corbusier, *Précisions sur l'état présent de l'architecture et de l'urbanisme* (Paris: Crès, 1930), pp 46, 48.

9 Le Corbusier, 'Bolche ou la notion du grand', *Prélude* (March 1932); later in *La Ville radieuse* (Paris: Editions de l'Architecture d'Aujourd'hui, 1935), p 182.

10 *L'Architecture vivante* (Autumn/Winter 1932): pp 2-14, 17-30.

11 Le Corbusier, *L'Oeuvre complète 1929-34*, 5th ed (Zurich: Les Editions d'Architecture, 1952), pp 123-124.

12 *L'Architecture vivante* (Autumn/Winter 1932): p 26.

13 See *L'Architecture vivante* (Autumn/Winter 1932): p 10.

Centrosoyus
Moscow, USSR 1927

15.906
Study sketch, perspective of the building. Pencil on sketching paper, 40cm x 54cm.

16.245 *Below left*:
Axonometric sketch of the building, sketch on reverse side. Pencil on sketching paper, 36 cm x 55 cm

16.246 *Below right*:
Drawing, axonometric of the building with keys, siting. Pencil on sketching paper, 46cm x 57cm.

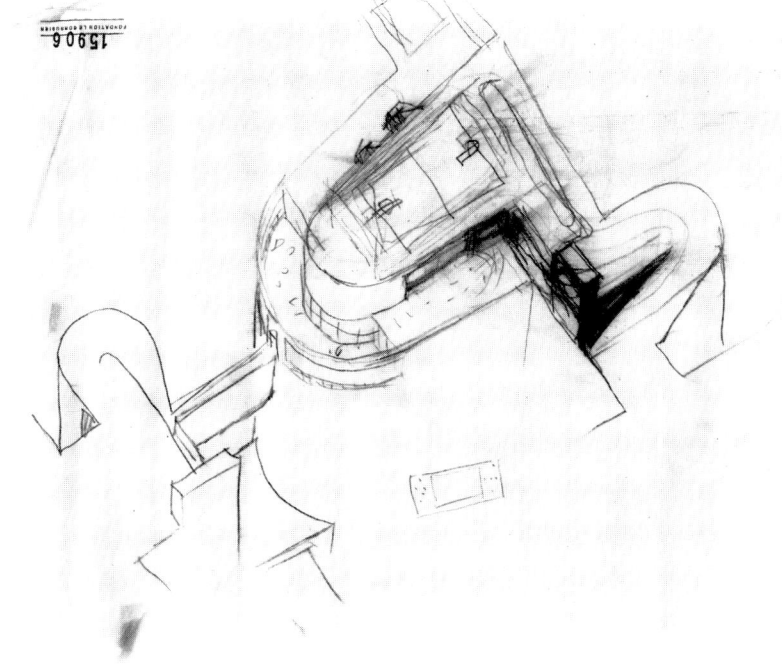

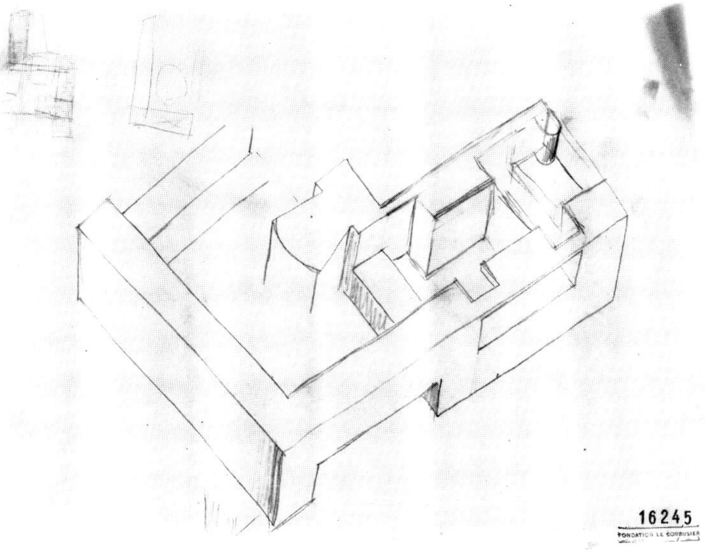

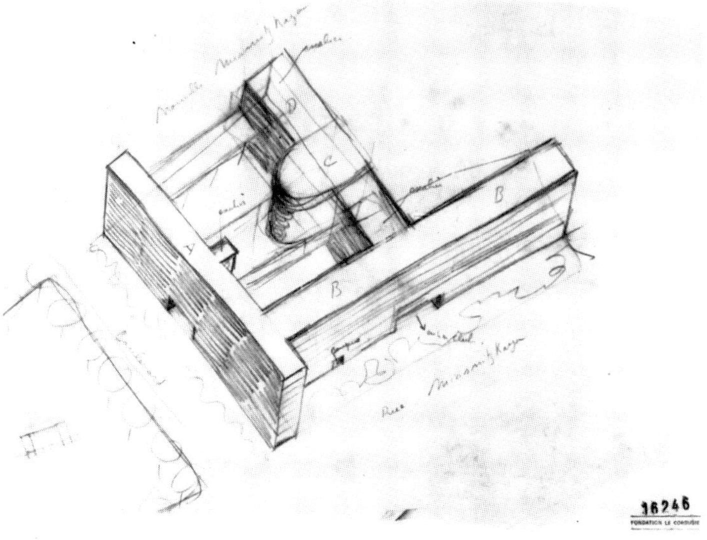

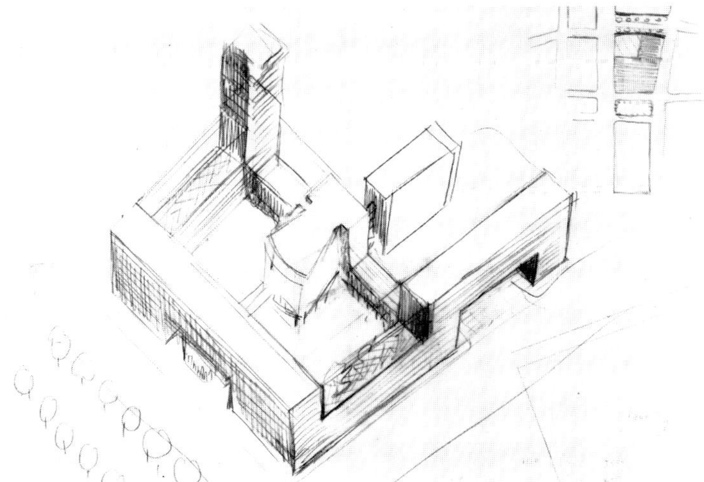

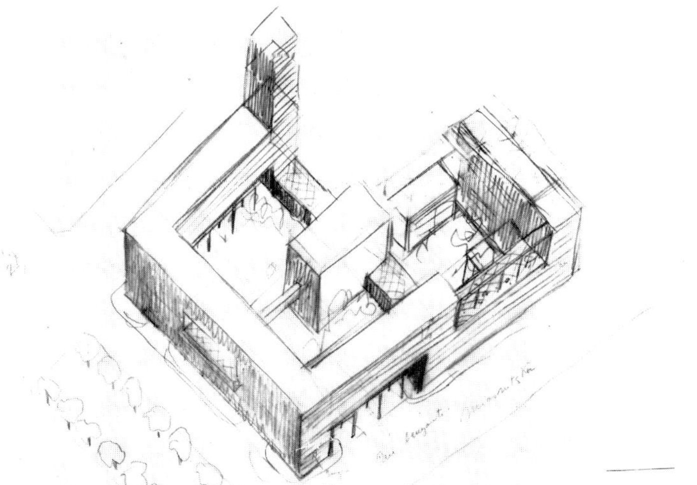

16.222 Sketch, axonometric of the building, calculations at the bottom right, sketch at the top. Pencil on sketching paper, 44cm x 55cm.

16.223 Sketch, axonometric of the building, keys. Pencil on sketching paper, 44cm x 56cm.

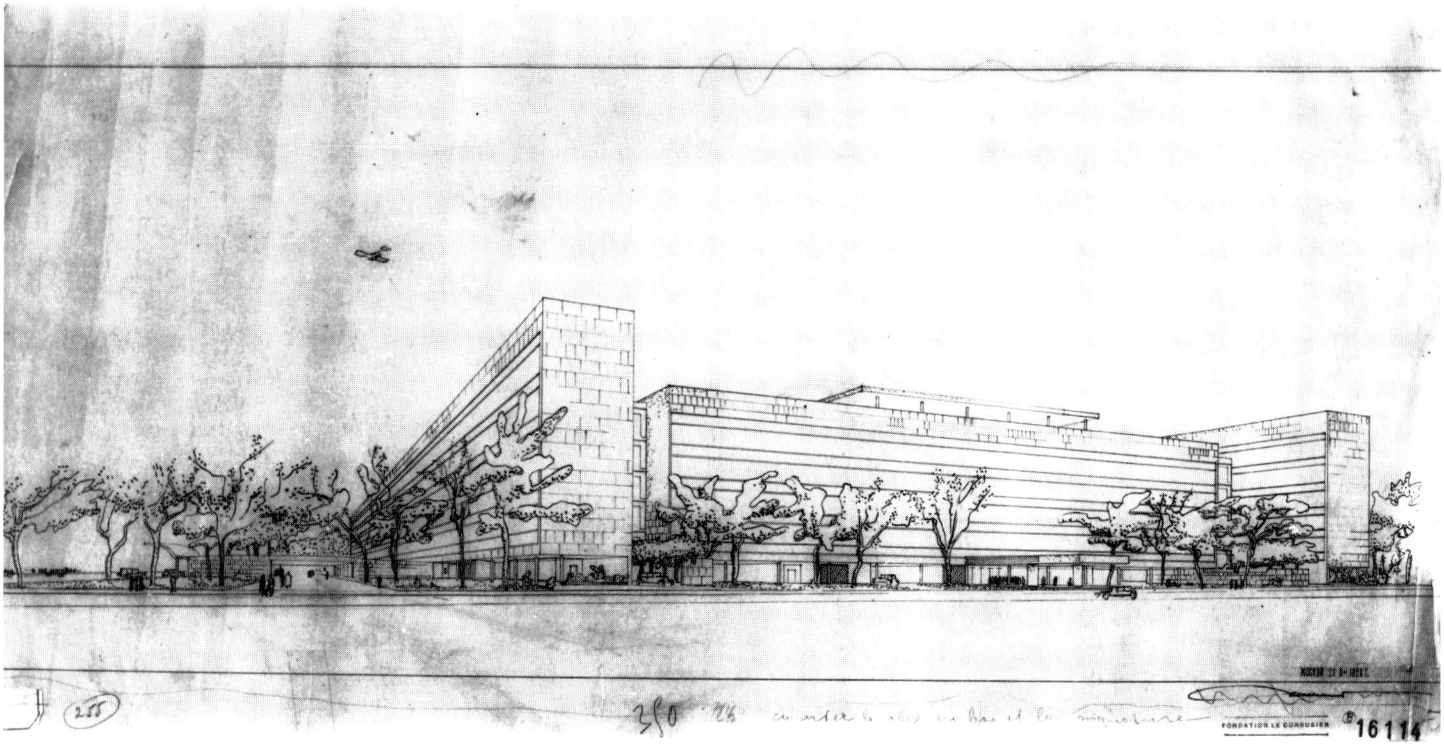

CS

10

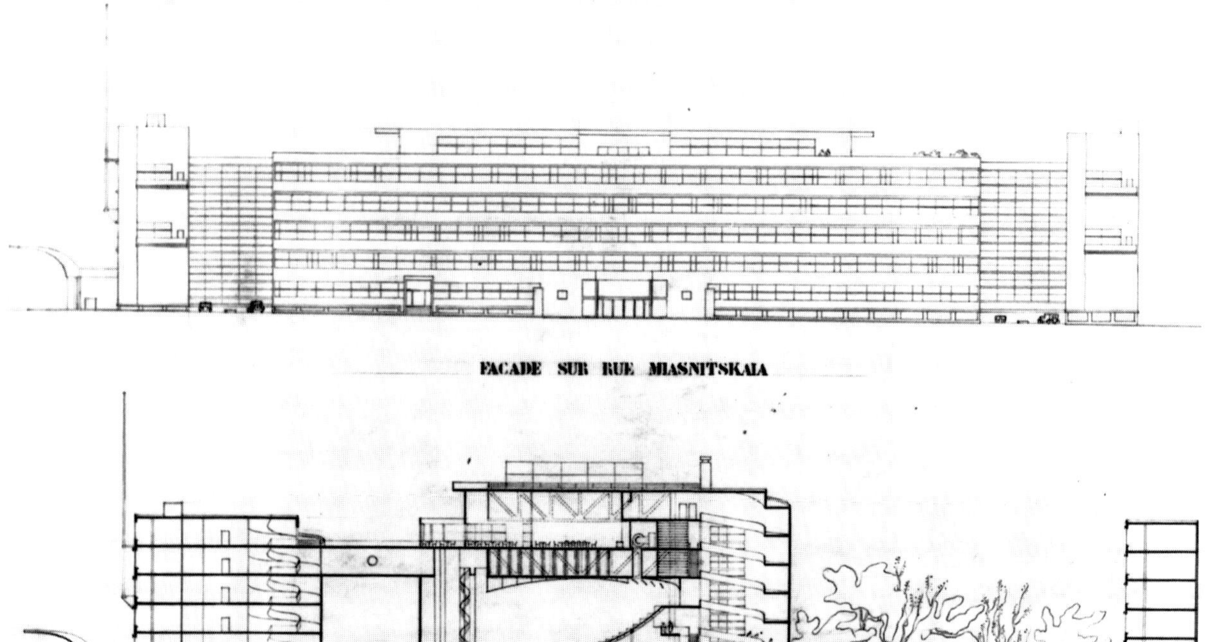

FACADE SUR RUE MIASNITSKAIA

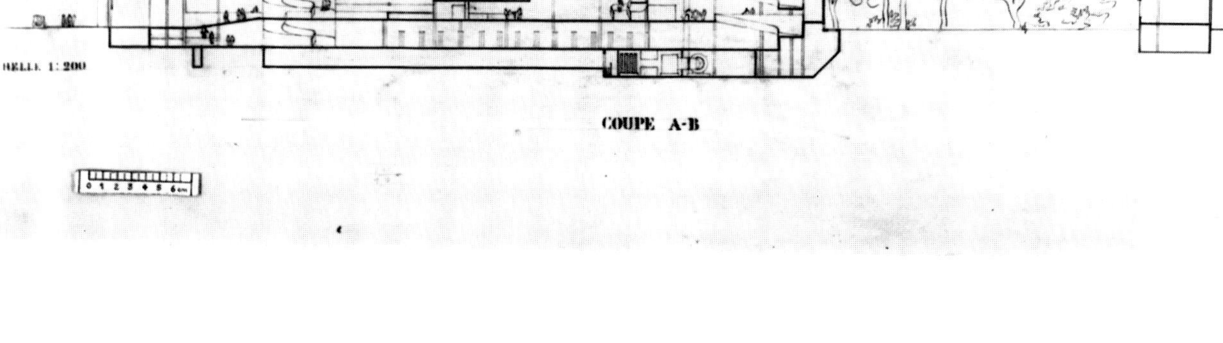

ECHELLE 1:200

COUPE A-B

16.114 *Left:*
Drawing and sketch, perspective of the building, with silhouettes, observation at the bottom, No 8 at the right and No 255 at the left on the label. Dated October 20, 1928. Indian ink, pencil and red pencil on vellum, 37cm x 75cm.

16.113 *Right*
Drawing, axonometric perspective of the building showing greenery, with a sketch at the top. Indian ink and pencil on vellum, 55cm x 77cm.

15.686 *Left:*
Study sketches: 1. elevation of the facade to Myasnitskaya Prospect; 2. A-B section of the building with silhouettes, cars and greenery: there is a gelatine print classified under the same number. Scale 1:200. Indian ink on vellum, 78cm x 110cm.

15.839 *Right:*
Facade, sketch and calculations on the right. Pencil and colouring chalk on tracing paper, 95cm x 109cm.

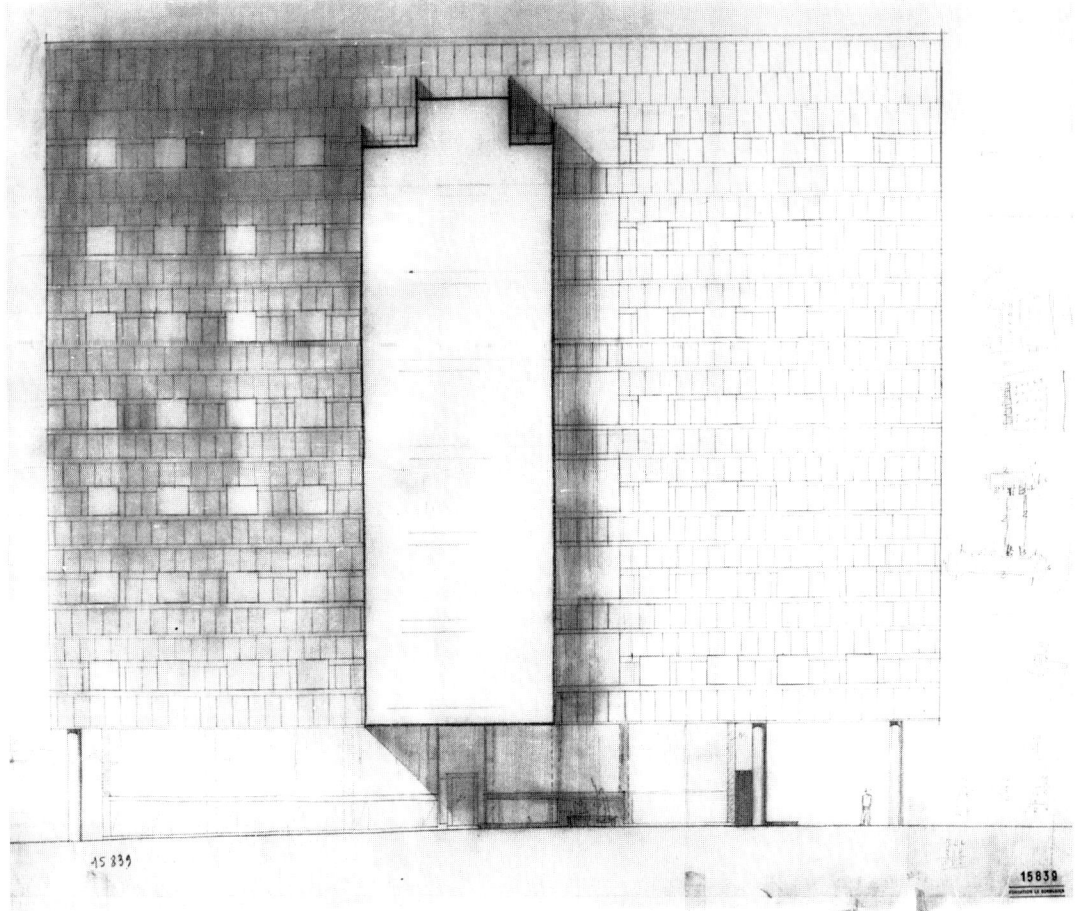

Palace of the Soviets
Moscow, USSR 1930

27.509 *Right:*
Study sketch, mass shaded plan of the building with notes and the stencil number 3 at the bottom left. Dated October 12, 1931. Charcoal and Indian ink on sketching paper, 47cm x 65cm.

27.515 *Far right:*
Sketch, shaded mass plan of the building with notes and the stencil number 8 at the bottom left. Dated November 22, 1931. Charcoal and Indian ink on sketching paper, 46cm x 93cm.

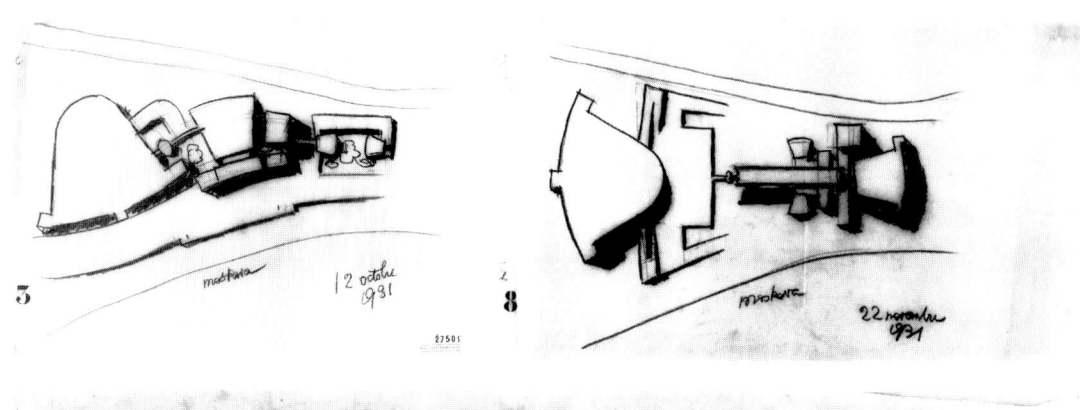

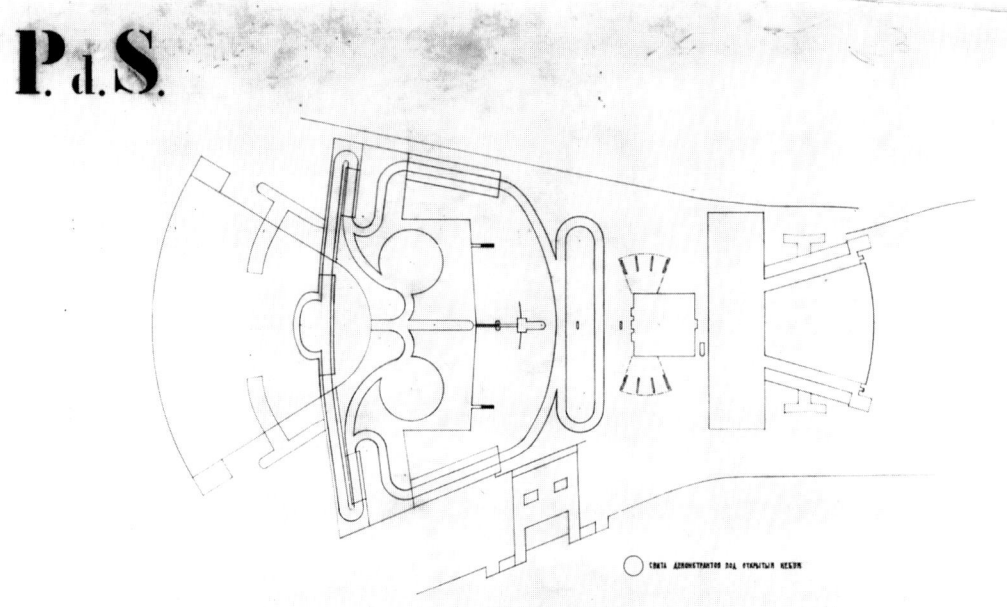

27.266
Plan of the Palace with key in Russian. Indian ink on vellum, 47cm x 71cm.

27.861
Study sketch, mass plan of the project as a whole with spot heights, keys, notes and calculations. Dated October 29, 1931. Pencil and coloured chalk on medium paper, 100cm x 132cm.

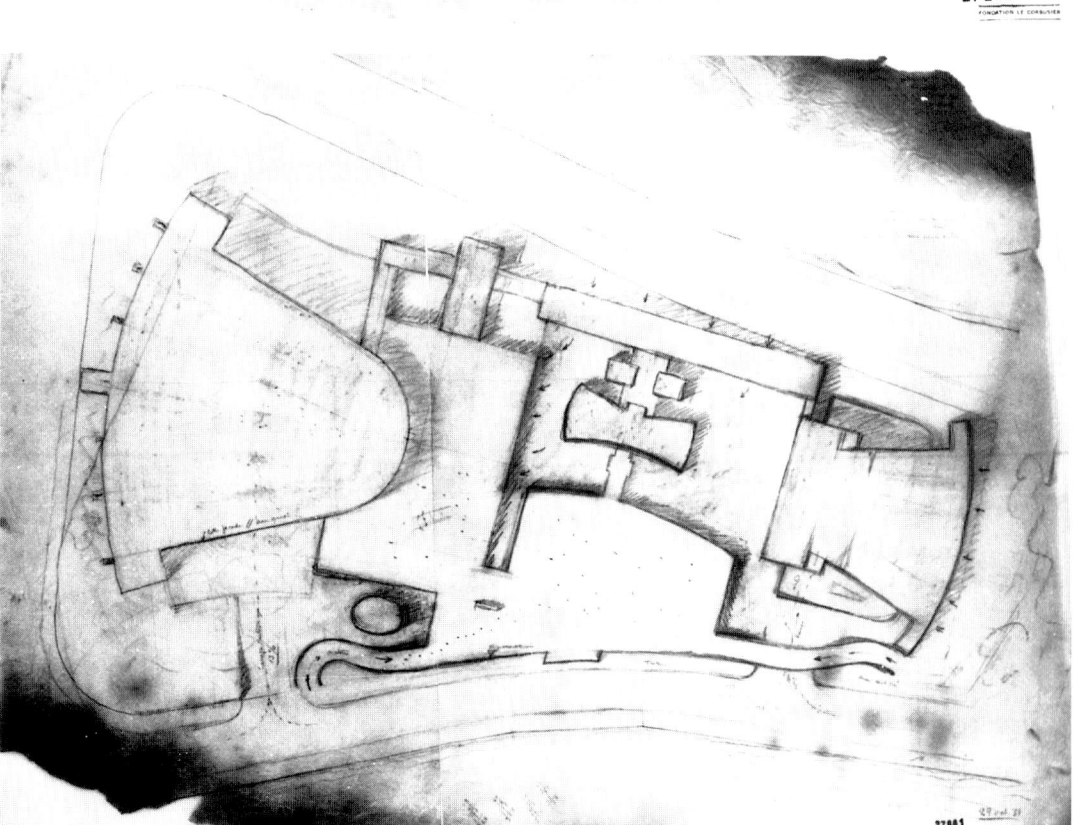

Timeless but of its Time: Le Corbusier's Architecture in India
PETER SERENYI

FOR LE CORBUSIER THE RESOLUTION OF OPPOSITES was a deeply felt need that elicited some of his most heroic architectural responses. He was certainly not alone among twentieth-century architects in this respect, for some of his greatest contemporaries, Frank Lloyd Wright and Mies van der Rohe, were equally obsessed by it. To create a resolution of opposites, Wright fused, whereas Mies neutralised, a building's constituent parts. This resulted in a state of interdependent individuality in the work of Wright, and a state of anonymity in the work of Mies. Le Corbusier, on the other hand, used juxtaposition as a means of attaining a resolution of opposites. In so doing, he succeeded in preserving the identity and at times even the separateness of a building's constituent parts.

For Le Corbusier the juxtaposition of diverse and often seemingly contradictory architectural elements was not merely a formal exercise, but rather a manifestation of a new kind of synthesis that brought together images of diverse cultural, historical, environmental, sociopolitical and psychological forces while permitting each to maintain its identity. He interpreted these forces in terms of a series of polarities that include: history and modernity, Mediterranean and Northern, mechanistic and folkloristic, utopian and pragmatic, puritanical and hedonistic, male and female. Although the resolution of these polar and often contradictory forces had obsessed Le Corbusier since his formative period, most notably since the creation of the Villa Schwob in 1916, this complex process found its richest and most subtle realisations in his late work, of which India received the largest share.

As is well known, Le Corbusier's name is linked with two cities in India: Chandigarh, the newly built capital of the state of Punjab, and Ahmedabad, the textile capital of India located in the state of Gujarat. Both cities are intimately tied to two of modern India's greatest statesmen: Mahatma Gandhi and Jawaharlal Nehru. Gandhi, a native son of Gujarat, had spent fifteen years in Ahmedabad laying the groundwork for India's independence. It was from here that he led the famous Salt March in 1930 that initiated the second phase of national non-violent resistance. Prime Minister Nehru, who supported Chandigarh both morally and financially, viewed the city as 'symbolic of the freedom of India, unfettered by the traditions of the past . . . an expression of the nation's faith in the future'.[1]

The price India had to pay for its independence from the British in July, 1947, was the loss of what is now Pakistan and Bangladesh. The people most affected by the partition of India were the Hindus of West Punjab and East Bengal who elected not to remain under Moslem rule but to resettle in India. In addition, Punjab lost not only its western part to Pakistan but also its old capital, Lahore, whose population was fifty-six per cent Hindu. What set the stage for the creation of Chandigarh was independence and partition, exhilaration and tragedy. Naming the city in honour of Chandi, the Hindu goddess of power, must be seen in this context.

Once the decision was made to build a new capital for East Punjab, Prime Minister Nehru seized the opportunity to make it the city of *his* India, liberated from the traditions of the past. As an initial act of commitment, Nehru recommended to the Punjab government that the American planner, Albert Mayer, whom he knew personally, be asked to draw up a master plan for the city. Although Mayer's plan was not carried out, Le Corbusier adopted many of its features when he prepared his own plan in Simla in February 1951. This plan was created only three months after P N Thapar and P L Varma, representatives of the Punjab government, had approached Le Corbusier in Paris and had offered him a contract as architectural advisor for Chandigarh.[2] Le Corbusier's biannual trips to India, a result of this contract, started on February 18, 1951. He left a permanent record of his thoughts and observations about India in his sketchbooks, which he carried with him during his many trips. These sketchbooks also contain visual imprints of his creative process, giving us a rare glimpse of his buildings in their formative stages.[3]

The two sketchbooks in which Le Corbusier recorded his first stay in India, extending from February to April 1951, give us the best indication of what he found most compelling and timely in the country's built environment.[4] It is revealing that the very first observation he made about India refers to Sir Edwin Lutyens and the Jantar Mantar, the astronomical observatory in Delhi built by Maharajah Jai Singh in 1719. He considered the observatory as 'leading the way: linking mankind with the cosmos'. In contrast, he found even the 'best qualities' of Lutyens' work in New Delhi less successful.[5] Yet both touched a familiar chord in his heart, the observatory being an example of what he described in *Towards a New Architecture* as 'pure creation of the mind' and Lutyens' New Delhi, with its axes and broad boulevards, being an evocation of Paris. It is not surprising that both reappear in Chandigarh.

Beyond this initial observation, these two sketchbooks encompass a wide yet predictable range of images of the Indian environment: the seventeenth-century Pinjore gardens near Chandigarh, Hindu and Jain temples in Ahmedabad, the Mogul-style Viceroy's garden by Lutyens in New Delhi, Bombay's Gateway of India of 1911, aerial views of Rajasthani villages near Jaipur, old courtyards in Ahmedabad, a water tower near Ambala and a factory in Ahmedabad. These and similar examples included in Sketchbooks E 18 and E 19 suggest that Le Corbusier's approach to absorbing a new culture had remained unaltered since his early travels spanning the years 1907-11, when he classified his observations into three categories: culture, folklore, and industry.[6]

The first two Indian sketchbooks also shed light on Le Corbusier's itinerary, which in turn sets the stage for initiating contact with all but one of his future Indian clients.[7] After his arrival in New Delhi on February 19, his first destination was Chandigarh and Simla. Already on March 19, he left for Delhi to fly from there to Ahmedabad. After a brief stay in Ahmedabad on March 22 and 23, he flew to Bombay to meet Bhabha Tata, the steel magnate and major owner of Air India.[8] On his way back to Chandigarh, he stopped in New Delhi on March 25 to be entertained in the presidential palace. Six days later he left Chandigarh to fly from Delhi to Bombay, whence he returned to Paris on April 2.

During these first six weeks in India, Le Corbusier gained a deeper understanding of the country's cultural, vernacular and industrial tradition, met most of his future clients from Pandit Nehru to the Sarabhais, and initiated ambitious projects ranging from the master plan of Chandigarh to a cultural centre for Ahmedabad. But why Ahmedabad? Such a question happily no longer needs to be raised about Chandigarh,[9] but still requires an answer with regard to the commissions he received in India's textile centre. There are few cities in the world that can claim more than three buildings by Le Corbusier, and Ahmedabad is one of them (after Paris, Chandigarh and La Chaux-de-Fonds), with the Museum, the Millowners Association Building, and the Sarabhai and Shodhan houses to its credit. Such major commissions, all initiated during Le Corbusier's first visit to the city, attest to Ahmedabad's intellectual climate and economic prosperity unrivalled in India for a city of its size. The events that contributed to these favourable circumstances have a long history whose highlights are worth mentioning here.[10]

Since its founding by Sultan Ahmed, Shah of Gujarat in 1411 AD, Ahmedabad had been a city of commerce and industry centred around textiles. After a period of great prosperity during the first hundred years of its existence, the city declined but recovered again when Akbar annexed it to the Mogul Empire in 1572. Its recovery prepared the way for Sir Thomas Roe's visit in 1618, which initiated the first commercial ties between Ahmedabad and England. The disintegration of the Mogul Empire during the eighteenth century brought in the Maratha from the south, who ruled it until 1817. During that year, and almost two hundred years after Sir Thomas' visit, Ahmedabad's ties with Britain were forcibly re-established by the East India Company.

Yet the British presence in Ahmedabad during the next hundred and thirty years was never too pervasive, largely because the economic base of its highly developed culture had always been trade and industry rather than agriculture. Hence, long before the advent of the modern era, the leading citizens of Ahmedabad were businessmen rather than landowners or men in the service of a court. This enabled the Ahmedabadis to take up the British on their own terms, and offer them stiff competition by mechanising the city's textile industry.

With the help of the city's Jain financiers, the modern textile industry of Ahmedabad was founded in 1861. One of the key factors behind the success of this industry is that since its founding it has been run largely by a close-knit group of Jain families who have valued cooperation rather than competition among themselves. Thus, as Kenneth Gillion has pointed out, 'the caste system and joint family system found new avenues of expression in a modern context'.[11] In addition to the social cohesion of the Jains, it was also their work ethic, their puritanical and frugal character, not to mention their entrepreneurial spirit, that contributed greatly to the success of Ahmedabad's modern textile industry. No wonder that by the turn of the century the city had become known as the 'Manchester of India'.

The economic growth Ahmedabad enjoyed since the 1860s was given a further boost by World War I, when the termination of British imports allowed the city's textile mills to supply India's needs more fully. After the war, the city utilised its unprecedented economic power by becoming, in Gillion's words, 'a financial and political base for the Indian National Congress and a leader and prototype of New India'.[12] While it was the mills which supplied the financial base for this new political movement, it was Mahatma Gandhi who provided the leadership.

The fact that Ahmedabad became Gandhi's home between 1915 and 1930 had powerful consequences for the city's political development, both in terms of its own affairs and its influence on the nation as a whole. Enjoying the respect of both industry and labour, Gandhi proved to be an effective arbitrator between the wealthy millowners and their workers during the city's labour unrests in the late 1910s and 1920s. Moreover, through his teachings, Gandhi disseminated those very ideals which made Ahmedabad such a success: puritanism, frugality and the ethic of hard work.

When India's independence was won in 1947, Ahmedabad could rightly claim an important share in its realisation. More importantly, however, it could claim that its unique blend of traditional values and modern technology could serve as an appropriate model for independent India. Conscious of this potential, the leaders of the city pursued a two-pronged approach to shaping its future: strengthening the achievements of the past; and moving into new directions. In pursuit of the former, they diversified the city's industry and helped make it, even if only temporarily, the state capital of Gujarat. In pursuit of the latter, they established it as one of the foremost cultural centres of India. In so doing, they revived an aspect of the city's past that had been lost since the seventeenth century.

Among the key leaders of the new Ahmedabad, four Jain textile millowners stand out: Kasturbhai Lalbhai, Chinubhai Chimanbhai, Surottam Hutheesing and Gautam Sarabhai. Mr Lalbhai, the wealthiest of the Ahmedabad industrialists, spent a considerable part of his fortune on establishing and supporting the city's new cultural and educational institutions through such organisations as the Ahmedabad Education Society and the Ahmedabad Textile Industry's Research Association. Chinubhai Chimanbhai, a nephew of Mr Lalbhai, was the city's energetic mayor who, during his tenure between 1950 and 1962, was instrumental in building such major undertakings as libraries, playgrounds, a stadium, an auditorium and a cultural centre. It was in fact the mayor who was largely responsible for inviting Le Corbusier to the city. Surottam Hutheesing, another nephew of Mr Lalbhai, was the president of the Millowners Association, the textile industry's powerful organisation, and it was he who was responsible for commissioning Le Corbusier to build the association's new headquarters. Gautam Sarabhai, a leading member of a family that had distinguished itself in the arts and sciences, was the founder, designer and first director of the National Institute of Design in Ahmedabad, which under his leadership became one of the foremost art schools of India. And it was Gautam Sarabhai's sister-in-law Manorama – a niece of Mr Lalbhai – who entrusted Le Corbusier with her house.

During Le Corbusier's first visit to Ahmedabad in March 1951, Mayor Chinubhai Chimanbhai gave him two commissions; the building of a cultural centre overlooking the Sabarmati River, and a house for himself.[13] Although the Chimanbhai house was never built by Le Corbusier and the cultural centre was only partially realised according to his plans,[14] he was at least given the opportunity to build the centre's museum according to ideas he had developed since 1929 (Figure 1).[15] In the museum of Ahmedabad Le Corbusier combined two concepts to express the notion of an environment that is both interdisciplinary and unlimited. Even if neither of these concepts was realised in the building literally, both were inherent in its design. The best explanation of these concepts is to be derived from looking at how they were first visualised.

The concept of an interdisciplinary cultural environment was first proposed by Le Corbusier in the project for the 'Mundaneum' World Museum of 1929. In this ziggurat-shaped building the visitor could have surveyed the physical manifestation of man's diverse achievements in a historical and geographical context.[16] The Museum of Unlimited Growth was first developed by Le Corbusier in 1931, when he envisaged such a building as a flattened-out ziggurat spiralling outwards in squares with the potential of being extended ad infinitum. Both of these prototypes find a partial realisation in Ahmedabad, where the

Figure 1. Museum of Ahmedabad.

Figure 2. Millowners Association Building, Ahmedabad.

Figure 3. Shodan House, Ahmedabad.

museum's exhibition space is treated as a continuous volume revolving around a central courtyard. This makes it possible to present works representing the broadest range of human activity in a contextual setting and in a continuous manner.

For the roof of the museum, Le Corbusier had planned a Mogul garden which he intended to fill with flowers, shrubbery and forty-five shallow reflecting pools arranged in straight lines. Had it been realised, this garden would have combined Le Corbusier's long-standing fascination with roof gardens with his admiration of India's own cultural tradition. Regrettably, however, only the concrete frames of the pools give the visitor a hint of the architect's original vision.

Although the cultural centre was not completed as originally planned and the museum is still under-utilised, Le Corbusier's original proposal – the creation of a stage where the arts could not only interact but could also relate to a broader contextual setting – is still a provocative concept. It is not surprising that it had such an appeal for Ahmedabad's energetic mayor, who was determined to make the city a symbol of the new India – not unfettered by the past as Nehru proposed, but rather continuing its past through its cultural institutions.

The second public building Le Corbusier designed for Ahmedabad was the headquarters of the Millowners Association, commissioned by its president, Surottam Hutheesing, in March 1951 (Figure 2). Planned for a site overlooking the Sabarmati River, the building was to serve a unique organisation whose essence Le Corbusier seems to have understood very well. Since its founding in 1891, the Millowners Association had provided an institutional framework for the close family ties that existed among the city's largely Jain textile millowners. Here Le Corbusier encountered a public institution whose very existence depended on personal relationships that resulted from caste and family ties. His response to this unique commission was to express the institution's dual character – the private and the public – through his concept of the house as a palace, which he developed during the 1920s and which he gave clearest expression in his book, *Une Maison – un palais*, published in 1928. There he defined the palace as 'a house endowed with dignity', which for him meant monumentality achieved by 'pure forms composed according to a harmonious law'.[17] One of the houses Le Corbusier singled out in his book to exemplify his concept of the house-palace was his Villa Cook of 1926, which offers important clues for understanding the internal organisation of the Millowners Association Building.[18]

The Millowners Association Building, like the Villa Cook, is defined by a richly symbolic front and back placed between two blind end walls. Within this exterior shell the Millowners Building contains a partly open ground floor for service and circulation, as did its antecedent. The second floor in both is intended for more private functions: bedrooms in the Villa Cook, boardrooms and offices in the Millowners Association. The third and fourth floors in both buildings are treated as double floors and intended for public functions: living room, dining room and kitchen in the Villa Cook, and lobby and auditorium in the Millowners Building.[19]

The lobby and the auditorium are the climactic points of the interior of the Millowners Building. It is here that Le Corbusier created the greatest dramatic tension by treating the lobby as an open space defined by harsh, angular forms and the auditorium as an enclosed space delineated by soft, curvilinear forms. 'This prodigious spectacle has been produced by the interplay of two elements, one male, one female: sun and water. Two contradictory elements that both need the other in order to exist.'[20] There are no better words than these, written by Le Corbusier many years before this building was ever conceived, to sum up the essence of these antithetical spaces. Here, as in most of his

Figure 4. Shodan House, Ahmedabad.

buildings, Le Corbusier achieved a resolution of opposites by juxtaposing rather than fusing diverse architectural elements so that each part retained its identity and separateness. With the male/female correlation as the central theme here, Le Corbusier imbued these spaces with a meaning that is analogous to the Indian attitude towards the sexes. This gives a special significance to the relationship between the lobby (male) and the auditorium (female) based on the notion of a strong sense of identity and separateness.

Besides the Millowners Building, Surottam Hutheesing also commissioned Le Corbusier to build him a house in the spring of 1951 (Figure 3).[21] The architect's task was to respond to the life-style of a wealthy bachelor, about to marry, who needed a variety of spaces to allow entertaining on a grand scale. After the plans were completed, however, Mr Hutheesing decided to sell these to a fellow millowner, Shyamubhai Shodhan. Notwithstanding the change in the site and the dissimilarity in his lifestyle, the new client wanted Le Corbusier to build him the very same house he had designed for Hutheesing.[22] Hence, in assessing it, the original functions intended for the house must be kept in mind.

For Le Corbusier the Shodhan house represented the culmination of his efforts in the field of domestic architecture that had evolved over a period spanning more than forty years. In order to understand its nature and meaning, we must examine the house in a dual context: how it grew out of the architect's own works, and how it is related to the traditional architecture of Ahmedabad.

The house is a cubical concrete frame structure whose exterior surface unfolds from a severe and forbidding entrance facade to an open and welcoming garden facade (Figures 3, 4). By treating each side of this classical cube differently, Le Corbusier juxtaposed the formality of the Mediterranean with the flexibility of the Northern approach to architectural design. The classical aspects of the house find their antecedents in Le Corbusier's earlier houses, going back to the one he designed for his parents in La Chaux-de-Fonds in 1912. Apart from its sharp and clear cubical mass, certain important details of the first design for the Jeanneret house find their way into the Shodhan house, as for example its flat roof defined by strong projecting cornices and the continuous band of windows beneath it. These are reinterpreted as the parasol roof and the continuous openings of the terrace in the Shodhan house.

Le Corbusier's most important house built in La Chaux-de-Fonds, the Villa Schwob of 1916, serves as a point of departure for the structure and personality of the Shodhan house. As one of the first concrete framed houses in Europe,[23] the Villa Schwob marked the beginning of Le Corbusier's use of this structural system, which reached a high degree of complexity in Ahmedabad. More interesting, however, is the way in which these houses reveal Le Corbusier's own personality. He was known to have had an 'impressive demeanour seemingly built for defence, behind which he appeared to withdraw'.[24] On the other hand, he was considered by his friends to be 'uncommonly generous and unselfish'.[25] Both houses convey these personal characteristics by the stark and almost forbidding demeanour of their street facades and the generous and accessible quality of their garden facades. As a result, they effectively ward off strangers while at the same time they welcome those who have been allowed to enter.

Although the Schwob and Jeanneret houses are important precedents for the Shodhan house, they play a far less significant role in this capacity than Le Corbusier's houses designed after 1919. In fact, in 1919 Le Corbusier initiated a new direction in architecture which he never abandoned afterwards. In the realm of domestic architecture the Maison Citrohan of

1920-22 and the Maison Monol of 1919 mark the beginning of this new direction.[26] The former, angular and firm, stands erect on the ground, dominating the setting, while the latter, undulating and soft, rests on the ground, absorbing the setting. Le Corbusier's description of what for him represented the masculine and feminine characteristics in architecture succinctly sum up the essence of these two projects.

> In the one, strong objectivity of forms, under the intense light of a Mediterranean sun: *male* architecture. In the other, limitless subjectivity rising against a clouded sky: *female* architecture.[27]

Having thus set the stage for a dual approach to domestic architecture, Le Corbusier used these two projects as the basis of all his later houses. When in 1951 he was called upon to design a house for Surottam Hutheesing, a bachelor wanting to entertain extensively, he understandably followed the model of the Maison Citrohan.

Among the many sources of the Maison Citrohan, two provide the best clues to an understanding of its nature and meaning. The inspiration for its exterior came from such Parisian artists' studios as those built by François Le Coeur in the rue Cassini in 1906, which Le Corbusier admired greatly.[28] Its double-storeyed interior, on the other hand, was based on the spatial organisation of the Café Legendre in Paris, which Le Corbusier frequented with Amédée Ozenfant (Figure 11).[29] The fusion of the artist's studio with the restaurant resulted in a new kind of house which so appropriately expresses the lifestyle of a growing segment of the urban population in the industrialised world: uprootedness and transience. The former is embodied in the artist's studio, the latter in the restaurant, and Le Corbusier understood both these states of mind from personal experience, for when he conceived the Maison Citrohan he was an uprooted artist whose family table became the restaurant table.

The most important link between the Maison Citrohan and the Shodhan house is the first project for the Villa Baizeau in Carthage, Tunisia, designed by Le Corbusier in 1928.[30] The significance of this design lies in two areas: a new approach to climate control, and a fuller use of de Stijl vocabulary. The former is exemplified by the parasol roof and the interlocking interior spaces providing shade and ventilation; the latter is expressed by the facade where the studio and ribbon windows – hallmarks of Le Corbusier's style of fenestration – are fused with the help of de Stijl vocabulary. As in Mondrian's paintings or especially as in Rietveld's Schröder house of 1924, the composition of the facade is based on compensation rather than symmetry achieved by a strong interplay between lines and planes, between verticals and horizontals, and between different colours.[31] All of these elements were given a more complete realisation in the Shodhan house. The design that provides the key connection between the villa at Carthage and the Shodhan house is Le Corbusier's house in Lannemezan of 1940 (Figure 5). This project was conceived as a cubical structure of exposed stone and wood. Here, as in his houses designed during the 1930s, Le Corbusier abandoned his favoured structural device, the steel or concrete skeletal frame, in favour of load-bearing walls to be constructed of natural materials. Moreover, instead of putting the house on stilts, he anchored it to the ground, thus imbuing it with a sense of rootedness which was so clearly lacking in his houses of the 1920s.

The decade of the 1930s represented a turning point in Le Corbusier's architecture for reasons too numerous to list, but mention must be made of the economic depression of the period, his questioning of the supremacy of technology, and his marriage to Yvonne Gallis in 1930. The direction he began to pursue in 1930 found its clearest architectural expression in his designs for houses ranging from the project of the Errazuris house to the house in Lannemezan. In them Le Corbusier established a close relationship with nature, the site, and the vernacular tradition that recalls his first three houses in La Chaux-de-Fonds.[32] These changes in fact paved the way for the formal and structural innovations made in his later buildings such as the Shodhan house.

As seen from the point of view of Le Corbusier's later buildings, the decade of the 1930s stands out for another entirely different reason: the invention of the sunbreaker, or *brise-soleil*. This device made its first appearance in 1933 with the project for an apartment house intended for a site in Algiers.[33] But it was only in his design for an office building conceived for Algiers between 1938 and 1942 that Le Corbusier gave it his first imaginative interpretation (Figure 25). From this project on, sunbreakers began to fulfil a number of complex functions in his design, ranging from the utilitarian to the symbolic: they provide protection from the sun, they help give scale and proportion to the building, and they serve as major conveyors of the building's symbolic significance.

In the Shodhan house the sunbreakers act in all of these roles. Dominating the southwest or garden facade of the house and forming an irregular concrete grille, they provide an effective screen against the summer sun without blocking out the winter sun on the most open side of the house. They also serve as visual connections between the observer and the house, between inside and outside, between the various parts of the house ranging from the very large to the very small. Most important, however, is the fact that they embody a major part of the personal and cultural significance of the house.

Le Corbusier likened the sunbreaker to a portico as well as to the aperture of a camera.[34] As a portico it acts as a container and definer of human action, and as an opening it links the outside with the inside in a defined and sequential way. As a photographer focuses the camera on a given target, Le Corbusier zeroed in on a specific view by giving a desired aperture and orientation to each concrete frame. Furthermore, if taken together, sunbreakers serve as conveyors of the life pattern that unfolds within the building. In their role as porticoes, the sunbreakers of the Shodhan house provide a more intimately scaled architectural environment within the framework of a palatial house; they act as houses within a house. As cameras, they focus on the sensuous shape of the swimming pool and the soft, grass-filled mound surrounding it; as such, they act as apertures between the angular interior and the soft exterior. Taken together, they convey a playful, spontaneous, almost dollhouse-like quality, thus effectively counteracting the formal setting. In all three roles, they help express the function Le Corbusier intended for the house: to be like a 'château of the Loire . . . for an intelligent prince'.[35]

On a cultural level, the sunbreakers link the Shodhan house with the architectural tradition of Northern Europe, whose asymmetrical, irregular and flexible design elements they incorporate. In a sketch of primitive huts of Ireland published in 1928, Le Corbusier captured these elements by highlighting their structural frame, which in turn foreshadows the sunbreakers of his later buildings.[36] More important, however, is the connection between the sunbreakers of the Shodhan house and a more recent manifestation of Northern architecture: de Stijl. As a comparison between the sunbreakers and Theo van Doesburg's project for an artist's house of 1923 reveals, Le Corbusier incorporated in his design such de Stijl elements as asymmetry, flexibility and plasticity (Figure 6). In the Shodhan house, however, these Northern elements are held in check by the restraining power of the classical cube, whereas in Van Doesburg's project they are expressed more freely. Having always remained a classicist at heart, it is not surprising that in this

Figure 5. House at Lannemezan.

Figure 6. Theo van Doesburg, project for an artist's house.

Figure 11. Café Legendre in Paris.

Figure 7. Hutheesing Jain Temple.

Figure 8. Old town house of the Shodan family.

Figure 10. Chunilal House interior.

house, as well as in most of his other buildings, Le Corbusier allowed the Mediterranean rather than the Northern tradition to dominate the design.

Le Corbusier's Mediterranean formalism and Northern flexibility served him well in India, where both of these cultural traits are manifested in the country's indigenous architecture. In the context of the exterior of the Shodhan house, two examples of traditional architecture in Ahmedabad stand out: the Hutheesing Jain temple, and the old town house of the Shodhan family (Figures 7, 8). The temple was commissioned by the wealthy Jain merchant Sheth Hutheesing in 1850, and Le Corbusier made reference to it in one of his sketchbooks during his first visit to Ahmedabad.[37] The temple is distinguished by its openness and flexibility, largely achieved by its numerous porches that are grouped around the main hall of worship. Like the sunbreakers and terraces of the Shodhan house of a hundred years later, the porches of the temple offer shade in the summer, sun in the winter, and breezes in every season.

The old town house of the Shodhan family located in the heart of the city provides an interesting clue to an understanding of the client's willingness to accept Le Corbusier's design exactly as it was intended for Surottam Hutheesing. Having been raised in a house which had *pilotis*, terraces, roof gardens and open facades, Shyamubhai Shodhan must not have found the designs for the house he was to buy too unusual. Coming from such an architectural environment, he was in fact better prepared to accept Le Corbusier's ideas than a Parisian client. One of the reasons why Le Corbusier's architecture was welcomed by his Indian clients was because they were accustomed to seeing classical buildings that, in addition to being open, were often characterised by irregularity and flexibility. Hence, in evaluating Le Corbusier's success with his Indian clients, the Northern element in his architecture is just as important to bear in mind as its more obvious Mediterranean element.

The focal point of the interior of the Shodhan house consisting of the great double-storeyed living room is also in keeping with Ahmedabad's own architectural tradition (Figure 9). The large houses of old Ahmedabad were usually built around a double-storeyed entry hall, or *chowk*, which signifies their symbolic and ceremonial centre. As seen in the eighteenth-century Chunilal house, this space was given the greatest artistic attention in terms of spatial organisation and decorative treatment (Figure 10). When Shyamubhai Shodhan first saw the designs for the double-storeyed interiors of his future house, he must have recognised in them a modern reinterpretation of a familiar symbol of status and wealth.

Apart from the coincidental connection between the Shodhan house's living room and the entry halls of Ahmedabad's old houses, the roots of Le Corbusier's double-storeyed space go back to his earlier architecture. As mentioned before, the inspiration for this space, according to the architect, originally came from the Café Legendre, where a balcony provided additional seating space (Figure 11). His first literal interpretation of this spatial arrangement occurred in the Maison Citrohan of 1920, whose interior can best be visualised through the Pavillon de l'Esprit Nouveau of five years later. There, the balcony does not merely connect two parts of the house, as it does in the Villa Schwob, but instead functions as an actual room, as in the Café Legendre.

During the 1920s, Le Corbusier gave the double-storeyed interior space a wide range of interpretations, but the one that stands out in relationship to the Shodhan house is the great entry hall of the Villa La Roche of 1923. Here, as in his later house, Le Corbusier organised the interior volume in terms of polarities that include public and private, formal and informal, and impersonal and personal, allowing each to preserve its

Figure 9. Shodan House, living room.

Figure 12. Shodan House, terrace.

discreet identity. In the living room of the Shodhan house the strong contrast between the public level of the main space and the private level of the balcony best exemplifies the architect's polarisation of spaces. The balcony, as in the Villa La Roche, functions as the study and den and provides an ideal setting for intimate gatherings enlivened by a striking view of the space below.

The most dramatic part of the house is the triple-storeyed terrace where Le Corbusier's definition of architecture as 'the masterly, correct, and magnificent play of forms in light' was fully realised (Figure 12). Created largely in response to Ahmedabad's intense sun, the terrace functions as a major part of the house's natural climate-control system by cooling the bedroom units during the day and serving as bedrooms during hot summer nights. Beyond this, it provides a stage where man, architecture and nature meet as active partners. Following a precedent established in the recessed terraces of the Immeubles-villas project of 1922 and first realised in the Villa Stein-Monzie of 1927,[38] Le Corbusier created a setting here where nature is invited to penetrate the body of the house through light, air and water, while being compelled to respond to the power of architectural form to shape nature. In the midst of this orchestrated interaction between architecture and nature, the observer is engaged as an active participant so that he/she can develop a heightened awareness of the experience of living.

As Le Corbusier's most ambitious example of domestic architecture, the Shodhan house represents a highly complex synthesis of forms and spaces resulting from a long process of selection, absorption and transformation. Although the constituent elements of his architecture have undergone major changes to suit new functions and express new meanings, they have retained their original identity. As the Shodhan house's double-storeyed living room illustrates, the key formal solutions which Le Corbusier developed during the 1920s remained an essential part of his late work. Yet notwithstanding the continuity of such forms and spaces, their characteristics and qualities changed dramatically over the years. As a comparison between his houses of the 1920s and the 1950s indicates, the frail, transient and uprooted qualities of the former were reshaped by Le Corbusier into the strong, durable and rooted qualities of the latter. This process was in no small measure reinforced by his encounter with India, where he found the right cultural and climatic setting for strengthening the direction he had initiated in the 1930s.

The second house Le Corbusier built in Ahmedabad was commissioned by Mrs Manorama Sarabhai in March 1951 who, after the death of her husband, wanted a secluded place for herself and her sons, aged ten and thirteen.[39] The site chosen for the house was a tree-filled area on the large Sarabhai estate in the Shahibag district of the city. In response to the site and his client's needs and personality, Le Corbusier designed an open and flexible house whose spatial organisation was determined by its dual function: to provide maximum comfort for adults and children alike. To this end, he planned a double-storeyed block for Mrs Sarabhai and a single-storeyed block for her children; these blocks, although adjoining, are divided by a built-in carport and a slide. The exterior of these blocks is defined by load-bearing concrete walls, while their interior is organised in terms of parallel bays crowned by low concrete barrel vaults (Figure 13). This structural solution ingeniously combines both of Le Corbusier's approaches to domestic architecture by utilising the angularity of the Maison Citrohan for the exterior, and the undulating quality of the Maison Monol for the interior.

By giving the Sarabhai house a hard, angular exterior and a soft, undulating interior, Le Corbusier juxtaposed what for him represented the masculine and feminine characteristics in

Figure 13. Sarabhai House, interior.

Figure 14. Royal Apartments of the Red Fort, Delhi.

architecture, without allowing either to lose its identity. To this end, he visually separated the exterior shell from the interior, so that the 'feminine' interior seems incomprehensible when seen from the outside, and the 'masculine' exterior becomes unintelligible when seen from within. The separation between the two is reinforced by the materials and colours: mostly grey concrete on the outside, and mostly red brick and multicoloured on the inside. For a house intended for a widow with two sons, the architectural imagery embodying the male/female symbolism seems most appropriate, especially as it was handled by Le Corbusier. Unlike the Shodhan house, whose masculine exterior is as important as its equally masculine interior, in this house everything emanates from within, making the feminine interior the *raison d'être* of the house. No wonder that its masculine exterior is reduced to a quasi-autonomous shield that offers some physical and psychological protection to the interior without, however, interfering with it.

The focal point of the interior is the open multipurpose public space which occupies most of the first floor of the main part of the house (Figure 13). Serving as a living/dining room and hall, this space is defined by low tile vaults resting on exposed concrete beams which in turn are supported by brick walls that are either exposed or covered by plaster or plywood. To add to this rich orchestration of materials, Le Corbusier used the three primary colours, plus black and white, for the walls covered by plaster. Hence each major part of the interior stands out visually, if not necessarily structurally, as an independent element. But to counteract this, he forged a spatial connection among the bays and between the inside and outside so as to achieve a greater sense of openness. To gain a clearer understanding of this spatial and formal organisation, we must examine, however briefly, some of its sources.

As we have seen, the interior of the Sarabhai house grew out of the project for the Maison Monol, which was planned as an earth-hugging structure with an undulating concrete roof held up by concrete columns. The first built version of this project was designed by Le Corbusier in 1935 for a suburban site in La Celle-St-Cloud, near Paris.[40] This weekend house represents the most important link between the Maison Monol and the Sarabhai house, largely because of the way in which the architect handled its form, space and materials. As in the Monol house, the space is anchored to the ground by low barrel vaults, yet the interaction between inside and outside is far greater here than in its prototype. These spatial characteristics were further developed in the Sarabhai house, where they acquired a sense of sheltered openness. In terms of form, the weekend house offers striking juxtapositions between the angular and curvilinear and between the smooth and the rough, yet the greatest amount of contrast is to be found in the handling of materials. Such diverse materials as concrete, stone, brick, glass and plywood are placed side by side so as to give each constituent part of the house a high degree of independence. This brings us only a short step away from the Sarabhai house where form, materials and colours are juxtaposed in an even more uncompromising manner.

The role fulfilled by the weekend house in preparing the way for the Sarabhai house is comparable to that played by the house in Lannemezan in relationship to the Shodhan house. The spatial and formal innovations made in both of these 'transitional' houses greatly facilitated Le Corbusier's encounter with India, where he was compelled, more than before, to respond to conditions set by nature. It is not surprising, therefore, that the weekend house's low, earth-hugging form, channelled space and roof garden reappear in the Sarabhai house, where they are eminently suited to the prevailing climate.[41] This leads to the question of whether the Sarabhai house was at all inspired by India's traditional architecture.

A comparison between the Sarabhai house and the royal apartments of Delhi's Red Fort shows that both are low, dark and sheltered architectural environments which shut out the summer sun yet let in the cooling breezes. Moreover, both spaces are primarily intended for the sitting position (Figures 13, 14). Yet the close kinship that exists between these two interiors is not necessarily the result of a direct influence from India's own architectural tradition; instead, it is largely the outcome of a long creative process that was decisively shaped by the natural and built environment of the Mediterranean world.[42] What India did offer to Le Corbusier was the right climatic and cultural setting for bringing his Mediterranean style to a full fruition.

If the formal and spatial qualities of the Sarabhai house are Indian only by coincidence, is there anything about the house that can be called uniquely Indian? The answer is yes: its naturalness. And this is precisely the quality that is so greatly valued by the followers of the Jain religion. The belief in the overriding importance of nature constitutes in fact a central tenet in Jainism. This is most eloquently manifested in the avowed commitment not to harm any living being and to interfere with nature as little as possible. Le Corbusier paid a profound tribute to Jain beliefs by making the Sarabhai house his most natural house.

In the concluding lines of *Le Poème de l'angle droit* (1955), Le Corbusier wrote:

With a full hand I have received
With a full hand I give[43]

There are no better words to sum up what Le Corbusier and Ahmedabad owe to each other, for what he created there was just as much the result of his clients' vision as it was of his genius. Whether the intention was to enrich the cultural life of the city or the personal life of a client, it took courage and insight to engage Le Corbusier in the process of restoring Ahmedabad's eminence in the cultural life of India. The most immediate effect of the reciprocal relationship between Le Corbusier and his Ahmedabadi clients was that it made the city aware that modern architecture could be used as a means to express its aspirations. Those who benefited from this were India's own younger architects, most notably Achyut Kanvinde of New Delhi, Balkrishna Doshi of Ahmedabad and Charles Correa of Bombay, who later became the country's foremost architects. Thanks to the patronage they received there from the mid-1950s on, they built some of their finest buildings in Ahmedabad, making the city the birthplace of India's indigenous modern architecture.

However important Le Corbusier's work in Ahmedabad, it was Chandigarh that brought him to India, and it was there that he created his most profound architectural statements. Thanks to the pioneering work of a number of scholars, it is possible today to offer a brief evaluation of Le Corbusier's achievement there without doing injustice to the subject.[44]

As indicated earlier, Le Corbusier was invited by the representatives of the Punjab government to become the architectural advisor for Chandigarh. In this capacity he was primarily responsible for the master plan of the city and the capitol complex. Later he undertook to design a major portion of the business centre and a few additional buildings for the city.[45] My discussion will focus on only a few salient characteristics of the executed buildings of the capitol complex: the Secretariat, the Assembly Building and the High Court, serving the executive, legislative and judiciary branches of government.[46]

The first of these to be erected was the High Court, a concrete structure defined by a large rectangular frame within which the different functions of the building are inserted, from the highest court on the left to the lowest on the right (Figure 15). The

Figure 15. High Court, Chandigarh.

significance of the Supreme Court is underscored by its separation from the rest by a giant portico whose massive pillars are painted green, yellow and red. Clues to an understanding of the nature and meaning of this building can be found in its sources and the development of its design.

The first sketch of the High Court that appears in Le Corbusier's sketchbooks shows that he envisaged the building as a monumental vaulted structure set against the backdrop of the Himalayas (Figure 16).[47] The spatial and formal configuration proposed here recalls two sketches the architect made fifty years apart, the first representing the Basilica of Constantine and the second the pavilion of the Pinjore gardens (Figures 17, 18). Appearing next to the High Court in his sketchbook, the sketch of the pavilion and its surroundings sets the stage for the siting of the capitol complex and the spatial relationships established in it.[48] Like the pavilion, the High Court is placed in a wide-open space linking the mountains with the observer. Although the position intended here for the High Court was soon given over to the Governor's Palace, Le Corbusier retained in the completed building the sense of isolation inherent in the sketch. In fact, a comparison between the High Court and the pavilion of the Pinjore gardens shows that the isolation of Le Corbusier's building is far greater than that of the pavilion. As in most Mogul palace gardens, the individual buildings in Pinjore are interconnected by landscaped processional spaces unmarred by overscaling. Le Corbusier, on the other hand, not only overscaled his processional spaces but also replaced landscaping with paving, thus forcing the High Court into an even greater sense of isolation (Figure 15). The High Court, more than the Assembly and the Secretariat, became in fact the victim of Le Corbusier's heroic attempt to fuse Parisian scale with Mogul processional spaces: mating the two without the mitigating power of Mogul landscaping resulted in failure.[49]

Figure 17. Basilica of Constantine, Rome.

If the Pinjore gardens gave the impetus for the initial siting of the High Court, it was the Basilica of Constantine as sketched by Le Corbusier during his first visit to Rome in 1911 that provided the point of departure for the design of the building (Figures 16, 17). As can be seen from his early sketches, Le Corbusier used the great barrel vaults of the Basilica as the most dominant element in his preliminary designs.[50] However, as the building evolved in his mind, the importance of Constantine's law court gradually diminished to give way to influences emanating from the North. Hence in the final design the lower parts of the massive Roman vaults were largely replaced by sunbreakers whose irregular concrete grille was inspired by de Stijl architecture (Figures 15, 6).

The facade of the High Court, consisting of a flexible framework of sunbreakers placed within a single monumental frame, sheds an important light on the symbolic significance of

Figure 16. Sketch of High Court, Chandigarh.

Figure 18. Sketch of the Pavilion of the Pinjore Gardens.

Figure 19. Assembly Building, Chandigarh.

Figure 21. The Red Fort, Hall of Public Audiences, Delhi.

Figure 20. Assembly Building, Chandigarh.

the building. As a classicist at heart and as a citizen of a country whose law still reflects the basic principles of Roman law, Le Corbusier first turned to a great example of Roman judicial architecture, whose most essential elements he retained even in the final design. He did so by joining the Basilica's arcuated and trabeated system in the building's exterior frame. By placing all the law courts within this all-embracing Roman frame, Le Corbusier reaffirmed the fundamental role that Roman architecture and Roman law have played in Western culture. Moreover, by imbuing the building in general and its great frame in particular with clarity, constancy and logic, he gave the High Court a sense of majestic unity. And it is precisely such a unity that constitutes the essence of Roman architecture and Roman law.

Yet within the High Court's formal, classical frame, Le Corbusier allowed the sunbreakers to act more freely and flexibly, in keeping with the architectural tradition of the North. He did so not only to provide better protection from the sun and give scale to the building but also to convey a major part of the building's symbolic significance. Although Roman law remained the primary basis of Western law, it was English common law that was brought into India by the British. As opposed to the codified law of Rome, common law has developed in England gradually and organically since the early Middle Ages. Based on custom and precedent, this law is known not for constancy and logic but rather for variety and flexibility. And these are precisely the qualities which characterise the sunbreakers of the High Court's facade.

In the High Court Le Corbusier juxtaposed the Mediterranean and Northern traditions of architecture by making the former the anchoring point and primary frame of reference of the building without, however, minimising the prominence of the latter. He embodied the Mediterranean tradition primarily in the clarity and constancy of the building's monumental frame, while he expressed that of the North in the variety and flexibility of the sunbreakers. In so doing, he created architectural forms possessing the very same qualities that characterise Roman law and English common law: majestic unity and organic quality, respectively. Hence, in the High Court the two great systems of Western law, Roman civil law and English common law, find, unwittingly perhaps, a most eloquent visual interpretation.

Facing the High Court across the 400 m-wide capitol square is the Assembly, whose exterior consists of three main elements: a square block, a portico and a superstructure, each of which has a distinct identity (Figures 19, 20). As early sketches of the Assembly indicate, Le Corbusier first envisaged it as a great arcuated building evoking the memory of such Roman structures as the Basilica of Constantine and the Pont du Gard.[51] But as the building evolved in his mind, the arcuated system was replaced by a trabeated system exemplified largely by a regular grille of sunbreakers.

The sources of the three main constituent elements of the Assembly's exterior provide important clues to an understanding of the nature and meaning of the building. Fronting the building is the monumental portico whose dominant feature is the upwards swooping curvilinear canopy that functions both as an umbrella and a gutter. This canopy rests on eight tautly stretched walls that cut the portico into clearly defined cubical bays whose distinctness is reinforced by the compositional organisation of the back wall. The climactic point of this wall is the 25 ft^2 enamelled ceremonial door, which depicts a complex set of images dominated by the sun.

The Assembly's monumental portico incorporates the spatial and formal qualities of two distinctly different strains of India's architectural past: the palatial and the folk. As a comparison with the Red Fort's Hall of Public Audiences shows, the repetitive rhythm, the sheltered openness, and the ceremonial dignity of this Mogul palatial building reappear in Le Corbusier's portico (Figures 19, 21). However, the surface treatment of his forms, whether in the Assembly's portico or in his other concrete buildings in India, shows a greater affinity to the country's folk architecture. He was fond of visiting the villages around Chandigarh to study their low, moundlike huts constructed of mud brick; these visits found their way into his handling of rough concrete, or *béton brut* (Figure 22). Even before his contact with India, Le Corbusier was fascinated by the possibility of making concrete look more like a natural material, and his work there greatly enhanced this process.

Le Corbusier reinforced the meaning of the portico with the enamelled doorway that links the outside with the columnar lobby. The primary function of this door is to provide a ceremonial entryway for the governor when he opens the Assembly once a year. Both sides of the door are decorated with a rich range of images that convey multiple meanings. The door's pictorial composition facing the portico is divided into two halves: the upper, representing the paths of the sun, and the lower, representing rivers, vegetation and animals; and both are interpreted in a spontaneous, almost childlike, manner. Hence the function and scale of the ceremonial doorway convey a formal and ritualistic order, while the imagery on its surface evokes the world of fantasy and folklore.[52] And both of these meanings are inherent in the portico.

Treating the great portico as a gateway to the building that houses the two legislative bodies of the Punjab government – the Assembly and the Governor's Council – it is fitting that Le Corbusier incorporated in it a broad range of India's architectural tradition: from the stately and ritualistic to the informal and rustic. In so doing, he expressed in it, unintentionally perhaps, some of the most salient characteristics of Indian society.

The main body of the Assembly Building is defined on three sides by large grilles of sunbreakers arranged in repetitive rows. This organisation reveals the nature of the spaces that lie behind them: scores of offices and committee rooms serving the members of parliament and their staff (Figure 20). On top of the Assembly's classical block is a superstructure which consists of three separate yet interrelated parts: a tower in the shape of a hyperbolic paraboloid, a tilted pyramid and a service tower (Figure 19). The basic function of the first is to provide light for the assembly hall, and that of the second to help illuminate the council chamber. The relationship between the hyperbolic tower and the main body of the building evokes the memory of French industrial architecture as exemplified by Züblin's coal-washer for the Société des Mines de Carmaux of 1928-29 (Figure 23). The Assembly's tower, like the funnel-shaped receptor of the coal-washer, is dramatically juxtaposed with the main part of the building, producing a strong sense of tension between the two. Juxtaposing a building's constituent parts in such a manner is not uncommon in industrial architecture but is quite exceptional in an honorific building. In fact, one of the most remarkable qualities of the Assembly is the daring contrasts created by Le Corbusier among the building's three major parts: the portico, the main block, and the superstructure. Without his deep admiration for the compositional solutions established in industrial architecture, this could hardly have been accomplished.[53]

The striking contrast between the Assembly's main block and the hyperbolic tower tends to suggest that the two are not functionally interrelated. Yet a closer examination reveals that the building's crowning feature is in fact a continuation of the large hyperbolic shell which serves as a container for the assembly hall. As Le Corbusier's sketch of June 1953 shows, the inspiration for this shell came directly from the cooling towers of the Sabarmati power plant in Ahmedabad.[54] By using the form of the cooling towers for both the interior shell and the protruding part of the assembly hall, Le Corbusier not only preserved the building's consistency but also reinforced a key aspect of the building's symbolic significance.

In the Assembly's interior the building's underlying theme of juxtaposing quasi-autonomous architectural elements is best exemplified by the way in which the hyperbolic shell of the assembly hall is related to its setting. Instead of treating this shell as a continuous part of the interior, Le Corbusier handled it as a building within a building. He did so by placing it inside a large hypostyle hall known as the forum, which in turn is surrounded by offices facing the outside. As a result, the assembly hall is just as clearly separated from the rest of the interior as the Assembly's tower is from the rest of the exterior, thus ensuring consistency in the building's formal organisation.

On the symbolic level, the isolation of the hyperbolic shell highlights the importance of the legislative assembly. Following the parliamentary system inherited from the British, the Assembly, like the lower house in Britain, enjoys a prime decision-making power in the government. Le Corbusier gave this political reality a powerful architectural interpretation by making the hyperbolic shell the focal point of the interior and the crowning point of the exterior. In so doing, he not only expressed the nature of the legislative assembly's power in Chandigarh, but also proclaimed the role that the lower house fulfils within a parliamentary system. In fact, never before has the role of the lower house been given such a forceful and eloquent architectural interpretation as in Le Corbusier's Assembly Building.

However, the inspiration emanating from the cooling towers of the Sabarmati power plant served Le Corbusier in other ways as well. With its obvious references to technology, the image of the cooling towers offered him an opportunity to pay tribute to one of Prime Minister Nehru's most fundamental beliefs summed up in one of his lectures: 'The essential and most revolutionary factor in modern life is not a particular ideology, but technological advance'.[55] Nehru put these general principles into practice by establishing a five-year plan whose primary aim was to develop industry and produce electricity on a large scale. Thus, the cooling towers of an electric power plant must have seemed to Le Corbusier a particularly appropriate symbol for expressing the social and political aspirations of his friend and patron. As a Ruskinian at heart, he may even have believed that by placing the legislators in an architectural environment that strongly resembled the cooling towers of a power plant, he could influence them to follow Nehru's commitment to technology.

The Assembly's conspicuously visible symbol of technology should not give the impression that Le Corbusier paid tribute to only one of India's great modern leaders, for in addition to Nehru, Gandhi's presence can also be found in the building. Gandhi's philosophy of rejecting technology and focusing on the importance of agriculture, handicraft and cottage industry finds many direct and indirect references in the Assembly. The handmade quality of the *béton brut*, the folk imagery on the ceremonial gateway, the wall decorations based on imprints made by the workmen, and the juxtaposition of the oxcart with the building in one of Le Corbusier's sketches all attest to a world view that shared a great deal with Gandhi's own. For Le Corbusier, Gandhi's philosophy of rural rejuvenation offered a felicitous balance to Nehru's technological bias, and how he agreed with both can be seen in two statements he made in his early Indian sketchbooks: 'Atomic energy is now a fact. Put it in the countries and in the homes'. But elsewhere he wrote: 'How the earth remains a primary, primeval primitive in spite of the works of Men'.[56] And one of Gandhi's aims was to keep it that way.

The Assembly Building represents a culmination of Le Corbusier's heroic efforts to give the most meaningful architectural

Figure 22. Village near Chandigarh.

Figure 23. Züblin, coal-washer for the Société des Mines de Carmaux.

Figure 24. Secretariat, Chandigarh.

interpretation to political institutions. This effort has a long history in his own career, going back to his projects for the League of Nations Building in 1927 and the Palace of the Soviets in 1931. In the former he combined Beaux-Arts composition with a technologically perfected structural system, while in the latter he allowed technology to triumph throughout the entire design. Intended for an international political body of the modern world, it is fitting that Le Corbusier imbued his project for the League with a sense of history and modernity. And by giving technology such a prominent presence in the Palace of the Soviets, he highlighted one of Soviet Russia's most deeply felt ambitions: to achieve technological superiority in the world. But to express the social, political and economic aspirations of newly independent India, Le Corbusier not only had to invent new forms but he also had to develop a new formal organisation that could convey architecturally the complexity of the issues at hand. He did so by turning to India's rich past and evolving present while fertilising these with his own creative memory. No wonder that the Assembly became one of the most probing and compelling architectural manifestations of the human spirit.

Looming behind the Assembly, the Secretariat is an 800 ft-long concrete slab consisting of six eight-storey blocks interconnected by a massive grille of sunbreakers (Figure 24). Originally Le Corbusier had envisaged it as a high-rise building, but when this was rejected he proposed the present solution. As an early sketch of the building shows, the architect first visualised it as a tall concrete slab defined by arches on its narrow ends. In a more developed design, he presented it as an even taller slab resting on *pilotis* and sheathed by a repetitive grille of sunbreakers.[57] The project that links this design with the final version is his Admiralty Building planned for Algiers between 1938 and 1942 (Figure 25).

Intended as an office building and hotel for Algiers' marine district, the Admiralty represents a major point of departure in Le Corbusier's approach to skyscraper design. Here he abandoned his earlier skin-and-bone technique in favour of achieving firmness, scale and functional clarity – a dramatic change directly attributable to his encounter with the skyscrapers of New York in 1936. In his account of his American journey he wrote:

> In New York, then, I learn to appreciate the Italian Renaissance. It is so well done that you could believe it to be genuine. It even has a strange, new firmness which is not Italian but American! The maritime atmosphere and the potential of the American adventure have lifted Tuscan graces to a new tone. The oldest skyscrapers of Wall Street add the superimposed orders of Bramante all the way up to the top with a clearness in moulding and proportion which delights me.[58]

The praise that Le Corbusier lavished on New York's skyscrapers may seem surprising after the diatribes against them in his earlier books, most notably in *Urbanisme*. But even during the 1920s he singled out a few American skyscrapers as worthy of emulation, for example, Albert Kahn's First National Bank Building in Detroit of 1922 (Figure 26). Illustrated in his book, *L'Art décoratif d'aujourd'hui*, he used the building as a frontispiece for a chapter devoted to utilitarian design.[59] But he had to come to America to appreciate its qualities fully.

The qualities that Le Corbusier ascribed to New York's Beaux-Arts Renaissance skyscrapers in the passage quoted above – clarity, firmness and proportion – can also be found in Kahn's building. Hence it can be used as a frame of reference for discussing the 'Americanisation' of Le Corbusier's approach to skyscraper design. Following the principles of the Beaux-Arts Renaissance style popularised by Daniel Burnham, Kahn divided his building into three major zones: the public for the lobby, the semi-private for the offices, and the private for the top executives. These three functional zones are clearly revealed in the building's exterior design with the help of columns, cornices and windows. Moreover, the building's firmness and proportion are expressed in its mass and articulation of parts, respectively.

In the Admiralty, Le Corbusier incorporated some of the key principles of the American Beaux-Arts Renaissance skyscraper style, most notably its emphasis on mass, proportion and hierarchical organisation. As a comparison between the Admiralty and the First National Bank Building in Detroit shows, he interpreted these principles with the help of large frames and sunbreakers to be built of concrete. In fact, from this project on, sunbreakers became the key conveyors of his design principles based on the American Beaux-Arts skyscraper. They gave his projects and buildings clarity by externalising the spatial and hierarchical organisation of the interior; they imbued his works with firmness by the sheer weight of their mass; and they helped achieve proportion by the articulation of their form. And all of these principles were fully realised in Chandigarh.

When it became clear to Le Corbusier that he could not build the Secretariat as a tall slab, he offered a horizontal version of it without, however, abandoning the principles he had developed

Figure 26. Kahn, First National Bank Building, Detroit.

in the Admiralty Building. The Secretariat, like its precursor, is divided into large rectangular blocks which are shielded by a massive grille of sunbreakers whose shape ranges from the simple to the complex. The simple, repetitive sunbreakers covering most of the building enfront the endless rows of bureaucratic offices, while the complex ones concentrated in the central block largely define the ministerial offices. The unprecedented complexity and monumentality of the ministerial block show that Le Corbusier wanted the sunbreakers to serve there as powerful witnesses to the functional and symbolic role fulfilled by the spaces that lie behind them.

If the Secretariat's firmness, proportion and functional clarity must be seen in part as a continuation of American Beaux-

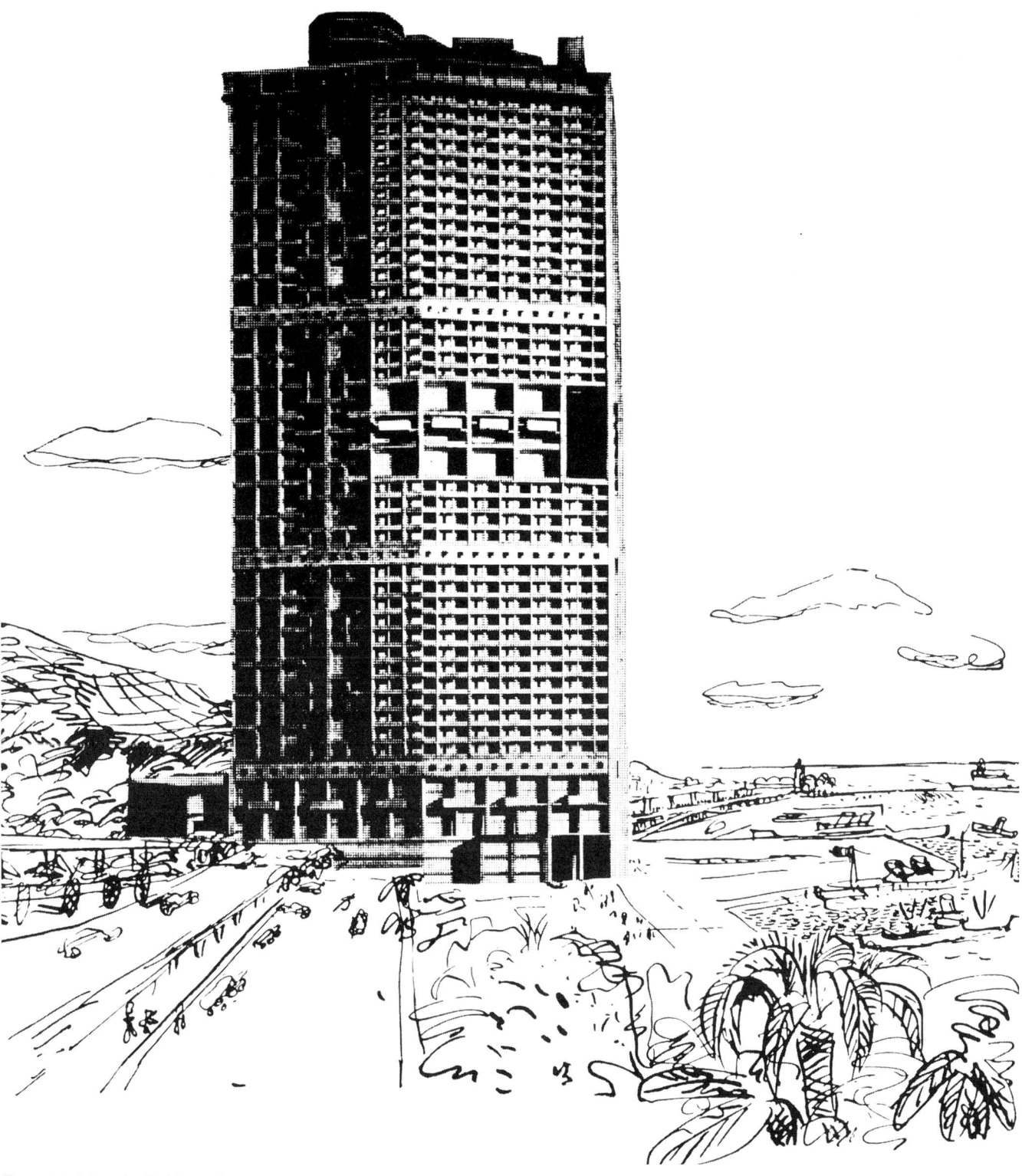

Figure 25. Admiralty Building, Algiers.

Figure 27. Ronéo file cabinet.

Arts skyscraper design principles, the form and composition of its sunbreakers should not. To find precedents for these one must turn to Le Corbusier's books, where illustrations of file cabinets will provide the clues. The two that stand out appear in his *L'Art décoratif d'aujourd'hui*, the first representing a Ronéo file cabinet system (Figure 27) and the second a file cabinet drawer.[60] Discussing these and other examples of office furniture, Le Corbusier singled out their efficiency, suitability and flexibility, qualities that he also expected of buildings. No wonder that he incorporated these when he designed an office building such as the Secretariat, whose overall composition shares a great deal with the built-in file cabinets (Figures 24, 27), while the sunbreakers fronting the bureaucratic offices reveal a striking similarity to file cabinet drawers. As a result, the building looks like a huge file cabinet system, with most of its 'drawers' lined up in an orderly fashion while its 'shelves' (porticoes) are left open in a random fashion.

By juxtaposing the firmness, proportion and functional clarity of the American Beaux-Arts office building with the efficiency and flexibility of the office cabinet system, Le Corbusier developed a new approach to the design of office buildings. The experience that had a decisive role in making this possible was his first visit to New York in 1936, when he saw the city's skyscrapers at first hand. Notwithstanding his oft-quoted statement that the skyscrapers of New York are too small, he learned to value them once he saw them. His most consequential immediate response to New York was embodied in the project for the Admiralty, in which he launched a new direction of skyscraper design. But the only country that benefited from this was India; there, he was given the opportunity to put his ideas into concrete form and thus enabled to realise his most eloquent architectural interpretation of modern bureaucracy.

In his first Indian sketchbook Le Corbusier wrote: 'Calm, dignity, contempt for envy: perhaps India is capable of *standing by them*, and establishing herself at the head of civilisation'.[61] These words clearly sum up what for Le Corbusier represented India's most lasting values: her moral force and potential for moral leadership. In the buildings of Chandigarh's capitol complex, Le Corbusier offered a powerful architectural interpretation of the moral force inherent in India's executive, legislative and judicial branches of government. He also expressed in them India's aspiration to become the foremost moral leader in the world, as envisioned by Gandhi and Nehru. No wonder that in his outline of the city's programme he noted that 'responsibilities of aesthetics and ethics equally dominate the work'.[62]

Le Corbusier believed that he was in an exceptional position to interpret India's needs and aspirations, for he was not bound by the issues of the day in which political leaders – including Gandhi and Nehru – are often enmeshed. In his third Indian sketchbook he wrote:

> Life has placed me in the position of an observer, giving me incomparable – and exceptional – means of judgment. I believe that this order of thought is not available to political leaders and that they live *in* the problem and hence do not see it.[63]

Viewing his role in this light, he spared no effort in giving the three great buildings of the capitol complex the most memorable form and the richest meaning possible. In so doing, he offered the newly independent India an architecture intended to outlast the contribution made even by the country's two greatest modern political leaders. Hence Le Corbusier's architecture there can justly be called timeless but of its time.

Notes

1 Quoted by B P Bagchi, *Chandigarh* (Chandigarh: New Horizons Press, 1965), p 1.
2 For an account of the birth of Chandigarh, see Norma Evenson, *Chandigarh* (Berkeley: University of California Press, 1966). For an interpretation of the city's symbolic significance, see Stanislaus von Moos, 'The Politics of the Open Hand: Notes on Le Corbusier and Nehru at Chandigarh', in *The Open Hand: Essays on Le Corbusier*, ed Russell Walden (Cambridge, Mass: The MIT Press, 1977), pp 412-57.
3 There are seventy-three sketchbooks covering the period from 1914 to 1964 in the archives of the Fondation Le Corbusier in Paris. These have been published by the Architectural History Foundation, New York, as:
Le Corbusier Sketchbooks Volume 1, 1914-1948 (1981)
Le Corbusier Sketchbooks Volume 2, 1950-1954 (1981)
Le Corbusier Sketchbooks Volume 3, 1954-1957 (1982)
Le Corbusier Sketchbooks Volume 4, 1957-1964 (1982)
4 These are Sketchbooks E 18 and E 19. See *Le Corbusier Sketchbooks Volume 2, 1950-1954*, no 309-414.
5 Ibid, no 329-330. It must be kept in mind, however, that Le Corbusier's reservation about Lutyens' work is made here in the context of an exceptional example of earlier Indian architecture. Elsewhere he was unequivocal in his praise of this British architect/planner. 'New Delhi (in Tuscan-inspired style), the capital of imperial India, was built by Lutyens over 30 years ago, with extreme care, great talent, and with true success. The critics may rant as they like, but the accomplishment of such an undertaking earns respect.' (Le Corbusier, *Oeuvre complète, 1952-1957*, published in Zurich by Girsberger, 1957, p 51). For Lutyens' influence on Chandigarh, see Allan Greenberg, 'Lutyens' Architecture Restudied', *Perspecta 12* (1969): 129-52.
6 Le Corbusier, *Le Voyage d'Orient* (Paris: Forces Vives, 1966). For an earlier published account of Le Corbusier's trip to the East, see 'Confession', in his *L'Art décoratif d'aujourd'hui* (Paris: Crès, 1925), pp 197-247, esp p 246).
7 The client whom he was to meet only in the fall of 1951 was Shyamubhai Shodhan.
8 During the next few years Le Corbusier repeatedly tried to convince Bhabha Tata to let him build the headquarters of the Air India Company, but without success. I am indebted to Charles Correa for this information.
9 L R Nair, *Why Chandigarh?* (Simla: Publicity Department, Punjab Government, 1950).
10 For the best study of Ahmedabad in English, see Kenneth L Gillion, *Ahmedabad, A Study in Indian Urban History* (Berkeley: University of California Press, 1968).
11 Ibid, p 94.
12 Ibid, p 153.
13 Except during the monsoon season, this river is reduced to a trickle, leaving the large riverbed exposed. For the project of the Chimanbhai house, see the drawings in this volume (FLC 6.313-6.397).
14 The unexecuted buildings include the Spontaneous Theatre, the Magic Box, the Library and the Art Studios. See Le Corbusier, *Oeuvre complète, 1946-1952* (Zurich: Girsberger, 1960), pp 160-61. Balkrishna Doshi's Tagore Theatre and Gautam Sarabhai's National Institute of Design were subsequent additions to the still incomplete cultural centre.
15 The Museum of Ahmedabad was first adumbrated in Le Corbusier's World Museum planned for his Mundaneum of 1929 (see 'Mundaneum', in *The Le Corbusier Archive*, ed H Allen Brooks (New York: Garland Publishing/Paris: Fondation Le Corbusier, 1982-), vol 7, *Villa Savoye and Other Buildings and Projects, 1929-1930* [forthcoming]). However, the most direct prototypes for this museum are the projects for the Museum of Contemporary Art, Paris, 1931 (see 'Centre d'Art Contemporaine', in the *Le Corbusier Archive*, vol 10, *Urbanisme, Algiers and Other Buildings and Projects, 1930-1933* [forthcoming]), the Pavilion for the Paris International Exhibition of 1937 (see *The Le Corbusier Archive*, vol 13, *Pavillon des Temps Nouveaux and Other Buildings and Projects, 1936-1937* [1983], pp 557 ff); and the Museum of Unlimited Growth planned for Philippeville, Algeria, in 1939 (see *The Le Corbusier Archive*, vol 14, *Buildings and Projects, 1937-1942* [1983], pp 577 ff).
16 See 'Mundaneum', in *The Le Corbusier Archive*, vol 7, and Paul Otlet and Le Corbusier, *Mundaneum* (Brussels: J Lebégue, 1928).
17 Le Corbusier, *Une Maison – un palais* (Paris: Crès, 1928), p 52.
18 Before the Millowners Building acquired its present form, it had undergone major changes during its lengthy design process, which included an earlier project with stone facing and only a few sunbreakers. See FLC 6.781, 6.788 and 6.789 in this volume.
19 In the Villa Cook Le Corbusier reversed the traditional organisation of the interior of a house by placing the public over the private floors. This concept was first realised in his Ozenfant house built in Paris in 1922, where the double-storeyed studio occupies the top two floors.
20 Le Corbusier, *The Radiant City* (New York: The Orion Press, 1967), p 78 (originally published as *La Ville radieuse* in 1933).
21 *Le Corbusier Sketchbooks Volume 2, 1950-1954*, E 18, no 359.
22 Le Corbusier, *Oeuvre complète, 1952-1957* (Zurich: Girsberger, 1958), p 134; and Balkrishna V Doshi, *Le Corbusier, Sarabhai House and Shodhan House, Ahmedabad, India* (Tokyo: ADA Edita, 1974) n p.
23 Reyner Banham, *Theory and Design in the First Machine Age* (New York: Praeger Publishers, 1960), p 221.
24 Maurice Jardot, 'Sketch for a Portrait', in Le Corbusier, *Creation is a Patient Search* (New York: Praeger Publishers, 1960), p 9.
25 Ibid, p 11.
26 For the importance of these two projects, see my article, 'Le Corbusier's Changing Attitude Toward Form', *Journal of the Society of Architectural Historians 24* (March 1965): 15-23, and reprinted in my *Le Corbusier in Perspective* (Englewood Cliffs, NJ: Prentice Hall, 1975), pp 68-73.
27 Le Corbusier, *The Modulor* (Cambridge: Harvard University Press, 1958), p 224.
28 Le Corbusier, *Oeuvre complète, 1910-1929* (Zurich: Girsberger, 1960), pp 13-14.
29 Ibid, p 31. Located at 32 rue Gogot-de-Mauroy, off the boulevard des Italiens, the Café Legendre is now called the Café Le Mauroy.
30 For the first critical discussion of this project, see my article mentioned in note 26. Le Corbusier makes reference to this project in Sketchbook E 18, no 360, by saying, 'Brother's villa roofing in manner of Baizeau Tunis'. Here he refers to the unexecuted house designed for Chinubhai Chimanbhai, which was almost identical with the early design for the Hutheesing/Shodhan house. Compare FLC 6.313 in the Villa Chimanbhai drawings with FLC 6.444 in the Villa Shodhan drawings, in this volume.
31 For the most thorough discussions of the Schröder house in Utrecht, see Theodore M Brown, *The Work of G Rietveld Architect* (Utrecht: A W Bruna & Zoon, 1958), pp 35-74, where he writes that, according to Mrs Schröder, 'Le Corbusier visited the house within a few years of its completion'. p 74.
32 These are the Villa Fallet, 1906, and the Villas Jaquemet and Stotzer, both of 1908. See Charles Jencks, *Le Corbusier and the Tragic View of Architecture* (Cambridge: Harvard University Press, 1973), pp 21-23.
33 See 'Maison locative', in *The Le Corbusier Archive*, vol 11, *Immeuble, 24, rue Nungesser-et-Coli and Other Buildings and Projects, 1933* (1983), pp 485 ff.
34 See Le Corbusier, *Oeuvre complète, 1946-1952*, p 109. For the camera analogy, see Christopher Rand, 'City on a Tilting Plain', *New Yorker*, April 30, 1955, p 56.
35 *Le Corbusier Sketchbooks Volume 3, 1954-1957*, J 39, no 451.
36 For this and other drawings of primitive architecture, see Le Corbusier, *Une Maison – un palais*, p 39.
37 *Le Corbusier Sketchbooks Volume 2, 1950-1954*, E 18, no 357.
38 For the Immeubles-villas project, see *The Le Corbusier Archive*, vol 1, *Early Buildings and Projects, 1912-1923* (1982), pp 353 ff; for the Villa Stein-Monzie see *The Le Corbusier Archive*, vol 3, *Palais de la Société des Nations, Villa les Terrasses, and Other Buildings and Projects, 1926-1927* (1982), pp 365 ff.
39 *Le Corbusier Sketchbooks Volume 2, 1950-1954*, E 18, no 361 and E 23, no 689.
40 See *The Le Corbusier Archive*, vol 12, *Buildings and Projects, 1933-1937* (1983), pp 391 ff.
41 Although a discussion of the roof garden of the weekend house lies outside the scope of this paper, it should be noted that it is there that Le Corbusier began to treat the roof garden as a more freely landscaped space. This new direction was given its fullest manifestation in the roof garden of the Sarabhai house.
42 In the context of the Sarabhai house the folk element of the Mediterranean tradition stands out. For earlier manifestations of this element in Le Corbusier's architecture, see his project for the Peyrissac house, near Cherchell, Algeria, 1942 (in *The Le Corbusier Archive*, vol. 14, *Buildings and Projects, 1937-1942* [1983], pp 733 ff), which is an important link between the weekend house and the Sarabhai house; and the projects for La Sainte-Baume, near Marseilles 1948 ('La Sainte-Baume', in *The Le Corbusier Archive*, vol 18, *Palais des Nations Unies and Other Buildings and Projects, 1946-1948* [forthcoming]), and Roq and Rob, Cap Martin, 1949 (in *The Le Corbusier Archive*, vol 19, *Projet Roq et Rob, Roquebrune-Cap Martin, and Other Buildings and Projects, 1948-1950* [1983], pp 47 ff).
43 Translation by Mary Patricia May Sekler, 'Ruskin, the Tree and the Open Hand', in *The Open Hand: Essays on Le Corbusier*, ed Russell Walden, p 73.
44 The most important scholars include: Norma Evenson, Stanislaus von Moos, Mary Patricia May Sekler and Alexander C Gorlin. For Evenson and Von Moos, see note no 2; for Sekler, see note no 43; and for Gorlin, see 'An Analysis of the Governor's Palace of Chandigarh', *Oppositions 19/20* (Winter/Spring, 1980): 161-183.
45 These are: the Museum and Art Gallery with the adjacent Lecture Hall (1964-68); the School of Art (1964-69); the School of Architecture (1964-69); and the Boat Club on Sukhna Lake (1963-65). For the best illustrations of these and the Business Centre, see *Le Corbusier: Last Works*, ed Willy Boesiger (New York: Praeger Publishers, 1970); for drawings, see *The Le Corbusier Archive*, vol 25, *Chandigarh: City and Musée* (forthcoming).
46 The original plan of the capitol complex also included the Governor's Palace, which was abandoned and replaced by the Museum of Knowledge in 1960. The museum has not yet been built. In addition to the buildings, Le Corbusier also planned certain monuments for the capitol complex, which are: the Monument of the Open Hand, the Tower of Shadows with the Trench of Consideration, and the Monument to the Martyrs of the Indian Partition. Only the last one has been built so far. See *Le Corbusier: Last Works*, pp 64-75, and Gorlin and Sekler. For the drawings, see *The Le Corbusier Archive*, vol 24, *Chandigarh: Capitole, Volume III: Palais du Gouverneur and Other Buildings and Projects* (forthcoming).
47 *Le Corbusier Sketchbooks Volume 2, 1950-1954*, E 19, no 391.
48 Ibid, no 392. The Pinjore gardens date from the seventeenth century and are located ten miles from Chandigarh at the foothills of the Himalayas. The Patiala gardens to which Le Corbusier makes reference here are the Baradari gardens in Patiala, which he visited on February 25, 1951. See ibid, E 18, no 331.
49 However, Le Corbusier applied the principles of Mogul landscaping in general and that of Pinjore in particular to the project for the garden of the Governor's Palace. See Le Corbusier, *Oeuvre complète, 1946-1952*, p 143.
50 For additional early sketches of the High Court, see Le Corbusier, *Oeuvre complète, 1946-1952*, p 126.
51 Le Corbusier referred to the Pont du Gard as 'among the very great works of architecture, and going far beyond mere mathematical formulae'. Le Corbusier, *The City of Tomorrow* (Cambridge, Mass: The MIT Press, 1971), p 57.
52 For a discussion of other aspects of the door's symbolic significance, see Richard A Moore, 'Alchemical and Mythical Themes in the Poem of the Right Angle 1946-1965', *Oppositions 19/20* (Winter/Spring, 1980): 111-39, esp pp 129-32.
53 Le Corbusier's reliance on the compositional solutions found in industrial architecture was preceded by the work of many architects, most notably by the Russian Constructivists.
54 For the sketch, see Le Corbusier, *Oeuvre complète, 1957-1965*, p 80.
55 Quoted by Stanislaus von Moos, p 418.
56 *Le Corbusier Sketchbooks Volume 2, 1950-1954*, E 23, no 662 and E 18, no 361.
57 See 'Capitole', FLC 5.144, in *The Le Corbusier Archive*, vol 22, *Chandigarh: Capitole, Volume I: Assemblée and Other Buildings and Projects* (forthcoming).
58 Le Corbusier, *When the Cathedrals Were White* (New York: McGraw-Hill Book Co, 1964), p 60 (originally published in 1947).
59 Le Corbusier, *L'Art décoratif d'aujourd'hui* (Paris: Vincent, Fréal, 1959), p 83 (originally published in 1925).
60 Ibid, pp 74 and 70.
61 *Le Corbusier Sketchbooks Volume 2, 1950-1954*, E 18, no 362.
62 Le Corbusier, *Oeuvre complète, 1946-1952* (Zurich: Girsberger, 1961), p 115.
63 *Le Corbusier Sketchbooks Volume 2, 1950-1954*, E 23, nos 662 and 663 (Translation by Agnes Serenyi).

High Court

Chandigarh, India 1950–65

4.911
Technical report. The studies refer to: 1 structures; 2 principle of fabrication of vaults; 3 principle of wind-resistance of a parasol; 4 natural ventilation; 5 dilation of the roof duct, questions of structure, the ramp, soundproofing; 6 overpass, etc. In total, there are eleven separate pages pasted onto three sheets of paper which all have the same number. Signed Le Corbusier, dated March 11, 1952. Coloured ink on typing paper on drawing paper, 50cm x 65cm.

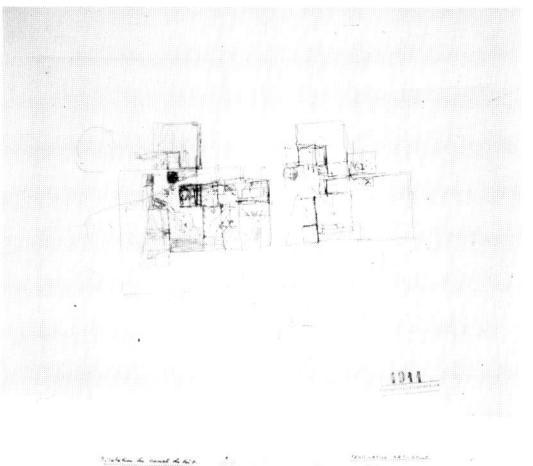
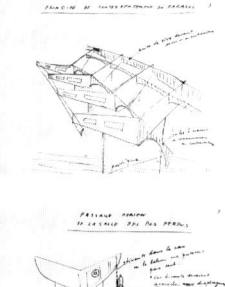

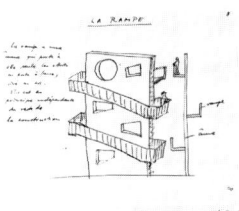

4.672
Perspective of the building with silhouettes and vegetation; there are two other gelatine prints with the same number. Signed Le Corbusier, May 3, 1951. Gelatine print on drawing paper, 76cm x 116cm.

4.675
Plan of level 2, numbering referring to the key on the right, orientation; there are two copies of this drawing, each bearing the same number. Scale 1:100. Signed Le Corbusier. Gelatine print on drawing paper, 75cm x 149cm.

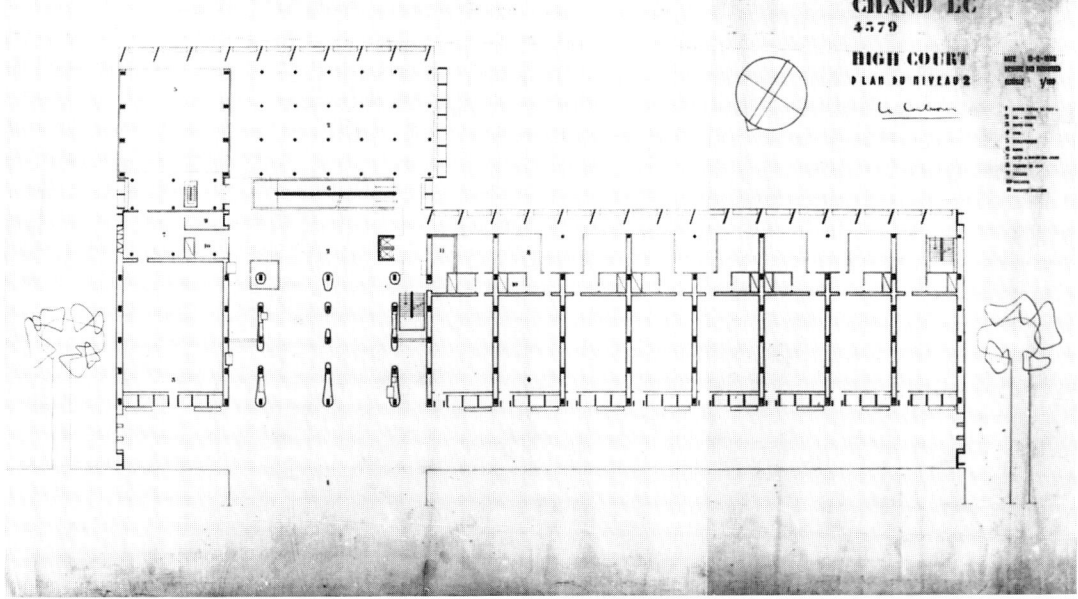

Capitol
Chandigarh, India 1951

5.160
Profile, elevation of the project as a whole. Charcoal sketch (profile of the Himalayas), drawn by Talati and dated April 23, 1957. Scale 1:200. Charcoal on heliotype, paper print, 42cm x 401cm.

Assembly Building
Chandigarh, India 1951

3.023
Study sketch, plan and section of the large room with silhouettes. Tobito. Pencil and colouring pencil on sketching paper, 66cm x 70cm.

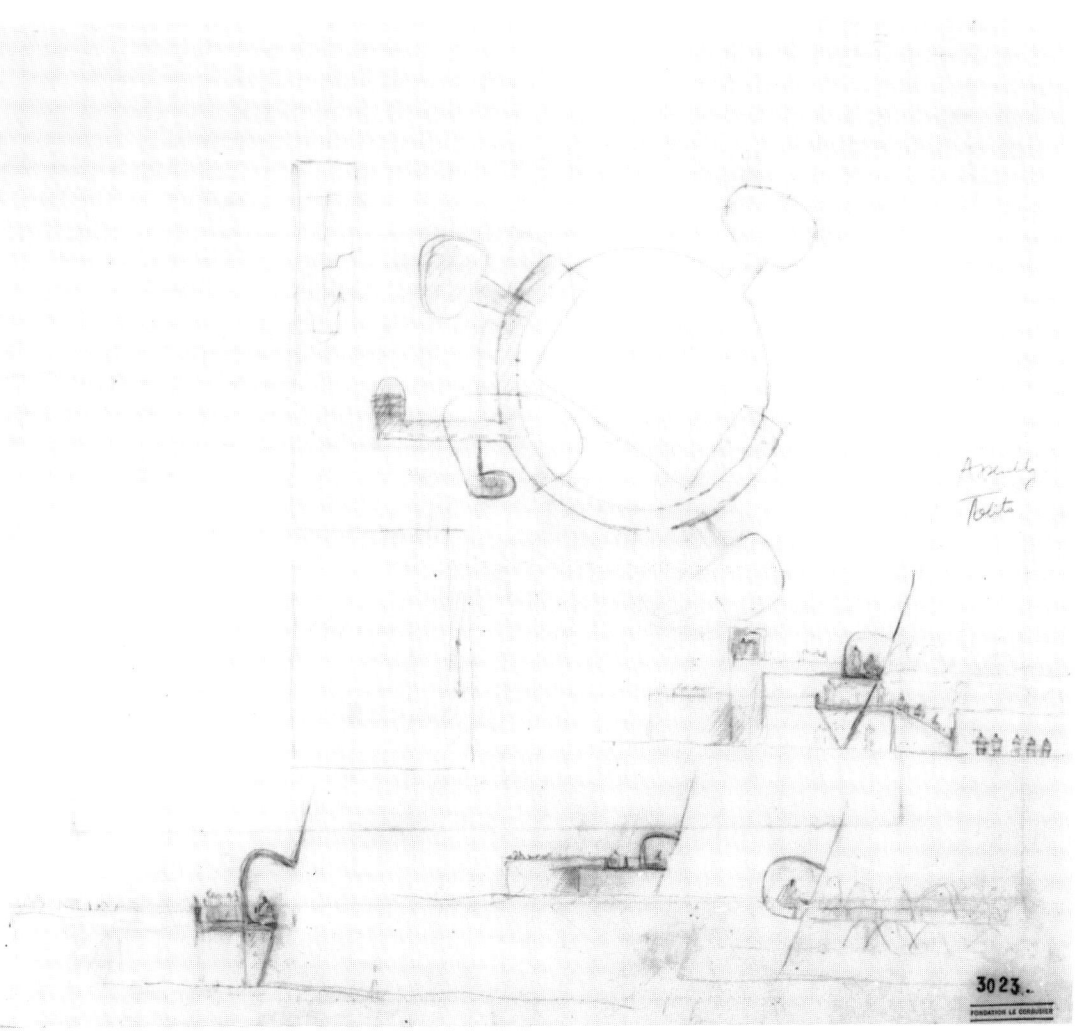

3.132
Study sketch, plan of the Assembly Building indicating floor levels and circulation in English. Pencil and yellow crayon on heliotype, paper print, 26 cm x 56 cm

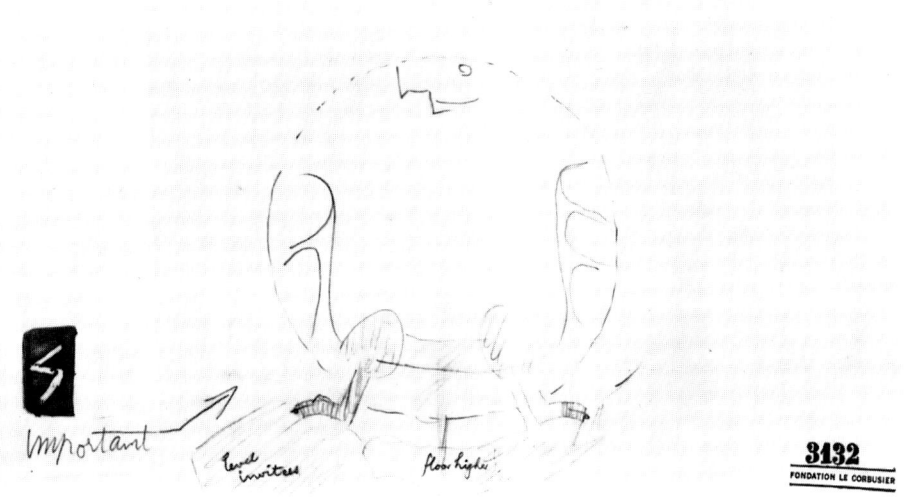

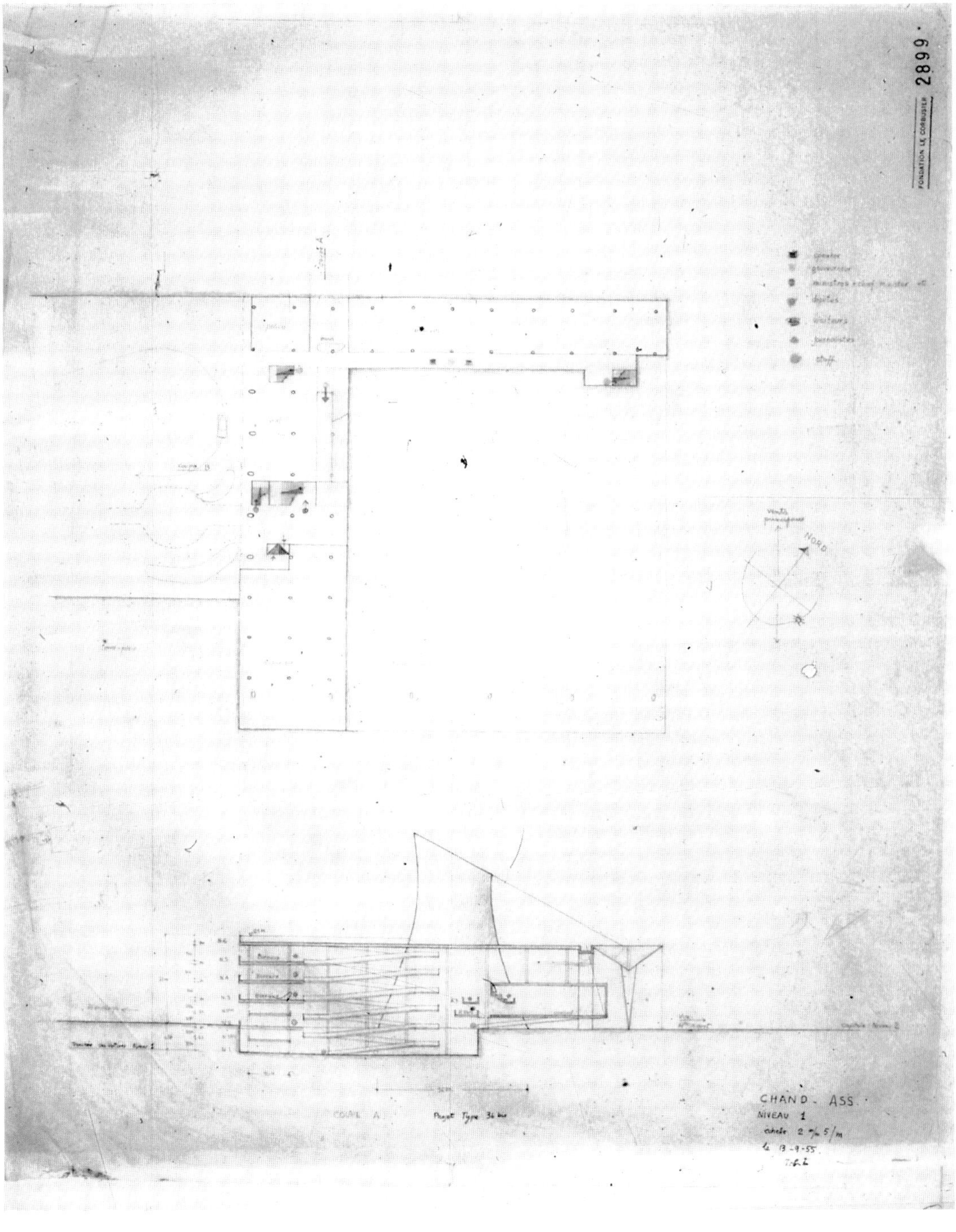

2.899
Drawing and plan of level 1 and section of the ramp between levels 1 and 5 showing the offices with a colour chart, top right, indicating the positioning of the different people working on this level of the building. Scale 1:2500, Tobito, 13.9.55. Pencil, colouring pencil and Indian ink on thick paper, 57 cm x 68 cm

3.186
Study sketch, plan of the entrance showing circulation, other notes and sketches. Pencil and coloured crayon on heliotype, paper print, 42 cm x 73 cm

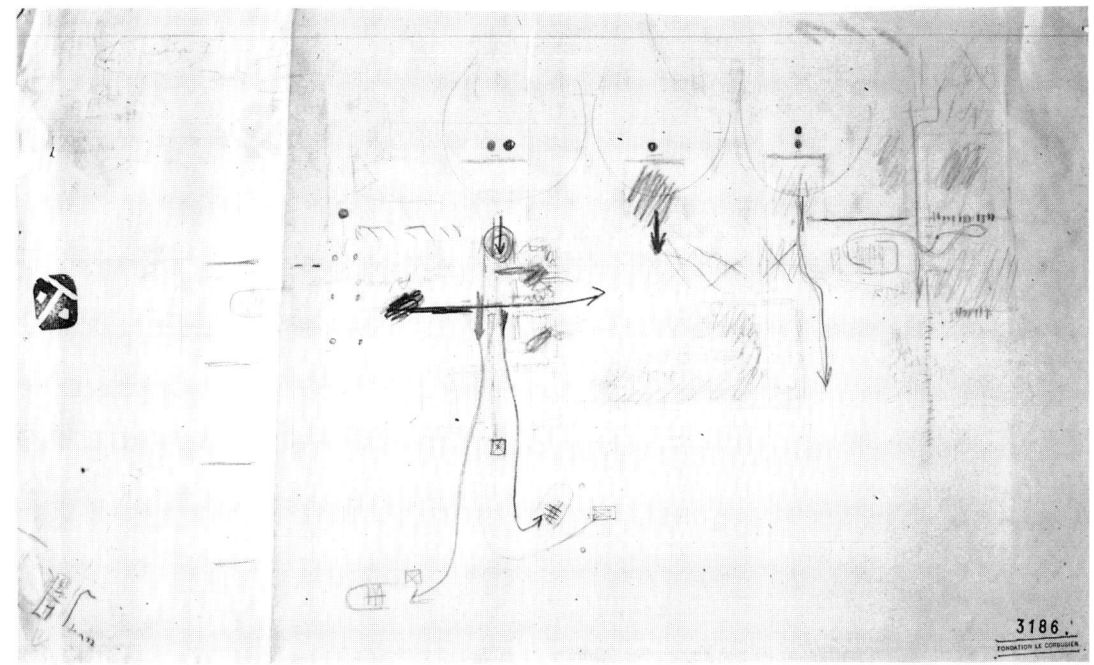

3.143
Study sketch, plan of the entrance portico, dated 16.4.56. Coloured crayons on heliotype, paper print, 36 cm x 43 cm

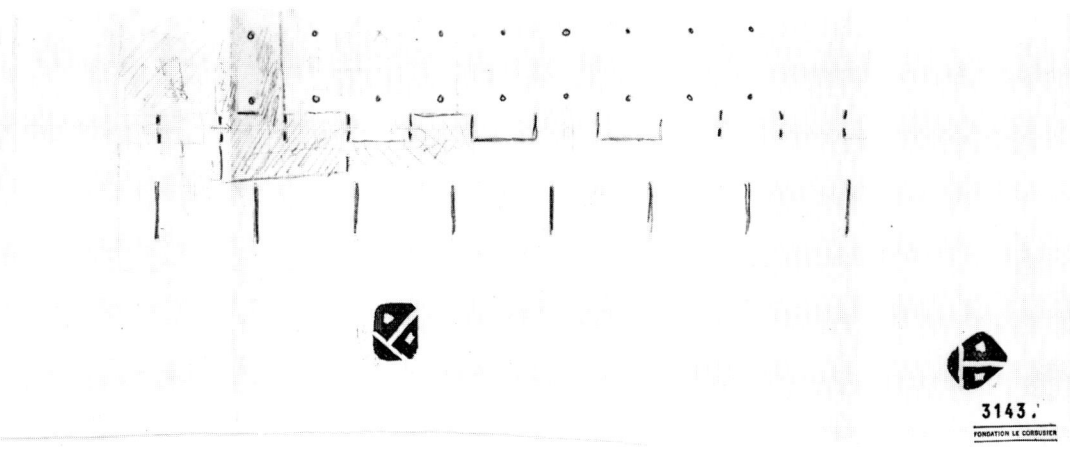

3.156
Study sketch, schematic plan. Coloured crayons on heliotype, paper print, 21 cm x 31 cm

3.105
Study drawing, plan with spot-heights, keys, *pilotis*, base line of a hyperbola. Volira, 25.8.60. Red pencil on heliotype, paper print, 71 cm x 125 cm

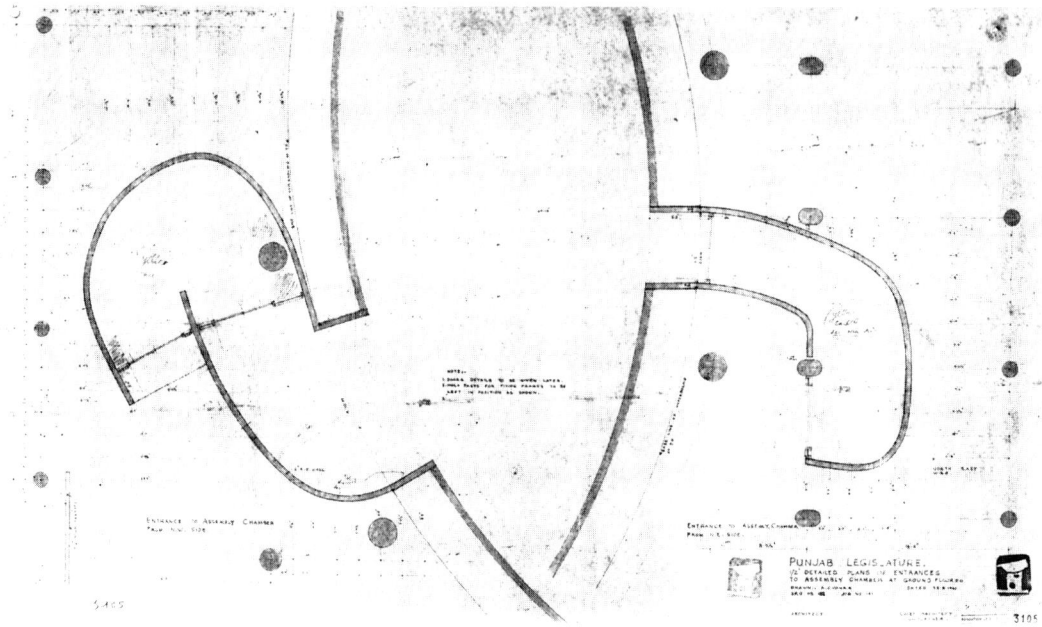

2.992
Study sketch, plan and schematic section with a small axonometric sketch and other sketches in pencil. Pencil, blue and yellow pencil on thick paper, 54cm x 46cm.

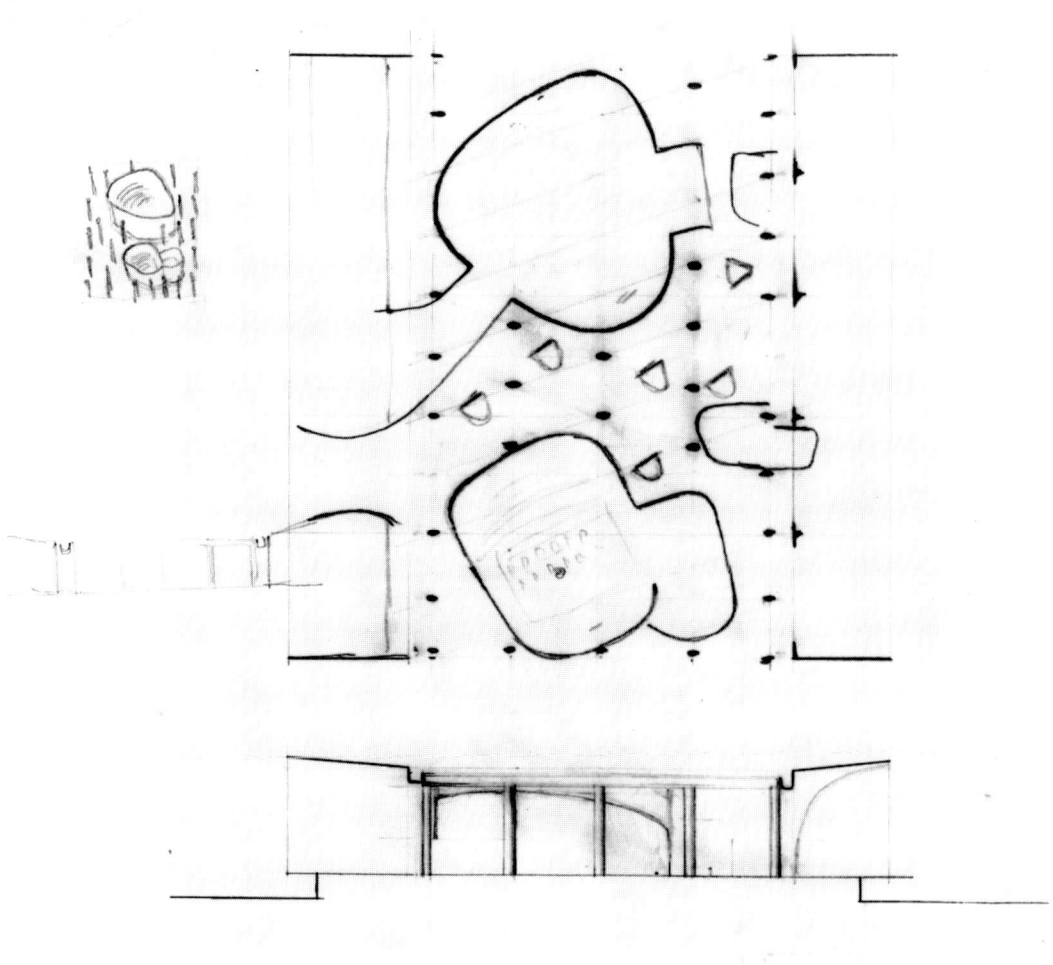

2.991
Study drawings, schematic plan and three sections through the building with small pencil sketches on the upper border. Pencil on thick paper, 69cm x 51cm.

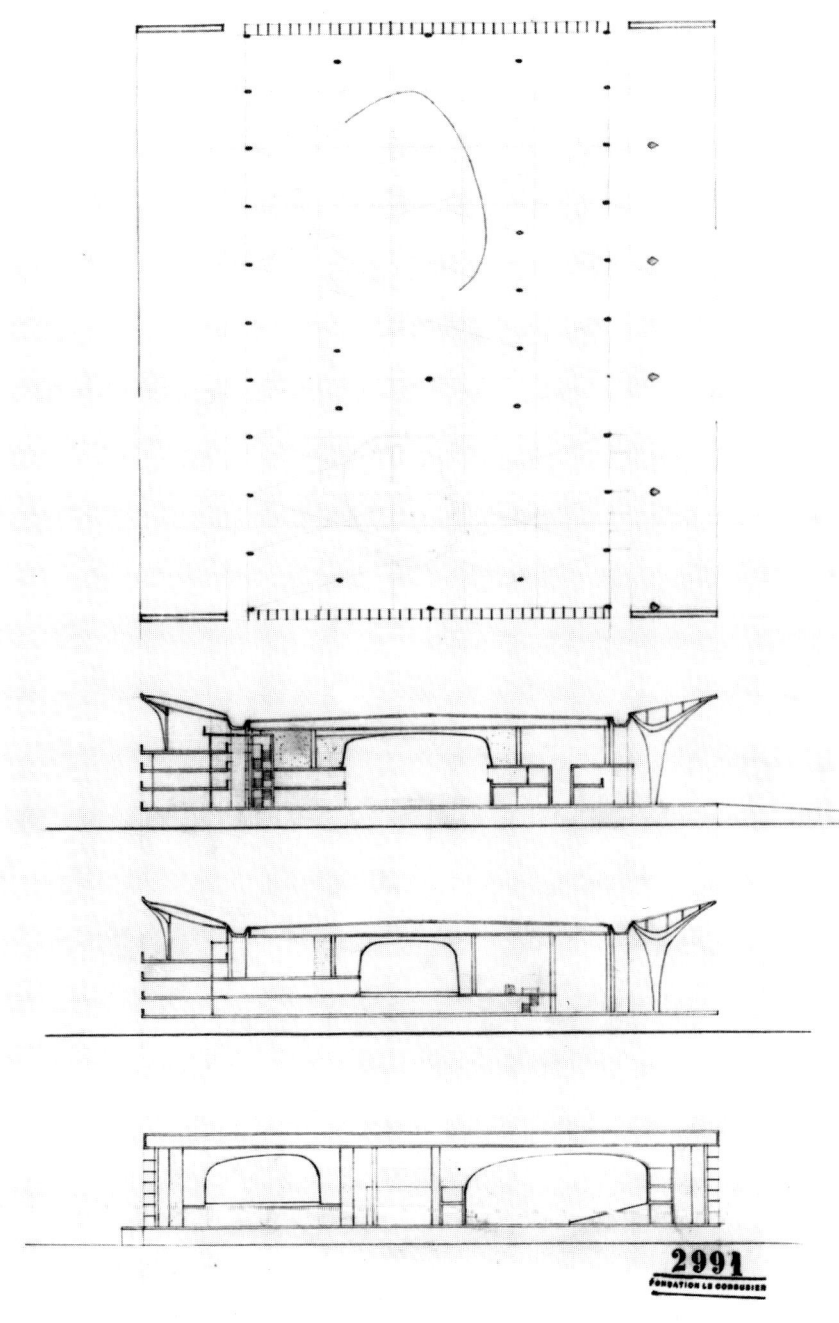

Secretariat

Chandigarh, India 1951

3.300
Level 1, basement, sketch No 2. Study sketch of the level, in several different places, and of circulation in the basement. Marked on the bottom left of the drawing is 'microfilm here between the two red lines', and on the bottom right, 'No 35'. Dated October 10, 1952. Pencil and colouring pencil on sketching paper, 49cm x 141cm.

3.323
Study sketch, plan showing *pilotis* and other areas. Pencil and red crayon on thick typing paper, 21 cm x 27 cm

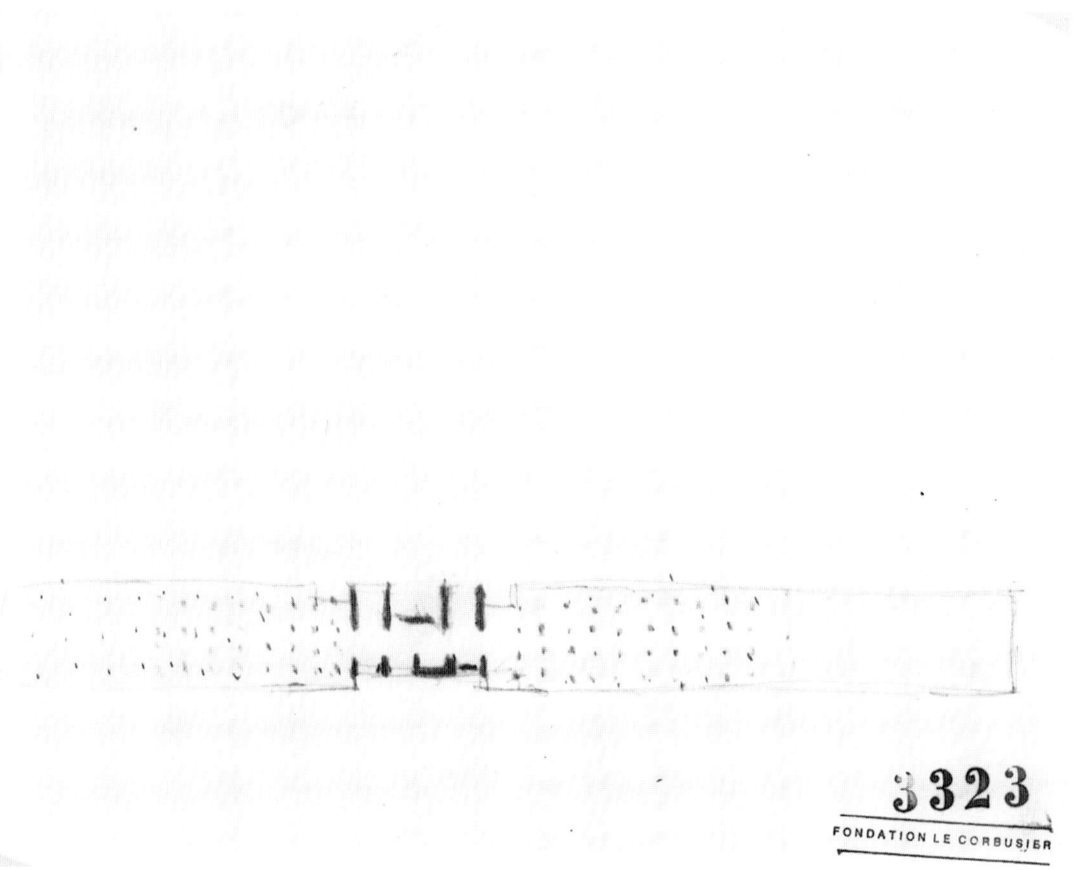

2.847
The ministry block, levels 2 and 6, plan of one block showing the stairways, offices, sanitation, entranceway etc, notes and spot-heights throughout, and observations, letters and angles marked in red pencil. Scale 1:50, Samper, 17.2.53. Indian ink, pencil and red pencil on thick paper, 91 cm x 133 cm

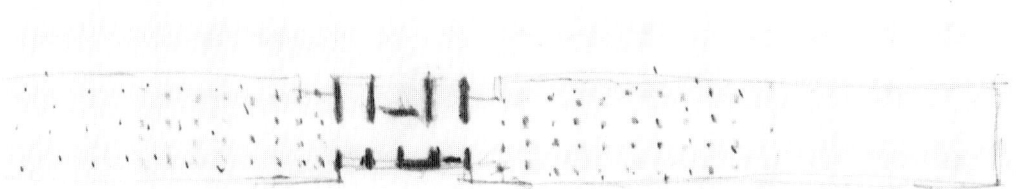

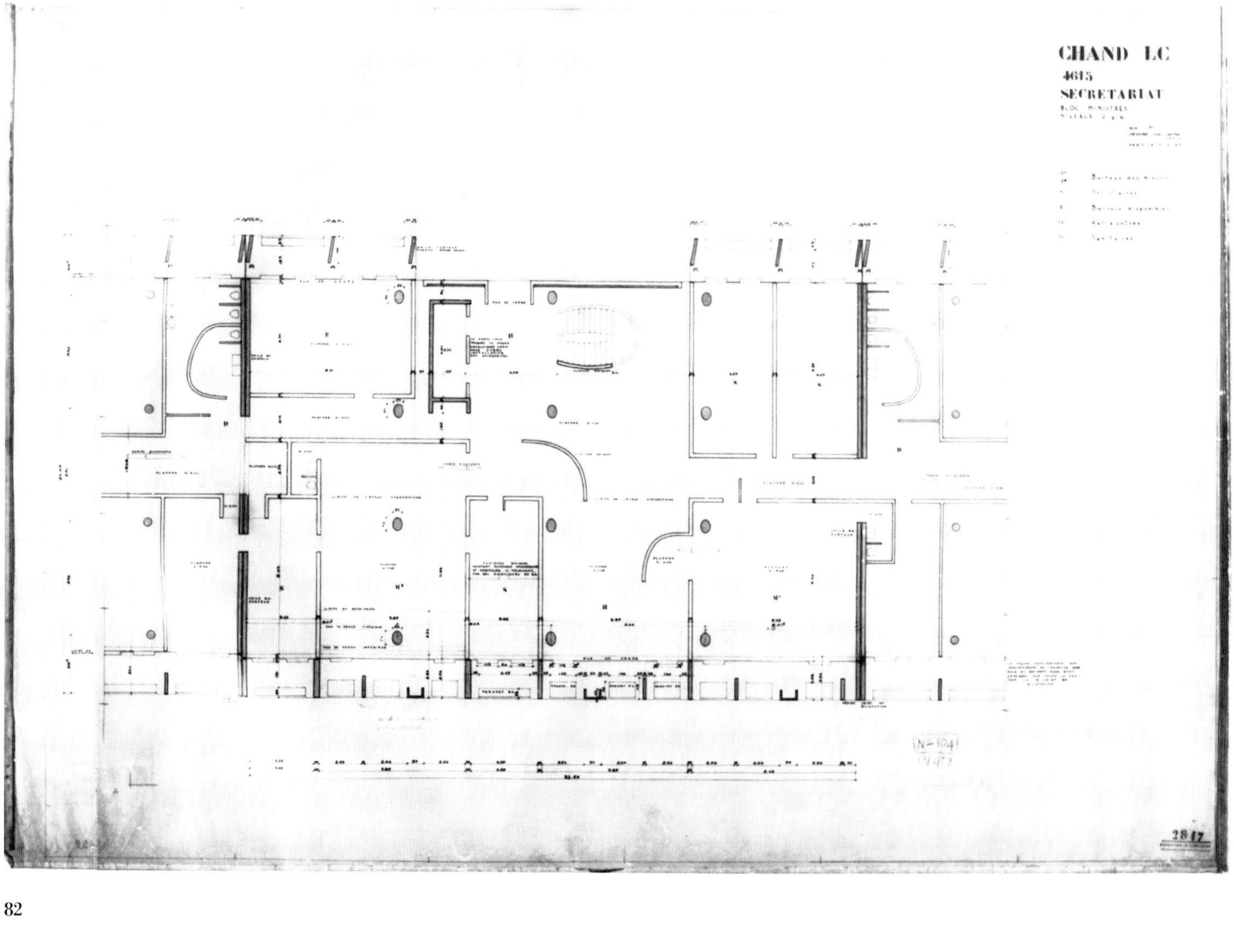

2.839
Plan sketch of the roof-terrace, study layout, keys. Samper, 29.3.53. Indian ink, black ink and red pencil on sketching paper, 30 cm x 28 cm

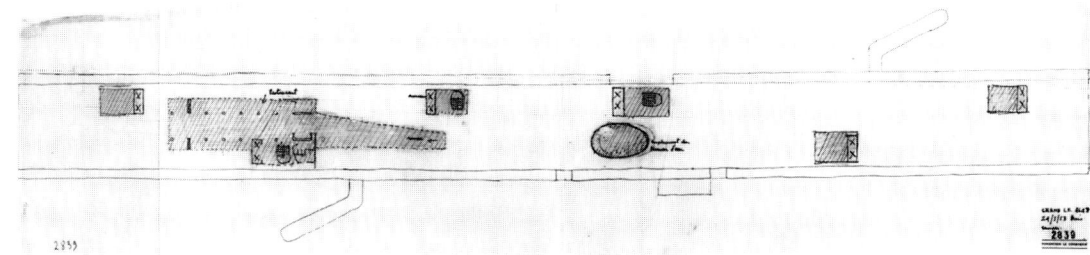

3.284
Study sketch of the facade with, bottom right, the letters 'No 22'. Dated May 27, 1952. Pencil and red pencil on tracing paper, 32cm x 45cm.

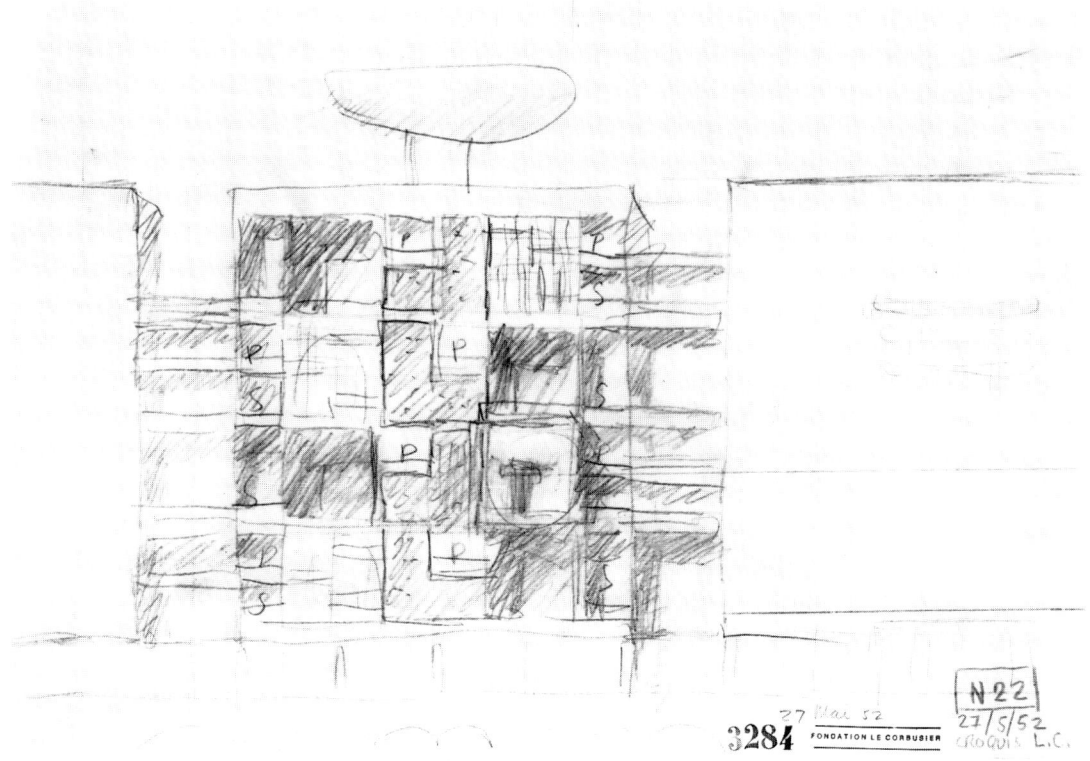

Millowners Association

Ahmedabad, India 1954

6.844
Study sketch, siting. Blue ink and colouring pencil on thick paper, 33cm x 45cm.

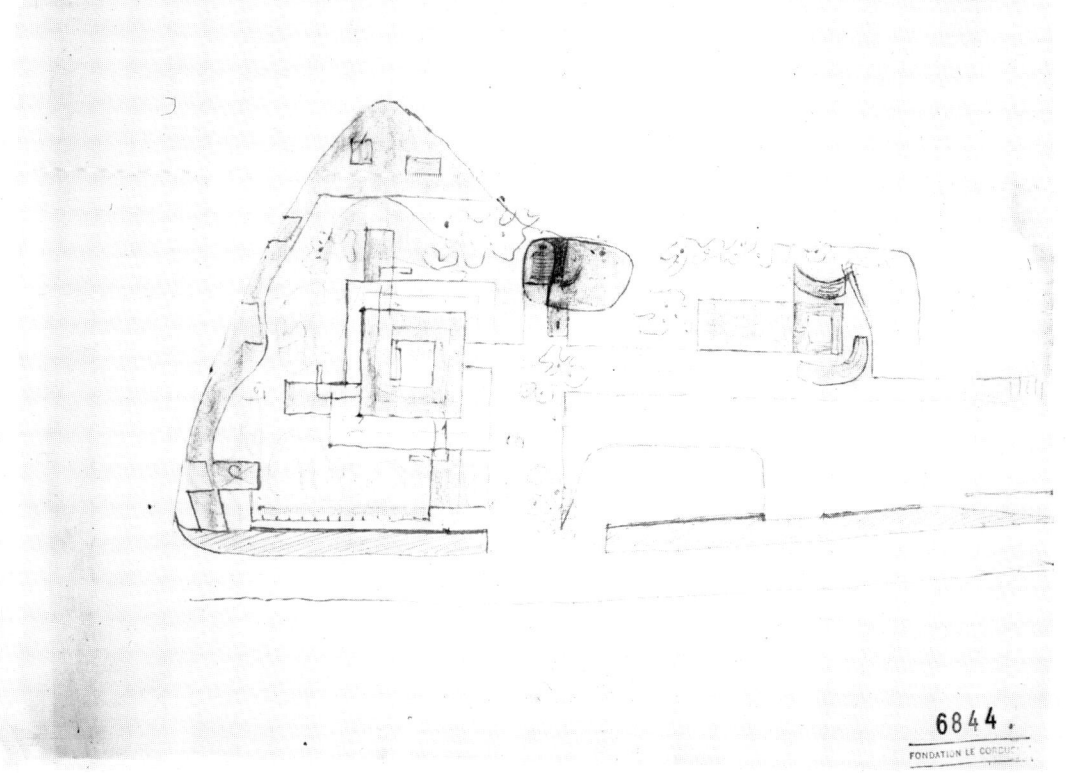

6.879
Level 4, study sketch, plan of level 4 showing the staircase, circulation and structure. Le Corbusier, October 9, 1952. Pencil and colouring pencil on sketching paper, 61cm x 74cm.

6.875
Various study sketches; plan, elevation with details of the main staircase. Pencil on sketching paper, 30cm x 46cm.

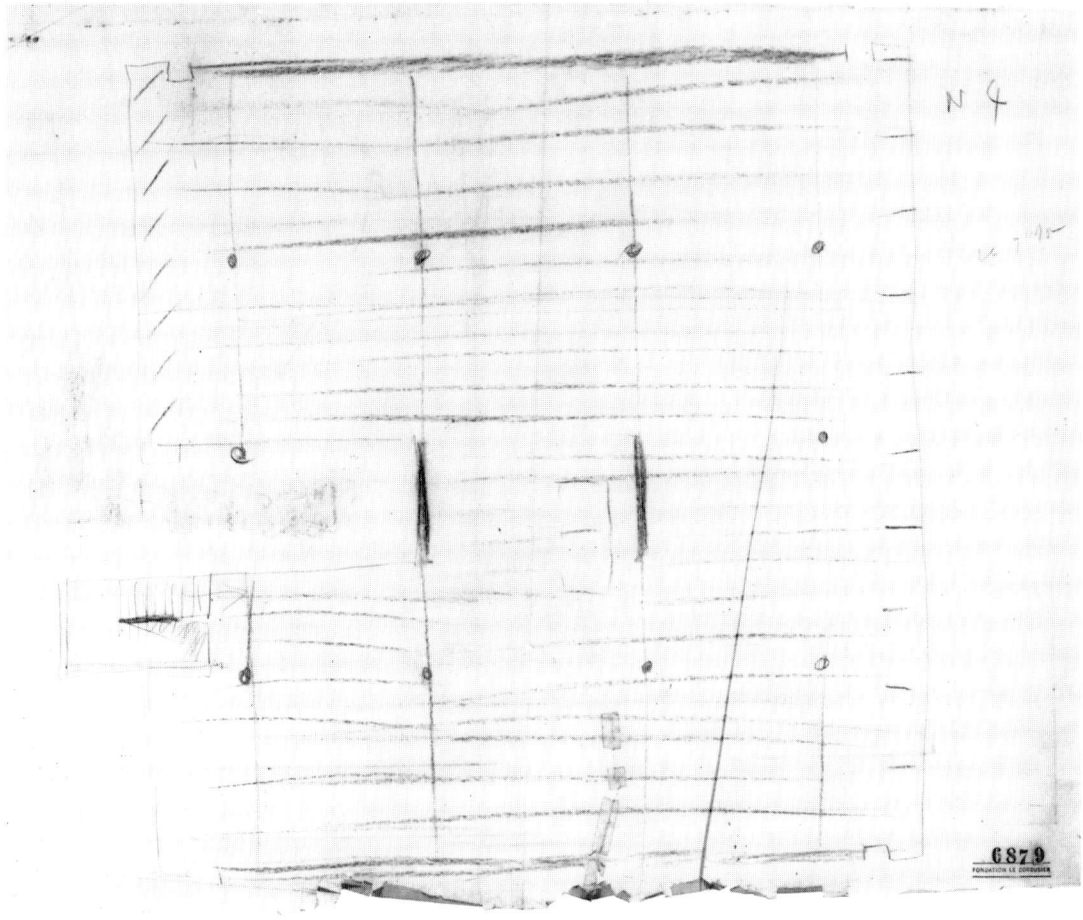

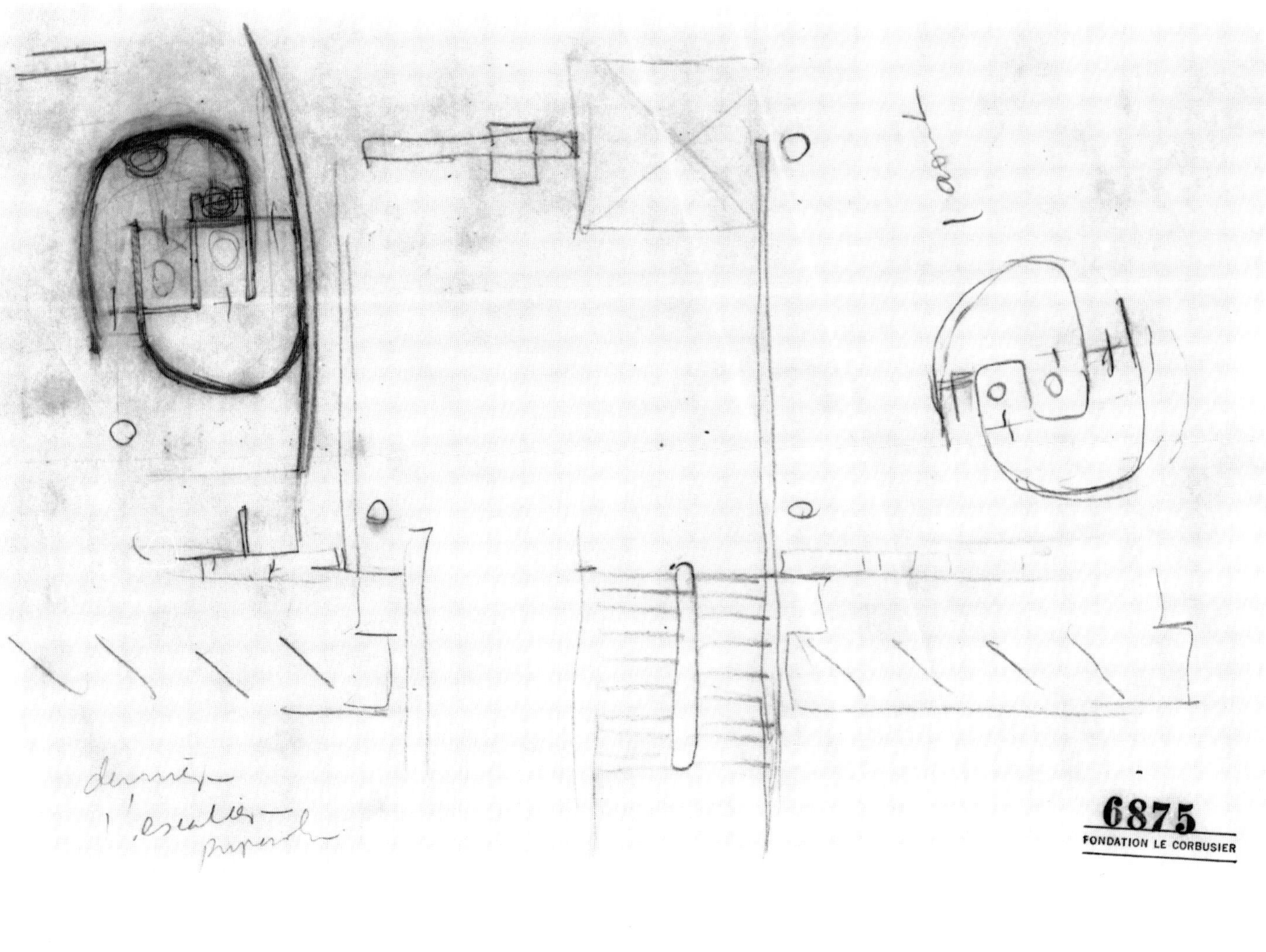

6.878
Level 5, study sketch, plan of level 5, on the left-hand side, sketch in pencil. Le Corbusier, October 9, 1952. Pencil and colouring pencil on sketching paper, 69cm x 75cm.

Ahmedabad Museum

Ahmedabad, India 1956

6.939
Ground level, plan of the levels with keys, orientation. Signed Le Corbusier, 'N1' on the print, drawn by Oubrerie 13 February 5, 1962. Scale 1:100. Pencil and colouring pencil on heliotype. Paper print, 85cm x 107cm.

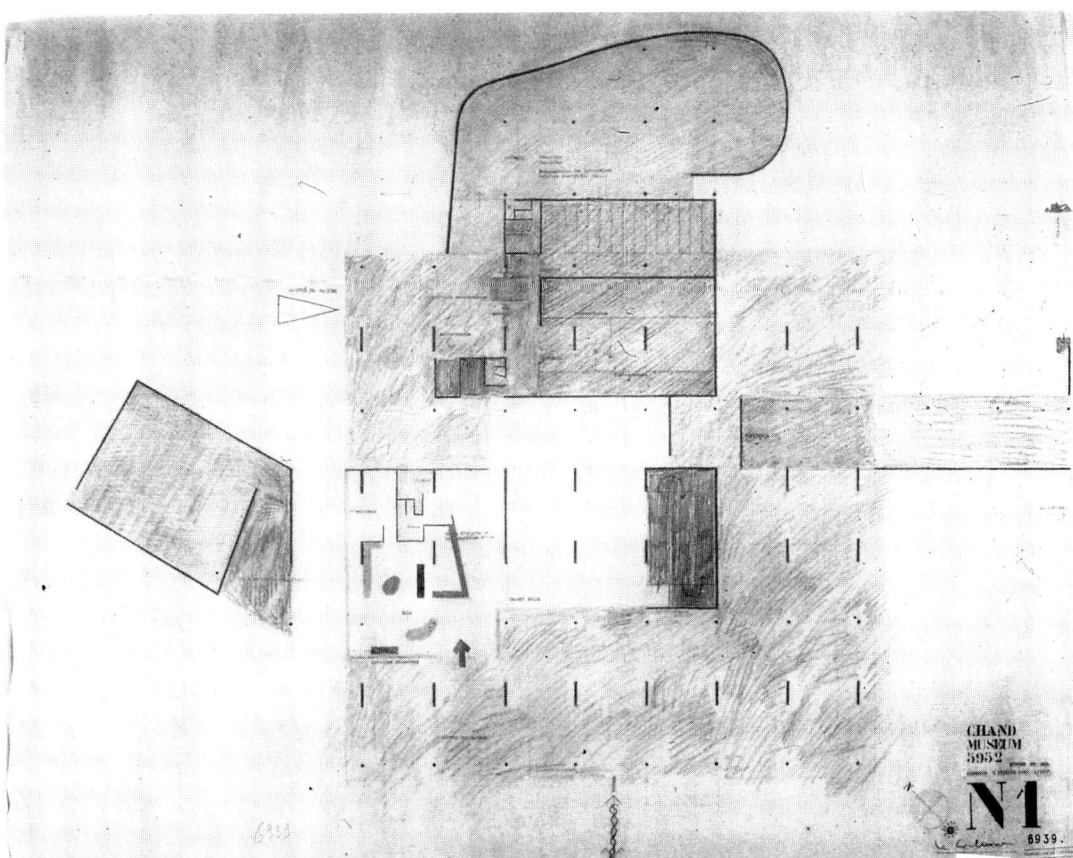

7.013
Study sketch, plan with layout of ground, access routes and siting of the buildings. At the bottom left, section and study for lighting on the stage, numerous sketches, silhouettes and notes. Le Corbusier, March 13, 1952. Pencil and colouring pencil, Indian ink on sketching paper, 41cm x 63cm.

Villa Sarabhai

Ahmedabad, India 1955

6.750
Plan of the building. Pencil and colouring pencil on sketching paper.

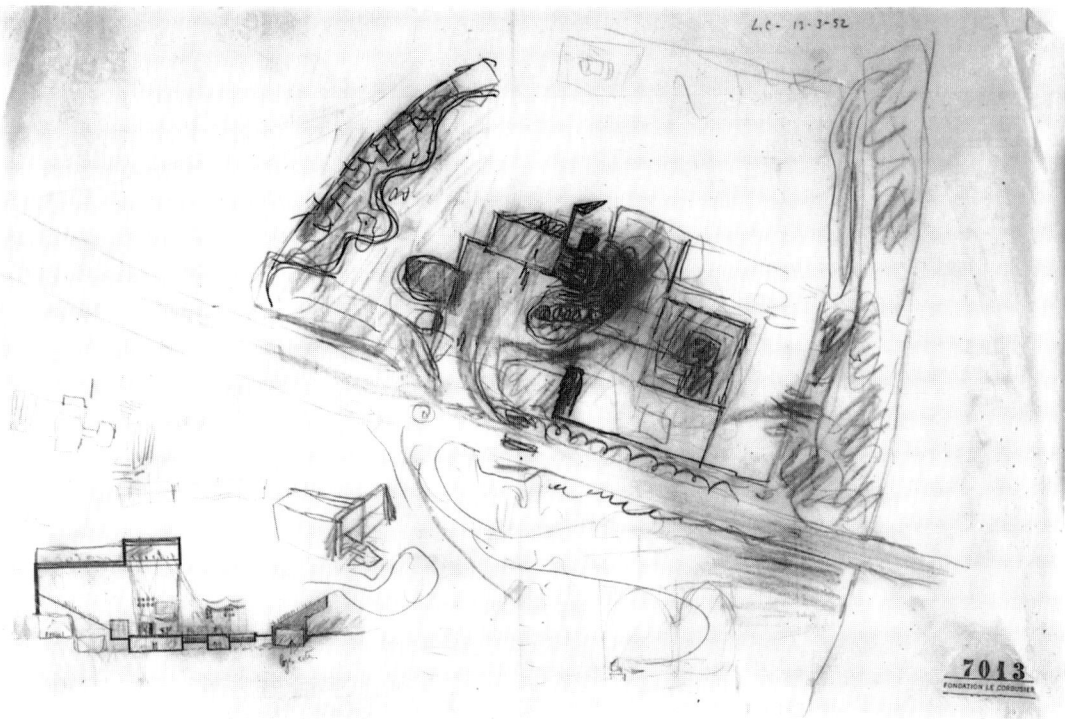

6.676
Various study sketches, modifications and notes added to a print: elevation of the facade and plan of the two levels showing bedrooms, rooms and structural elements, openings, etc. Drawn by Maisonnier and dated March 7, 1952. Black ink, pencil and colouring pencil on a print, paper print, 67cm x 72cm.

Villa Shodan
Ahmedabad, India 1956

6.454
Study sketch, perspective. Dated February 25. Pencil and colouring pencil on sketching paper, 30cm x 51cm.

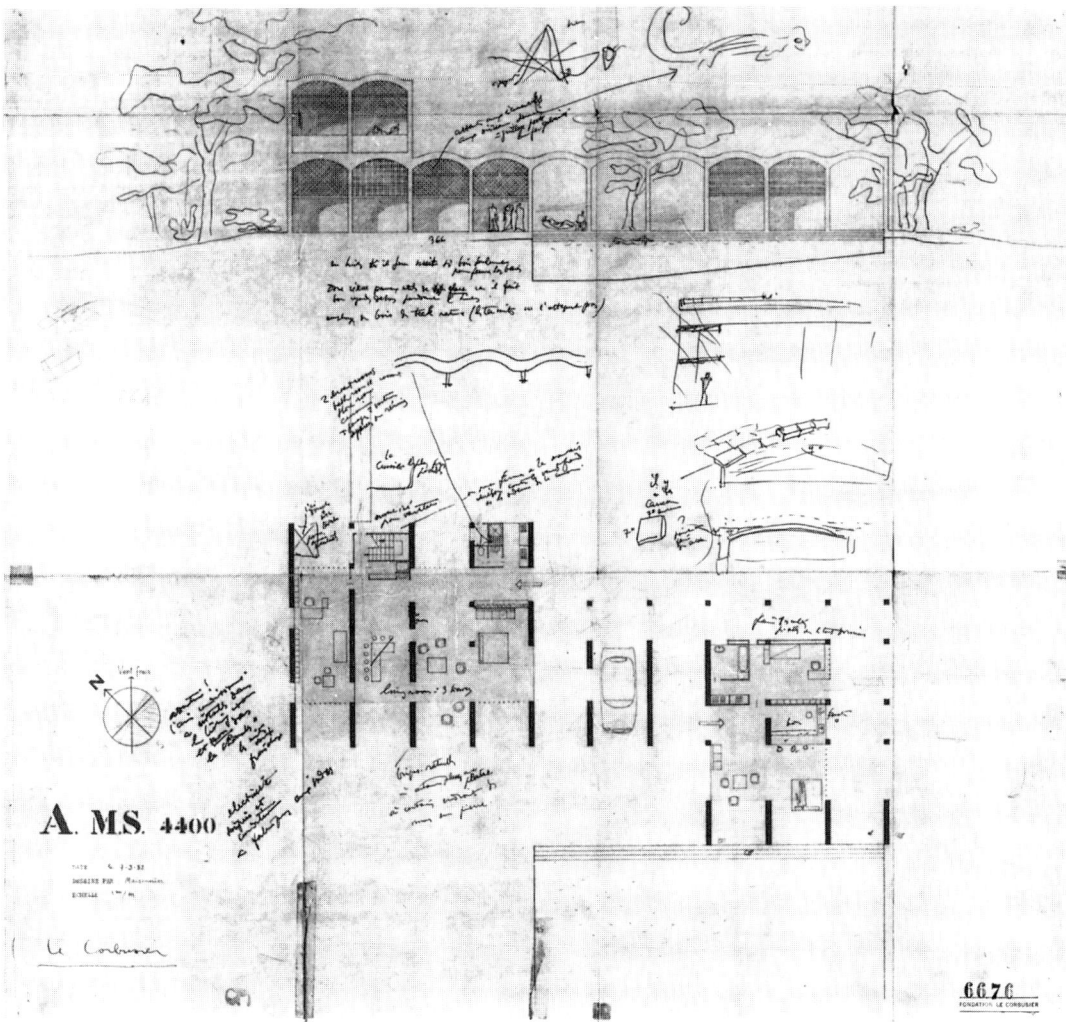

The Fondation Le Corbusier

SHORTLY BEFORE HIS DEATH, LE CORBUSIER ESTABlished a Foundation to which he left everything in his possession. Recognised as a public institution on July 31, 1968, the Fondation Le Corbusier is located in the Jeanneret and La Roche villas, on the Square du Docteur Blanche in Paris (75016).

According to its statutes, the aims of the Foundation are:
— To receive, acquire, restore, conserve and make known to the public by appropriate means (exhibitions, publications, conferences, colloquiums, films, etc) all of Le Corbusier's original works, notes, manuscripts, documents and miscellaneous objects, notably those given by Le Corbusier, the Association for the Fondation Le Corbusier, or by third parties with an interest in the dissemination of the thinking of Le Corbusier and of his architectural and literary work.
— The preservation and administration of the 'Maison La Roche' given to the Foundation by the Association, which in turn received it for this purpose from its Honorary President Raoul La Roche, who died on June 15 1965; and to preserve all furnishings that the Foundation can acquire.
— To encourage by all appropriate means research in the spirit defined in the written and built work of Le Corbusier.
— To accomplish, in a general manner, all acts corresponding to the objectives listed above, on the condition that a disinterested character is maintained.

The Foundation houses the largest collection of original documents of Le Corbusier's architectural studies in the world, including major archives of writings, drawings, paintings, tapestries, enamels, and sculptures. The Foundation assures the conservation of these objects, and from year to year improves their classification and viewing conditions.

The Foundation has organised or participated in the organisation of many exhibitions. It is willing under certain conditions to lend original works and documents, or copies of them. It advises owners of buildings designed by Le Corbusier on their maintenance and restoration. It has endorsed the integral publication of *The Sketchbooks* of Le Corbusier, as well as *The Le Corbusier Archive*.

Maison La Roche-Jeanneret, Paris, 1023 (FLC 15.111)